PRAISE FOR

Neurodiversity-Affirming Schools

"*Neurodiversity-Affirming Schools* is a book that needs to sit on *every* educator's desk. Amanda Morin and Emily Kircher-Morris's voice and wisdom holistically embrace how schools can build learning environments where all students thrive. Full of practical and inspiring information, this book is a catalyst for educators to build a learning environment that truly honors the humanity of each child. *Neurodiversity-Affirming Schools* activates us to assume our roles as advocates for learning environments that deeply support students who are neurodivergent."
—**Juliana Urtubey**, NBCT, 2021 National Teacher of the Year

"Emily Kircher-Morris and Amanda Morin have created a sensitive and insightful manual to understanding, supporting, and ultimately affirming neurodivergent kids in their process of learning and development. After nearly 20 years supporting kids in schools, I feel like I finally have that one book I can share with parents, teachers, and colleagues alike to help create inclusive and affirming schools for our kids. Spoiler alert . . . it's not nearly as hard as you think!"
—**Dr. Andrew Kahn**, licensed psychologist, neurodiversity specialist/consultant

"I have taught for 28 years and traveled the country trying to express how schools need to do a better job understanding neurodivergent learners, expanding their ideas of what inclusion and instruction can be, and listening to kids. I can confidently say that Emily Kircher-Morris and Amanda Morin's *Neurodiversity-Affirming Schools* is an invaluable resource to help educators change their practices and mindsets and create schools where neurodivergent—and all—students feel seen and have tools for self-advocacy. Informed by research, and written with care, thoughtfulness, and understanding, this is a book all educators need."
—**Kareem Neal, M.Ed.**, special education teacher, 2019 Arizona Teacher of the Year, 2022 National Teachers' Hall of Fame inductee, and inclusive practices trainer

"As someone who has worked with educators nationwide and parented a neurodiverse child, I can attest to the urgent need for the wisdom contained in this book. Emily Kircher-Morris and Amanda Morin skillfully blend theory and practice in an essential guide for creating truly inclusive classrooms. Their neurodiversity-affirming approach challenges educators to move beyond mere accommodation to celebration of cognitive differences. This book is a must-read for any educator committed to empowering ALL students to thrive."
—**Cindy Johanson**, executive director, George Lucas Educational Foundation

"There are many approaches to being an effective and equitable educator: being trauma informed, being culturally responsive-sustaining, and being committed to linguistic justice. Part of our work also involves creating learning spaces and schools that are neurodiversity affirming. Emily Kircher-Morris and Amanda Morin show us how all these approaches are connected. They offer practices for us to dream and realize a version of schools where both our neurodivergent and neuro-normative students and teachers can thrive. Kircher-Morris and Morin challenge us to reflect on practices such as behavior, communication, and development of IEPs and refine them in a way that truly supports kids' unique differences. This book is a necessary read for anyone who strives to cultivate a sense of student belonging."
—**Lauren Jewett**, NBCT, exceptional needs

"*Neurodiversity-Affirming Schools* is essential reading for educators committed to true inclusion. Emily Kircher-Morris and Amanda Morin advocate for a system that adapts to the learner and gets there through gradual and sustainable change. Every child deserves to feel like they belong, and this book takes us one step closer to schools that do just that."
—**Tim Villegas**, director of communications, Maryland Coalition for Inclusive Education

Neurodiversity Affirming Schools

Transforming Practices So All Students Feel Accepted & Supported

EMILY KIRCHER-MORRIS and **AMANDA MORIN**

Copyright © 2025 by Emily Kircher-Morris and Amanda Morin

All rights reserved under International and Pan-American Copyright Conventions. Unless otherwise noted, no part of this book may be reproduced, stored in a retrieval system, or transmitted in any form or by any means, electronic, mechanical, photocopying, recording, or otherwise, without express written permission of the publisher, except for brief quotations or critical reviews. For more information, go to freespirit.com/permissions.

Free Spirit, Free Spirit Publishing, and associated logos are trademarks and/or registered trademarks of Teacher Created Materials. A complete listing of our logos and trademarks is available at freespirit.com.

Library of Congress Cataloging-in-Publication Data
Names: Kircher-Morris, Emily, author. | Morin, Amanda, author.
Title: Neurodiversity-affirming schools : transforming practices so all students feel accepted and supported / Emily Kircher Morris and Amanda Morin.
Description: Huntington Beach, CA : Free Spirit Publishing, an imprint of Teacher Created Materials, Inc., [2025] | Includes bibliographical references and index.
Identifiers: LCCN 2024027019 | ISBN 9798885543972 (paperback) | ISBN 9798885543996 (ebook) | ISBN 9798885544016 (epub)
Subjects: LCSH: Children with mental disabilities--Education. | Neurodiversity. | Inclusive education.
Classification: LCC LC4601 .K546 2025 | DDC 371.92--dc23/eng/20241009
LC record available at https://lccn.loc.gov/2024027019

Free Spirit Publishing does not have control over or assume responsibility for author or third-party websites and their content. At the time of this book's publication, all facts and figures cited within are the most current available. All telephone numbers, addresses, and website URLs are accurate and active; all publications, organizations, websites, and other resources exist as described in this book; and all have been verified as of July 2024. If you find an error or believe that a resource listed here is not as described, please contact Free Spirit Publishing.

Permission is granted to reproduce the figures in this book for individual use only. Other photocopying or reproduction of these materials is strictly forbidden. For licensing and permissions information, contact the publisher.

Edited by Cassie Labriola-Sitzman
Cover design by Courtenay Fletcher
Interior design by Michelle Lee Lagerroos

Printed by: **995**
Printed in: **U.S.A.**
PO#: **PO15762**

Free Spirit Publishing
An imprint of Teacher Created Materials
9850 51st Avenue North, Suite 100
Minneapolis, MN 55442
(612) 338-2068
help4kids@freespirit.com
freespirit.com

Dedication

Emily: To Dave, who juggles our podcast production and my endless "big ideas" with unwavering support and love, and to our three neurodivergent children, Grayson, Maggie, and Trevor, who remind me daily why this work matters.

Amanda: To Jon, who believes in me even when I don't believe in myself, and to Benjamin, Jacob, and Megan for teaching me what it's like to be a neurodivergent parent with neurodivergent kids.

Contents

List of Figures x
Foreword by Ellen Braaten, Ph.D. xi

- **INTRODUCTION: Now Is the Time to Build Neurodiversity-Affirming Schools** 1
  - Why We Wrote This Book 2
  - Working Toward the Ideal 4
  - Small Changes, Not Seismic Shifts 5
  - A Word About Terms 6
  - The Double Empathy Problem 9
  - About This Book and How to Use It 11

- **CHAPTER 1: The Neurodiversity-Affirming School** 15
  - A Brief History of the Neurodiversity Movement 17
  - Neurodiversity vs. Neurodivergence 19
  - Who Is Neurodivergent? 20
  - Learner Variability and Neurodiversity-Affirming Schools 26
  - Destigmatizing Neurodivergence 31
  - Neurodiversity-Affirming Language 34
  - What to Remember 37

- **CHAPTER 2: Understanding Your Neurodivergent Learners** 39
  - A Linear Spectrum Is Too Shallow 40
  - Understanding Neurodivergent Labels 44
  - What to Remember 68

- **CHAPTER 3: Dismantling Ableism and Creating a Neurodiversity-Affirming Culture** **69**
  - Conceptual Models of Disability **71**
  - Understanding and Confronting Ableism **72**
  - Where to Start When Creating a Neurodiversity-Affirming Culture **76**
  - Engaging Families **81**
  - Trauma-Informed and Neurodiversity-Affirming Practices **82**
  - Burnout in Neurodivergent Students **85**
  - Collaboration Between Staff and Co-Teaching **87**
  - What to Remember **95**

- **CHAPTER 4: Universal Design for Learning as a Neurodiversity-Affirming Practice** **97**
  - Defining Universal Design for Learning **98**
  - Universal Design's Influence on UDL **98**
  - The Principles of UDL **100**
  - How UDL Supports Neurodivergent Learners **104**
  - UDL in the Classroom **108**
  - Accommodations for All **111**
  - Examining Barriers to Learning Through a UDL Lens **115**
  - Why Use UDL **118**
  - What to Remember **118**

- **CHAPTER 5: Camouflaging, Masking, and Authenticity** **119**
  - Understanding Camouflaging **120**
  - Short- and Long-Term Effects of Camouflaging **127**
  - Authenticity as the Antidote **130**
  - Neurodiversity-Affirming Supports for Unmasking and Authenticity **133**
  - What to Remember **136**

CHAPTER 6: Rethinking Behavior in the Classroom 137
- Moving Beyond Behaviors and Using Co-Regulation 139
- Co-Regulation Before Self-Regulation 152
- Demand Avoidance 156
- Rejection Sensitivity 161
- What to Remember 164

CHAPTER 7: Building Emotionally Competent Classrooms 165
- From Self to Students: The Impact of Teacher Emotional Regulation 166
- Using the CASEL 5 Framework to Examine Your and Students' Skills 167
- Understanding Family Emotions and Concerns 182
- The Four Es Framework 182
- What to Remember 187

CHAPTER 8: Meeting Sensory Needs 189
- Building Awareness of Sensory Integration Differences 190
- Emotional Regulation and Somatic Awareness 200
- Supporting Sensory Needs in Schools 201
- Seeing Stimming as Purposeful 206
- "Whole-Body Listening" Is Not Neurodiversity-Affirming 208
- What to Remember 209

CHAPTER 9: Neurodiversity-Affirming Communication 211
- What Is Neurodiversity-Affirming Communication? 212
- Setting the Stage for Neurodiversity-Affirming Communication 214
- Neurodivergent Communication Styles 221
- Fostering Peer Support and Understanding 225
- Social Acuity Over Social Skills 226
- What to Remember 228

CHAPTER 10: Strengths-Based Instruction ... 229
  What Is Strengths-Based Instruction? ... 230
  Neurology Justifies Strengths-Based Supports ... 230
  Starting with Strengths ... 231
  Mastery-Based Learning ... 242
  Novelty ... 243
  What to Remember ... 252

CHAPTER 11: IEPs, 504 Plans, and Other Personalized Learning Plans ... 253
  About Individualized Education Programs (IEPs) ... 254
  About 504 Plans ... 257
  Do Neurodivergent Students Need IEPs and 504 Plans? ... 259
  What to Look For in an IEP or 504 Plan ... 259
  Rethinking Least Restrictive Environment ... 263
  Rethinking IEP Goals to Be Neurodiversity-Affirming ... 266
  Personalized Student Learning Plans ... 269
  Creating Neurodiversity-Affirming Learning Plans ... 272
  Engaging Students in Creating Learning Plans ... 277
  What to Remember ... 278

CHAPTER 12: Mental Health Needs ... 279
  The Connection Between Neurodivergence and Mental Health ... 280
  Sorting Out Emotions from Diagnoses ... 281
  Misdiagnosis of Neurodivergence and Psychological Conditions ... 284
  Considerations for Counseling Interventions ... 285
  Suicidal Ideation and Nonsuicidal Self-Injury Behavior ... 289
  Assessing Risks and Creating Neurodiversity-Affirming Safety Plans ... 293
  What to Remember ... 295

CONCLUSION: Building the Future Together ... 297

Acknowledgments ... 301
References ... 303
Index ... 321
About the Authors ... 332

List of Figures

Figure 1.1 Frequency of Google Searches for *Neurodiversity*, 2011–2022 .... **17**
Figure 1.2 Neurodivergent Diagnoses vs. Psychological Diagnoses **22**
Figure 1.3 What Is Your Learner Variability? **29**
Figure 2.1 Autism as a Linear Spectrum **40**
Figure 2.2 Autism as a Web **41**
Figure 2.3 ADHD as a Web **42**
Figure 3.1 Ableist vs. Non-Ableist Language **73**
Figure 4.1 The Seven Principles of Universal Design **99**
Figure 4.2 Typical Classrooms vs. UDL Classrooms **109**
Figure 6.1 Interpreting Behavior as Communication **141**
Figure 6.2 The Cycle of Co-Regulation **153**
Figure 6.3 Examples of Using Declarative Language **155**
Figure 7.1 A Look at CASEL's Core Competencies **168**
Figure 7.2 Reaction vs. Response **171**
Figure 7.3 Uncovering the Hidden Curriculum **173**
Figure 8.1 Impact of Unmet Sensory Integration Needs **191**
Figure 8.2 Sensory Systems and Examples of Processing Differences **192**
Figure 8.3 Accommodations and Tools for Sensory Needs **203**
Figure 11.1 A Look at SMART IEP Goals **262**
Figure 11.2 Typical vs. Neurodiversity-Affirming IEP Language **267**
Figure 11.3 Comparing Typical Goals to Neurodiversity-Affirming Ones **269**
Figure 11.4 Deficit-Based vs. Strengths-Based Perspective for Common **275**
Neurodivergent Traits
Figure 12.1 Overlapping Neurodivergence and Mental Health Needs **282**

Foreword

by Ellen Braaten, Ph.D.

Teaching students is one of the most challenging and important jobs in our world today. And it's a profession that, I would argue, has become more complex and less supported over the decades I have been involved in the field of education. Teachers are expected to be nurturers and disciplinarians, counselors and role models. They navigate systemic issues, complex bureaucracies, and diverse needs—all while striving to give each student the supports they need to thrive. Even so, some students are left out and overlooked, including neurodivergent kids.

Meanwhile, people are discovering the importance of neurodiversity in schools, work, and life. Folks are beginning to see how neurodivergent people bring perspectives and ways of thinking that can lead to new ways of solving problems. And educators are recognizing how neurodivergent students can enhance learning in the classroom, as all students benefit when they have opportunities to learn from each other's skills and experiences.

Imagine a world where educational systems are equitable and where each student, including those who are neurodivergent, has access to the resources and supports they need to thrive. Imagine a resource for educators that offers a scientifically sound foundation for understanding why they should create this type of system and how to do it. This guide would explain how to structure classrooms that embrace students' unique learning styles. It would provide information to help teachers leverage the strengths and understand the needs of a neurodiverse student population. It would be written in an empathetic, collaborative style, understanding the ever-increasing pressures on educators and acknowledging how change is often difficult within educational systems. And it would be clear, engaging, and compassionate—educating and inspiring at the same time.

In *Neurodiversity-Affirming Schools,* Emily Kircher-Morris and Amanda Morin have delivered that book. With decades of professional expertise and personal experience,

Emily and Amanda translate current research on neurodiversity and share practical advice and concrete ideas for how to create neurodiversity-affirming schools where all students can thrive.

Meeting the needs of an entire student body is not an easy task, particularly in a post-pandemic world where students are feeling more anxious, less academically prepared, and less motivated than ever. Many teachers I speak to complain of burnout—due to polarized politics, less autonomy in the classroom, and what seems like a more complex student body, among other reasons. Students, teachers, and parents frequently say they do not feel heard, respected, or valued. Rethinking the one-size-fits-all approach to education in the way this book describes could go a long way in addressing causes of teacher burnout while simultaneously providing students, particularly neurodivergent learners, with the respect they so greatly deserve.

In this paradigm-shifting book, readers will discover how each student has a unique way of processing information and how to remove hurdles in the learning process and accommodate the diverse needs of neurodivergent students. The book offers ideas for how to develop personalized learning plans and strategies, as well as how to foster positive peer interactions. It shows how embracing neurodiversity in the classroom and creating more equitable and inclusive learning environments helps all students thrive.

The book begins by providing a history of the neurodiversity movement, explains how to best understand and talk about neurodivergent learners, and describes how to design schools and systems that are neurodiversity-affirming. Later chapters delve into more specific topics—from neurodiversity-affirming learning plans to neurodivergent communication styles to tips for encouraging student authenticity. Case examples, along with the authors' stories of their own journeys with neurodivergence, help readers make connections to their own situations. Questions to ponder and key takeaways to remember challenge readers' assumptions and encourage critical thinking. This important book offers a comprehensive way of not only understanding neurodiversity in the classroom, but also *thriving* as an educator in an ever-evolving and complex world and navigating the work of creating neurodiversity-affirming schools with wisdom, humility, empathy, and mastery.

This book is a gift to us all.

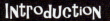

Now Is the Time to Build Neurodiversity-Affirming Schools

The needs of the students in classrooms today are very different from the needs of students even just a decade ago (NCES 2022). In a post-COVID world, students are facing increasing rates of anxiety, and schools are seeing increased absenteeism and the effects of COVID learning loss. As one teacher recently said to Amanda: "At the beginning of the pandemic, teachers were heroes. Now we're zeroes."

Everything from the charged political climate to students with higher needs has increased the pressure teachers feel every day. You may even be feeling like the teacher who said, "I don't know what to do anymore. The twenty-five students in my classroom feel like fifty students. I'm trying to help all of them, but I'm tired, I'm numb, and I don't have the professional development to do it better. I don't feel effective anymore."

It sounds dire, but it's also a moment to reconsider how to construct educational systems so that the burden of change doesn't fall solely on teachers. How *do* you go from feeling like a zero to a hero? What can you do to better understand the needs of all those students, so you can help them *and* feel effective? How can school districts prioritize this work and support your professional development?

It's time to rethink the one-size-fits-all approach to education and embrace the work of creating equitable education systems where each person has access to the resources and supports they need to thrive. It's important work, especially at a time when society is attuned to everyone feeling heard, valued, and respected, including—and maybe especially—educators. Equity challenges the notion of one-size-fits-all solutions and acknowledges that what works for one learner may not work for another—and that's okay. Transforming schools to be neurodiversity-affirming is part of this work. Here's why it matters now:

- Neurodiversity-affirming practices recognize that individuals have different needs and provide resources and support tailored to those needs. For your neurodivergent learners, this might mean specialized learning tools, flexible work environments, and teachers who have a better understanding of how their students interact with the world.
- Being neurodiversity-affirming means creating environments that are supportive of all neurotypes within a school. This is more equitable than a one-size-fits-all approach because it doesn't force neurodivergent students—or teachers—to conform to standards and practices that do not suit their needs. Instead, it adapts environments to be more welcoming and accessible to all.
- Neurodiversity-affirming practices focus on leveraging the unique strengths and talents of each person. This equitable approach doesn't just aim for equal participation but seeks to empower everyone in a school community to excel in their areas of strength.

By affirming neurodiversity, you move toward reducing stigma and discrimination against those with neurological differences. When your job is to create an environment where everybody feels a sense of belonging, there's no shame in asking for the training, knowledge, and information you need to create it. A neurodiversity-affirming school *demands* that everyone in the school develop a deeper understanding and acceptance of neurological differences—from school district officials, to administrators, to teachers and students. And it ensures that all learners receive appropriate differentiation, not just to support them but also to support you, the educator, and our global community.

We can't talk about creating equitable education systems for neurodivergent students without also acknowledging how discussions about equity and equality are closely tied to topics like race, ethnicity, socioeconomic differences, sexual orientation, and gender identity—to name a few. The intersection of these identities with neurodiversity is an important aspect to consider, and one we don't want to sweep under the rug. We recognize that someone's financial resources are closely tied to their ability to access an evaluation for a neurodivergent diagnosis and that a person's race or culture may influence how safe they feel to exhibit characteristics of their neurodivergence. The research shows that neurodivergent people are more likely to be nonconforming in their sexual orientation and gender identity, and that this can be weaponized against them (Dewinter, De Graaf, and Begeer 2017; Weir, Allison, and Baron-Cohen 2021; Warrier et al. 2020; Walsh et al. 2018). As you embark on the work of creating neurodiversity-affirming schools, we encourage you to always take a holistic view of each student when adopting new practices and consider how their unique experiences and intersecting identities may be influencing them.

Why We Wrote This Book

We met online, through shared professional learning communities. Emily is the host of *The Neurodiversity Podcast*, and at the time we met, Amanda was director of thought leadership at Understood.org. As we shared more of our own stories in these communities, we realized how much we had in common in our personal experiences as neurodivergent people, parents, and educators. When the pandemic hit, as we each worked on authoring separate books, we had the opportunity to support each other through the isolation of social distancing, stay-at-home orders, and writing a book (which can be a rather solitary activity).

As Amanda appeared frequently on *The Neurodiversity Podcast*, we realized that we had something to say about how schools and society could better support learner variability. As neurodivergent former students ourselves, we recognized the ways we wished we'd been supported by teachers. As parents to neurodivergent children and teens, we recognized the ways we hoped our own children would be supported in school. And we came to realize that our current system isn't there yet.

Our opinions about education were too verbose to be articulated with fidelity within the constraints of the platform-formerly-known-as-Twitter. Our online community grew as more parents and educators began to understand how neurodiversity could be better supported in schools. Then one day, Emily called Amanda while waiting for a plane in the St. Louis airport—Amanda had just left her position at Understood.org and had moved toward consulting in the neurodiversity space—and the idea for this book was born.

We come from different backgrounds in education. Amanda started in early intervention special education, and Emily worked in the gifted education classroom and as a school counselor. Our perspectives complement each other, and our experiences beyond the classroom as a special education advocate and a clinical mental health counselor, respectively, add another dimension to our understanding of how schools can better serve neurodivergent learners.

The resources and tools that are currently available aren't describing the type of paradigm shift we feel is necessary to move the needle toward neurodiversity-affirming practices that will allow the neurodivergent students in our schools to thrive and belong. With this book, we hope to help move that needle.

Working Toward the Ideal

People often wonder why "all of a sudden" there are so many more neurodivergent people. The truth is that they've always been here. The perception of a growing population of people with labels like autism, ADHD, or dyslexia is due to a few factors:

- The diagnostic processes for and understanding of neurodivergent diagnoses have improved. There is earlier identification of neurodivergence, and assessments are catching those who may have gone unidentified in the past.

- The stigma surrounding neurodivergent diagnoses is (very) gradually waning. Many people are no longer afraid to disclose their diagnoses and are talking about them publicly, bringing awareness of neurodivergence to expanding circles of influence, whether that is their family and friends or a broader audience through social media or other avenues.

- The "first wave" of neurodivergent children who were diagnosed in the 1990s and 2000s are reaching adulthood and leading the charge on the frontlines of the neurodiversity movement (Leadbitter et al. 2021; Kapp 2020). They are the parents, teachers, researchers, and advocates who have the voice and power to get people to listen. And behind them are the younger neurodivergent Gen Zs and Gen Alphas who have grown up with a greater understanding of themselves and an expectation of acceptance.

While, overall, acceptance and understanding of neurodivergence is growing, some environments are more progressive than others when it comes to neurodiversity-affirming practices. The tech industry, for example, leads the way with neurodiversity hiring initiatives and an understanding of the strengths of folks who learn and think differently. The education system, however, is lagging. Schools often value conformity. Curriculums are created to teach to the middle. And neurodivergent students fall through the cracks, especially students who don't qualify for special education services. They have "spiky" cognitive and affective profiles, with strengths and struggles that are, at times, difficult to understand.

Schools often have a hard time adapting to the needs of neurodivergent learners. They tend to view difficulty with staying organized or "reading between the lines" as a moral failing. "Have you tried using color-coded folders?" is code for "You are lazy." "How did you not understand what I meant?" often means "You are self-centered." When these difficulties are viewed through the context of neurodiversity, however, it is easier to understand that the way a person's brain is wired drastically impacts how they operate in the world. Part of being neurodiversity-affirming means understanding that it is much more effective to work *with* a person's differences than it is to try to change the way their brain works.

The ideal of a neurodiversity-affirming school (and world) is one that we all can work toward. We can work to remove the behavior management practices that teach neurodivergent learners to mask and camouflage their traits. We can understand that communication is a two-way street and that those with nonnormative styles of communication aren't the only ones who should modify the way they communicate. We can work with students' strengths and use them as a starting point for support, rather than isolating students and focusing solely on their areas of difficulty. By doing these things, we can empower neurodivergent students and help them grow into independent adults who recognize and understand their strengths and struggles and who live authentic, contented lives.

Small Changes, Not Seismic Shifts

The push toward neurodiversity-affirming schools is relatively new and has been a ground-up movement (Carey, Block, and Scotch 2019; Armstrong 2012; Armstrong 2017; den Houting 2019; Kapp et al. 2019; Shaw et al. 2022). Parents are advocating for accommodations for their neurodivergent children. Neurodivergent teachers are using self-disclosure as a tool to connect with students and bring about change in their schools. And a greater understanding of Universal Design for Learning provides a framework for thinking about different ways to support learners.

But change happens gradually, and you might face resistance from systems that are not used to big change or mindset shifts. It is important to know that the path toward neurodiversity-affirming schools is not all-or-nothing. Small changes in your classroom practices or short conversations with your colleagues lay the groundwork for bigger ones.

You may feel frustration as you pursue these small changes. We know we have—patience in these two neurodivergent people is in short supply. (From a strengths-based perspective, we would reframe this as an eagerness for progress.) But keep going. Your students will notice, their parents will trust you, and the system will begin to accommodate differences.

A Word About Terms

Throughout this book, we talk a lot about the language of the neurodiversity movement and the terms neurodivergent individuals use and prefer. However, we want to make a few notes about language up front, particularly around the use of the words *different*, *differences*, and *neuro-normative*.

The language surrounding neurodiversity is complex and evolving, and preferences can vary widely among individuals. The words *different* and *differences* can be perceived and used in varying ways by neurodivergent individuals. Some use these words to describe feeling on the periphery or left out, and some use them as a way to describe their neurodivergent traits.

There are strong opinions about whether these words are euphemistic terms for *disorder* or *disability* or are used for neurodivergent traits that are viewed as inherently problematic or less desirable. Using *differences* can be seen as unnecessarily highlighting distinctions between neurodivergent and neuro-normative traits, fostering a sense of otherness or separation. Adding to this sense of otherness is the common use of the word *neurotypical* to describe people and traits that aren't neurodivergent. Because *neurotypical* implies that there's a way of being that is usual or ordinary, we've chosen to use the word *neuro-normative* throughout this book instead. It advances the idea that there are standards or societal "norms" that are widely thought to be the way people should think or act but challenges the concept that those norms should be adhered to by a "typical" person.

Some neurodivergent individuals prefer to use the words *different* and *differences* to describe themselves, instead of using terms like *neurodivergent*, *neurodiverse*, or even specific diagnostic labels. For some, embracing *differences* is a form of personal empowerment, and it gives them a way to positively own their unique traits and experiences and acknowledge them as integral parts of their identity.

We use the words *different* and *differences* in this book because they avoid pathologizing and instead acknowledge that we all have variations of experiences. They're terms we use neutrally to describe the unique cognitive and perceptual experiences of all individuals. We think that respecting individual preferences around terms and language is crucial, and we believe that different is simply different, not less. The box below shares other neurodivergent terminology we use in this book.

Neurodivergent Terminology

allistic: Often used by members of the #ActuallyAutistic community, *allistic* (sometimes used interchangeably with *nypical*) refers to all nonautistic people, including both those considered to be neuro-normative and neurodivergent people who aren't autistic.

affirm: To affirm something means to validate it or to show a belief in or dedication to it. An affirming environment is one that accepts an individual as they are and works to help them operate within the world as their authentic self, rather than trying to change them to fit into certain situations or environments. An affirming relationship allows a person to express themself in a way that feels comfortable to them.

AuDHD: *AuDHD* (or *AuDHDer*) is a term used to describe people who are both autistic and diagnosed with ADHD. Since it's estimated that anywhere from 30 to 80 percent of autistic people also have symptoms of ADHD, and up to 50 percent of people with ADHD may also have symptoms of autism, this overlap in terminology makes sense (Kernbach et al. 2018).

identity-first language: Many neurodivergent people have reclaimed the label of their neurodivergence, asking to be called an autistic person, a dyslexic student, or an ADHDer to acknowledge how their neurodivergence is a part of who they are and that, without it, they would no longer be themselves. Using identity-first language embraces a person's neurodivergence. Though we default to using identify-first language in this book, we know that some neurodivergent individuals prefer person-first language instead. It's important to always respect individual preferences, and we implore you to default to following your students' lead in how they speak about themselves.

neurodiverse: All of humanity is neurodiverse; the concept of neurodiversity encompasses the varied ways the human brain can be wired. It recognizes that there are many ways for a brain to function and that variation does not mean a person is mentally ill or broken. Rather, it means that their brain operates in a way that is different from the majority. No single person is neurodiverse; only a group of people can be neurodiverse.

neurodivergent: Sometimes abbreviated as ND, *neurodivergent* is used to describe a person who experiences one or more variations of functioning in their brain, such as (but not limited to) autism, ADHD, dyslexia, or Tourette syndrome.

neuro-spicy: This portmanteau of *neuro* (as in neurodivergent) + *spicy* (as in strong and spirited) has taken off on social media as a self-descriptor for people who consider themselves neurodivergent. It's used both as a rejection of the perceived deficit of being identified as neurodivergent and as a way for people who identify as ND but don't have an official diagnosis to share their allegiance.

social model of disability: The social model of disability (see page 71) asks people to reconsider how they understand disability and the way the environment interacts with a person's needs. It posits that a person isn't disabled until society fails to make accommodations. *(Note: The social model of disability is useful in the context of a conversation about neurodiversity; however, like anything, it is an imperfect model to apply to all situations.)*

The Double Empathy Problem

Before you can set out to create neurodiversity-affirming schools, it is important to understand the double empathy problem, as it offers a critical lens through which to understand the communication challenges faced by neurodivergent individuals. Coined by Dr. Damian Milton, the double empathy problem suggests that misunderstanding between neuro-normative and neurodivergent individuals goes both ways (2012). In essence, just as neurodivergent individuals may struggle to fully understand and connect with the neuro-normative world, neuro-normative individuals also face challenges in understanding and connecting with the neurodivergent world.

The pressure to adapt, however, has disproportionately fallen on the shoulders of neurodivergent individuals. From early education to workplace environments, neurodivergent people are often expected to conform to neuro-norms and standards, sometimes at great personal cost. This pressure to fit in can lead to feelings of isolation, heightened stress, and even the suppression of one's genuine self (Radulski 2022; Evans, Krumrei-Mancuso, and Rouse 2023; Fotheringham et al. 2023; Chapman et al. 2022). By perpetuating these conformist expectations, society has inadvertently sent a message that neuro-normative ways of being and communicating are the standard, thereby marginalizing and devaluing neurodivergent experiences. Recognizing the double empathy problem is a step toward rectifying this imbalance and ensuring that the responsibility of understanding and adapting is shared more equitably among individuals, regardless of their neurological makeup.

In the classroom, the double empathy problem can manifest in numerous ways. A teacher might misinterpret a neurodivergent student's behavior as noncompliant or disruptive when, in reality, it's a communication method or coping mechanism. Conversely, a neurodivergent student might find typical classroom instructions confusing or vague, not because of a lack of understanding on their part but because the instructions aren't attuned to their way of processing information.

Addressing the double empathy problem requires a reevaluation of how you approach classroom communication. Rather than seeing communication differences as deficiencies, educators and students alike need to recognize them as just that—differences. This shift in perspective opens opportunities for mutual learning. Educators might explore alternative ways of presenting information, while neurodivergent students might share insights into how they process and understand the world, offering their peers and teachers a fresh perspective.

The classroom serves as a microcosm of the broader society, and what students learn there shapes their perspectives for a lifetime. In addition to educators understanding the double empathy problem, teaching neuro-normative students about it, as well as about neurodivergent communication styles, is important. It's not just a matter of academic enrichment; it's foundational to building inclusive communities both within and outside school walls.

By understanding the double empathy problem, neuro-normative students gain insight into the mutual misunderstandings that occur between them and their neurodivergent peers. It dispels the myth that communication challenges are solely a neurodivergent issue, and instead fosters the realization that true understanding is a shared responsibility. With this knowledge, neuro-normative students are more likely to approach interactions with neurodivergent peers with patience, openness, and a genuine desire to connect.

Furthermore, educating students about neurodivergent communication styles is crucial for dismantling preconceived notions and biases about there being "right" and "wrong" ways to communicate. When neuro-normative students recognize that there are many valid ways to communicate and process information, they're less likely to misinterpret or dismiss behaviors that don't align with their own ways of being.

This education can also have a broader societal impact. As neuro-normative students grow and move into various roles in society—whether as employers, colleagues, friends, or community leaders—their understanding of neurodivergence will inform their actions, decisions, and attitudes. They can become advocates for inclusivity, recognizing the value of diverse minds and pushing against systems that inadvertently sideline people.

In creating neurodiversity-affirming schools, it's essential to integrate education on the double empathy problem and neurodivergent communication styles. By doing so, we can equip the next generation with the tools and perspectives they need to build more understanding and inclusive societies. It's an investment in a future where neurodiversity isn't just acknowledged but genuinely understood as part of our collective human experience.

About This Book and How to Use It

This book includes ideas for philosophical shifts and practical ways to implement them. Chapters 1 through 4 provide a framework to better understand what a neurodiversity-affirming school is, while the remaining chapters address various topics that may be of unique importance based on the students you serve. You may prefer to read the book in its entirety, or you may jump right in with the chapters that are most relevant to you. Here's a quick look at what's included in each.

Chapter 1: The Neurodiversity-Affirming School provides a brief history of the neurodiversity movement and an exploration of what it means to be neurodivergent. It also describes some of the primary methods teachers can use to destigmatize neurodivergence in schools.

Chapter 2: Understanding Your Neurodivergent Learners answers the questions of what neurodiversity is and who is neurodivergent. In addition to discussing who neurodivergent students are, this chapter looks at how being neurodivergent can influence a student's school experience. Differences between medical diagnosis and educational identification of neurodivergent labels are also explained.

Chapter 3: Dismantling Ableism and Creating a Neurodiversity-Affirming Culture examines the idea of belonging within the concept of neurodiversity-affirming schools, the impact of ableism, and strategies to collaborate with your colleagues to create neurodiversity-affirming environments. It also includes the "Neurodivergent Learners' Bill of Rights" and accompanying "Neurodiversity-Affirming Teachers' Compact of Shared Beliefs."

Chapter 4: Universal Design for Learning as a Neurodiversity-Affirming Practice conceptualizes Universal Design for Learning (UDL) as a practice that can be leveraged to support neurodivergent learners. It provides examples of what neurodiversity-affirming practices grounded in UDL look like and troubleshoots barriers that might stand in the way when attempting to implement these practices.

Chapter 5: Camouflaging, Masking, and Authenticity considers the various ways students hide their neurodivergent traits, often to the detriment of their mental health. It provides ideas for how to create an environment that provides safety in unmasking and authenticity for all learners.

Chapter 6: Rethinking Behavior in the Classroom prompts critical consideration of what behavioral and disciplinary systems are in place in your classroom and how they impact neurodivergent learners. It reframes what has historically been considered "behavioral problems" through the lens of neurodivergence and suggests alternative ways to support learners.

Chapter 7: Building Emotionally Competent Classrooms looks at emotional regulation from the perspective of how teachers influence the emotional regulation of their students and provides guidance for developing expectations and strategies for emotionally competent classrooms.

Chapter 8: Meeting Sensory Needs analyzes the neurologically driven sensory differences experienced by neurodivergent learners and their impact on communication, emotional regulation, and learning. It provides tools and ideas to create a sensory-friendly classroom.

Chapter 9: Neurodiversity-Affirming Communication reassesses the methods and styles of communication that are expected in the classroom and identifies ways that neurodivergent communication may differ. It recognizes that neurodivergent communication may vary from the "norm" but isn't inherently wrong, and it provides ideas to help facilitate communication between neurodivergent students and those who communicate in more neuro-normative ways.

Chapter 10: Strengths-Based Instruction offers ideas to move away from focusing on deficits and toward leveraging strengths to support neurodivergent learners. It applies ideas beyond interest-based learning to understand the varied ways that the strengths of neurodivergent learners are an asset in the classroom.

Chapter 11: IEPs, 504 Plans, and Other Personalized Learning Plans discusses whether every neurodivergent student needs a formal learning plan to work toward their goals. It provides guidance on how to develop neurodiversity-affirming, rather than deficit-focused, goals for these types of plans.

Chapter 12: Mental Health Needs looks at the overlap between neurodivergence and mental health/psychological diagnoses, recognizing that unsupported neurodivergence often contributes to mental health concerns. It also includes a brief framework for counseling and clinical considerations when supporting neurodivergent students.

Each chapter begins with three **Points to Ponder**—guiding questions designed to encourage you to think deeply about the topics the chapter covers. The questions are open-ended and thought-provoking and are intended to prompt your learning. You may not find the exact answer to each question in the chapter, and that's the point—they're meant to challenge assumptions, provoke analysis, and stimulate critical thinking on your part. **What to Remember** sections close each chapter, sharing three key takeaways. We challenge you to reflect on these big ideas and how you might apply your learning in your school or classroom.

Throughout the book, you'll also find various recurring features. These callouts provide further insight and nuance on various topics.

Double Empathy Problem sections help you understand the miscommunications that can happen in your classroom by giving you a look inside the perspectives of a neurodivergent student and their neuro-normative peers on various situations. By providing both perspectives, these callouts show how the burden of change shouldn't fall solely on the shoulders of neurodivergent kids. Possible follow-up ideas provide guidance for how the situation may play out in a neurodiversity-affirming environment.

Unpacking Neurodivergence sections share our perspectives on evolving conversations in the neurodiversity movement. Leaning into our backgrounds as podcasters, these callouts are modeled as conversations, and they provide an example of how you can have productive discussions about neurodivergence with others in your school community. If you enjoy these callouts, be sure to check out the *Creating Neurodiversity-Affirming Schools Podcast* we host.

Intersecting Identities callouts address the impact of intersecting identities on neurodivergent learners, as well as the unique barriers they may face. And **student and classroom vignettes** share real-world examples of neurodivergence and neurodiversity-affirming practices in action.

Finding a Like-Minded Community

There is strength in numbers, and having other advocates to connect, brainstorm, and problem-solve with is crucial in moving schools toward becoming neurodiversity-affirming spaces. After all, that's how this book was born. If you are looking for opportunities to find other change-makers, the online space offers many. *The Neurodiversity Podcast* has over 250 episodes, most of which directly provide ideas and tools for educators to support their learners.

We also recorded a webinar together on the "Neurodiversity-Affirming Teachers' Compact of Shared Beliefs" (see chapter 3), and you are invited to watch us discuss how we developed this list of ideas. Additionally, if you would like the opportunity to connect directly with other neurodiversity-affirming educators, you are invited to the Neurodiversity University Educator Hub. You can find these resources and more at neurodiversityaffirmingschools.com.

To connect with other neurodiversity-affirming advocates in your school, you may wish to use the book as part of a professional learning community. The Points to Ponder and What to Remember sections in each chapter can support your group's reading and guide your conversations.

As you progress through this book, you may find yourself experiencing slight discomfort with some of the ideas that challenge the status quo. When this happens, we encourage you to take the advice you likely give students every day: Lean into the discomfort. As you know, discomfort is often a productive struggle, and it's where some of the best growth can happen. We feel confident that you'll recognize how shifting your current practices in the ways we suggest can be life-changing for the neurodivergent learners in your classroom—and for you as well.

—Emily and Amanda

Chapter 1

The Neurodiversity-Affirming School

 Points to Ponder

- What impact does a neurodiversity-affirming school have on neurodivergent students?
- Why do some people prefer identity-first language over person-first language?
- How can you begin to destigmatize neurodivergence in your community?

What words would you use to describe the way your students feel in your classroom? What words would your students use? Do the two align?

We all hope students describe their classrooms as places where they feel calm, accepted, included, seen, and understood. We want students to feel not just comfortable but confident in being their authentic selves, seeking support, and knowing they'll be treated with respect. But getting there requires creating a culture in classrooms and schools where students feel safe to take both academic and social risks.

While some students do feel safe to take risks, there are groups of students who don't, in large part because they do not experience the privilege of authenticity. Students who come from marginalized backgrounds are frequently asked to bend or hide their identities to fit within a school model that wasn't created with their needs in mind. Many students need to code switch between the language they use with their friends and family and the more formal language of academia. And neurodivergent students may mask and camouflage their differences to engage in "expected" behaviors.

Educators have made strides toward creating more inclusive environments for students from diverse backgrounds and continue to do this work today. But we are just beginning to gain an understanding of neurodivergent students and how we can structure our schools to support them.

This chapter shares a brief history of the neurodiversity movement, names which conditions fall under the definition of neurodivergent in this book, and explores ways students might be identified (as well as barriers to identification). It also places learner variability in the context of neurodiversity and shares strategies for destigmatizing neurodivergence and using neurodiversity-affirming language in your school community.

A Brief History of the Neurodiversity Movement

The term *neurodiversity* was first used in the 1990s and was originally attributed to sociologist Judith Singer. Recent discussion and research instead show that the term was collectively developed in the mid-1990s by autistic members of an email list known as Independent Living (Botha et al. 2024). However, most people remained unfamiliar with the term until the mid-2010s, when the neurodiversity movement really began to take off. Google Trends for *neurodiversity* since March 2011 (figure 1.1) shows a relatively steady line until 2019, when the frequency of searches begins to grow rapidly.

While the concept of neurodiversity encompasses a variety of diagnoses, it was initially embraced in the autism community. In 1994, the American Psychological Association added the diagnosis of Asperger's to the fourth edition of the *Diagnostic and Statistical Manual of Mental Disorders* (*DSM-IV*). This new categorization provided an opportunity for more children who previously may have received no diagnosis to be identified and receive support. Practitioners were trained in understanding Asperger's, and better tools were developed to help identify it. Concerns about the increasing rates of diagnosis were wrongly attributed to environmental influences, when really improved awareness and better diagnostic processes were behind the increase in numbers.

In 2013, the fifth edition of the *DSM* (*DSM-5*) was released, and Asperger's was absorbed under the diagnosis of autism spectrum disorder. (In the UK, the diagnosis is called autism spectrum condition, a much more affirming term in our view.) The children who were initially identified in the late 1990s and early 2000s were reaching adulthood and became the first strong advocates asking for a shift in the way they were treated and viewed. Since, prior to the *DSM-IV*'s addition of Asperger's, most people diagnosed with autism were nonspeaking and had high support needs in many areas, this "Aspie" generation was the first to really understand their own needs and begin advocating for the autism community at large. They used the term *neurodiversity* to help others understand that just because autistic people operate in the world in a way that is deemed different, this doesn't mean their way of being is wrong.

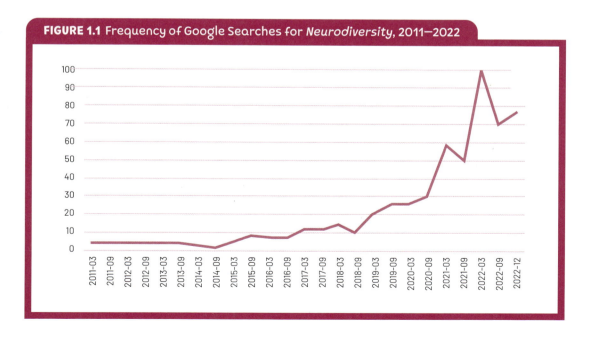

FIGURE 1.1 Frequency of Google Searches for *Neurodiversity*, 2011–2022

The term was then gradually adopted by other groups. People diagnosed with ADHD, dyslexia, dysgraphia, Tourette syndrome, OCD, and more, began to embrace the concept of neurodiversity. These folks began shedding labels of "dumb," "lazy," "weak-willed," or "crazy" and claiming the label of "neurodivergent." This recognition—that one's brain may be wired to experience the world in a unique way—has liberated so many from the belief that there is something wrong with them. They began healing from the trauma of growing up in a world where they were not only misunderstood but often punished for being different.

The COVID-19 pandemic also had a hand in accelerating the neurodiversity movement. The complete disruption of daily life that it caused led many people to question the status quo. Some parents watched their children attempt to complete online school and noticed previously unobserved signs of inattention or difficulty with reading, math, or another subject. Some neurodivergent adults, suddenly able to work from home, realized how much effort they'd expended camouflaging their differences in the workplace and how much their overall wellness improved once they were able to let down their masks and complete their work in a comfortable environment that accommodated their sensory needs. Students who were extremely stressed and dysregulated in the general classroom setting showed improvements in their academic performance when they weren't forced to navigate the social world of peers.

People began asking questions and seeking out information about neurodiversity, and for the first time, the general public began to listen. Neurodiversity became a mainstream topic, through social media, blogs, podcasts, and the media. Notable individuals, from actors to tech gurus to politicians, began identifying themselves as neurodivergent and sharing these labels with their followers and fans. When the time came to return to school and work, not only did people feel empowered to self-advocate for their needs in a way they hadn't before but some schools and workplaces were also beginning to understand how to respond to those needs. Today, the voices of neurodivergent people seem to finally be heard.

The neurodiversity movement is truly a political movement. It is a disability rights movement. It is the recognition that just because someone doesn't fit the definition of "typical," this doesn't mean that they are broken and in need of fixing. The leading edge of the neurodiversity movement focuses on the importance of changing the environment and culture that has held back neurodivergent people for too long.

While there is no specific organization that is responsible for the neurodiversity movement, we have identified are some common goals that unite advocates. These include the following:

- destigmatizing the process of seeking and receiving a diagnosis
- building awareness in the general public about the needs of neurodivergent people
- depathologizing characteristics of neurodiversity and viewing them outside the context of the medical model
- improving services and support for neurodivergent people in schools, workplaces, and the community
- creating a sense of community and belonging for neurodivergent people

Neurodiversity vs. Neurodivergence

As people have begun to seek out more information and talk about neurodiversity in mainstream conversations, it's become part of the business world too. Companies like Microsoft, JPMorgan Chase, Goldman Sachs, and Dell Technologies have all launched work initiatives and programs designed to recruit neurodiverse talent and thinkers. LinkedIn now has a skill badge of "Dyslexic Thinker." While these programs promote awareness of the neurodiversity movement, some advocates are concerned they make it easy to lose the distinction between neurodiversity and neurodivergence, and even when to use the words.

The word *neurodiversity* does not mean neurological disability. It's akin to the idea of biodiversity, which means that there's a variety and variability of life forms in the world and that some thrive in certain environments while others thrive in different ones. Looking at it from this perspective, all spaces that contain people—including schools—are neurodiverse because all people have nervous systems with degrees of variation of needs and abilities.

The term *neurodivergence* refers to the variation in the human brain regarding socialization preferences, learning, attention, mood, and other mental skills. When the needs of someone's nervous system differ from what we consider to be "typical," that can make it more difficult for them to navigate those spaces than the general public would expect.

Who Is Neurodivergent?

Some neurodivergent individuals may exhibit differences that are distinct from societal standards of "normal." These differences have come to be embraced by many as natural variation in human cognition. However, the concept and classification of neurodivergence can be controversial, particularly concerning which diagnoses fall under this umbrella.

Because the terms *neurodiversity* and *neurodivergence* are relatively new to many people, the language surrounding them and what they mean has evolved quickly over the last decade and continues to evolve (see page 7 for a list of terms we use). People get stuck in circular conversations about what neurodiversity is, what diagnoses or labels should be included under the umbrella of neurodivergence, and where the line is between neurodivergent (neurodevelopmental) and mental health (psychological) diagnoses—if there is one.

When we think about neurodiversity as a disability rights issue, the difficulty in identifying which diagnoses are officially neurodivergent fades into the background. Different people have different needs, and when we work to create supportive environments that meet those needs, the changes benefit everybody. How many nondisabled people have used a ramp instead of a set of stairs? The ramp was created for wheelchair-users and others with impaired mobility as a tool to improve accessibility. Yet by having it available, everyone benefits. The neurodiversity movement recognizes the value of all people, regardless of their ability or "contribution" to society.

The idea of not needing diagnoses and labels to get students the support they need in school (or to get anyone the support they need in general) is our vision for a future utopian world. In the meantime, we recognize that discussions about neurodivergent labels in school are useful, because the education world is full of labels. Having certain diagnoses or identifications entitles a student to a variety of supports, from individualized education programs (IEPs) to Section 504 plans to gifted education services.

For educators, understanding neurodivergence, especially in terms of neurodevelopmental diagnoses, is highly relevant. By recognizing neurodivergence as a variation of "normal," rather than a pathology, you can create learning environments where all learners belong. Educators already know that learners have many ways of processing information; this understanding helps them provide individualized and effective teaching strategies tailored to students' unique cognitive styles. A broader view and greater understanding of neurodivergence works in a similar way, helping reduce the stigma associated with neurodivergent labels and fostering more empathy and acceptance. This, in turn, helps educators (and students themselves) develop a more holistic understanding of each student's capabilities and needs, rather than focusing solely on their deficits or differences.

For the purposes of this book, we have settled on defining certain labels as neurodivergent. This is a conservative conceptualization compared to how some advocates identify neurodivergence. We specifically limit our definition to neurodevelopmental labels that are lifelong and persistently influence how someone learns, communicates, or operates in the world. Autism, attention deficit/hyperactivity disorder (ADHD), specific learning disabilities (dyslexia, dysgraphia, and dyscalculia), cognitive giftedness, dyspraxia, Tourette syndrome, and intellectual disabilities are some labels that clearly fit within the definition of neurodiversity used in this book.

A psychological diagnosis is often episodic, triggered environmentally, and/or mitigated with therapy or medication. It is often treatable through therapy or medication and may "go away" (temporarily or permanently) as the person gains strategies for managing it. Generalized anxiety disorder and major depressive disorder are more clearly aligned with psychological diagnosis. While they can indeed be disabling, they don't typically impact how a person processes information or learns. However, in some cases, they can be lifelong and/or disabling, aligning them more closely with neurodivergent labels. Diagnoses such as obsessive-compulsive disorder (OCD), bipolar, social anxiety, and post-traumatic stress disorder (PTSD) straddle the space between neurodivergent diagnoses and psychological ones. Figure 1.2 on the next page outlines the differences between neurodivergent and psychological diagnoses.

Of course, none of this is without nuance. We understand that someone who, for example, experiences anxiety daily for years will feel the impact in almost all areas of their life. And the long-term chronic stress associated with experiencing anxiety like this is, indeed, life-changing. Suffice it to say, these people would benefit from greater understanding from the general public and accommodations made available at school or work. Our hope is not to draw a line in the sand between neurodivergent and neuro-normative or to be exclusionary toward those who identify as neurodivergent but don't have one of the labels we've identified for this book. We recognize that the conversation is constantly evolving.

For the purposes of this book, we primarily look at the labels that are clearly neurodevelopmental, as well as those that straddle the space between neurodivergent and psychological diagnoses. We'll also address some outlying labels, like oppositional defiant disorder and pathological demand avoidance, and contextualize them within the neurodiversity framework. Whether we address a specific diagnosis or not, we enter into this work with the inclusive perspective that a neurodiversity-affirming school is good for *all* students.

FIGURE 1.2 Neurodivergent Diagnoses vs. Psychological Diagnoses

	Neurodivergent Diagnoses	**Psychological Diagnoses**
Labels	autism, ADHD, specific learning disabilities (dyslexia, dyscalculia, dysgraphia), cognitive giftedness, intellectual disabilities	OCD, PTSD, social anxiety, bipolar, generalized anxiety, depression
Nature of the condition	characterized by variations in the brain or neurological functioning	generally connected to thought processes, behaviors, and emotions (as opposed to structural neurological variation)
Onset and duration	typically present from birth or early childhood; long-term and often lifelong	can develop at any stage of life, depending on various factors such as trauma, stress, etc.; may be short-term, chronic, or episodic, depending on the condition and individual circumstances
Types of support	Services (as opposed to treatment) typically focus on educational support, accommodations, and skill building for areas of difficulty. The goal is to find a path of support rather than to "cure" the individual of the diagnosis.	Treatment may involve therapy or medication, with the goal of resolving the areas of concern.

Medical Diagnosis vs. Educational Identification of Neurodivergence

A medical neurodivergent diagnosis is provided by a health-care professional, such as a clinical psychologist or psychiatrist. It is based on a comprehensive evaluation that includes clinical observations and standardized assessments. An educational identification, on the other hand, is typically made by a team of school professionals, including special education teachers, school psychologists, speech therapists, and others. Rather than focusing on medical aspects and impact, an educational identification evaluates how the student's neurodivergence affects their ability to learn and function in an educational setting. An educational identification is needed to identify the specific learning needs and challenges that a student might face and to develop an IEP to support that student's success in the classroom. While the medical diagnosis seeks to categorize and understand the disorder itself, the educational identification aims to provide information that allows for tailoring education to meet the unique needs of the student. It takes a functional approach by focusing on how a student's neurodivergent characteristics impact their ability to learn and participate in the educational environment.

For families who do not have the advantage of a private evaluation or assessment of their student, school-based evaluations to determine educational identification for support may be the first opportunity they have to gather assessment information about their children's needs. However, parents may not be aware that they have the right to request a school evaluation if they have concerns, and this lack of awareness can be a big barrier to students accessing services. Because of this, it's important that teachers feel confident to start the referral process themselves by having conversations with parents about what they're seeing. In those conversations, it's key to share how everyone would benefit from more information about how the student learns and about their strengths and struggles. It's also important to walk parents through the process of requesting a school evaluation, to acknowledge any cultural views around disability, and to assure parents that your commitment to creating a neurodiversity-affirming environment means that their student has some support already built in.

In a neurodiversity-affirming school, medical diagnosis and educational identification are understood as complementary perspectives that center students' unique needs. A student may not meet the precise medical criteria for a specific neurodivergent diagnosis but may still display learning and behavioral challenges that resemble those seen with that diagnosis. In this case, the educational team might still provide support and interventions that align with those used for students with medical diagnoses. Conversely, a student with a medical diagnosis may not require special education if there isn't a significant impact on their educational performance. Autism diagnoses are a frequent example: a child is given a diagnosis in a medical setting, yet may not qualify for services in the academic setting. Students with learning disabilities sometimes face this same problem, although the families of students who receive an educational identification of a specific learning disability may not seek out a medical diagnosis if they're not seeing an impact outside of school.

These varying labels emphasize the importance of collaboration between medical and education professionals and recognize the individuality of each student. The goal is not to fit the student into a category but to understand and support their unique educational needs within the context of neurodiversity.

Barriers to Identification

Many barriers exist to accessing a medical diagnosis for a neurodivergent label. The diagnostic process can be costly and time-consuming, making a family's socioeconomic status and income a major barrier. A family's "cultural capital" can pose another barrier to access. Finding an assessment provider for families whose primary language is not English, for example, can be difficult. Families who have immigrated recently and do not yet have a wide community network also face unique barriers to finding a medical diagnosis, such as not understanding the reasons around why to seek one.

Even with a medical diagnosis, it's not necessarily the case that educational identification will follow. Federal law says that schools have to consider the results of a private evaluation when assessing for an IEP, but they don't necessarily have to act on it, especially if there's not sufficient evidence that a student's medical diagnosis is affecting their school performance (Individuals with Disabilities Education Act 2004).

Medical diagnosis or no, an educational identification begins with a parent or school referral. After this, a comprehensive evaluation will be done to see if a student has a disability (as defined by *IDEA* or Section 504—see chapter 11) and whether they need specialized instruction, accommodations, and other support to fully benefit from their education.

The educational identification of neurodivergent students is crucial, not only to ensure that these students receive appropriate educational services but also to support them in forming their identity, understanding themselves and their neurodivergence, and learning to self-advocate for neurodiversity-affirming practices. There are barriers to educational identification that can prevent or delay the recognition of neurodivergent traits and needs. Some common ones include the following:

- **Parents and educators lack awareness and understanding about the signs of neurodivergence** or even the diversity of signs within certain neurodivergent conditions. When parents and educators aren't aware of how neurodivergence can show up, signs can sometimes be misinterpreted as "behaviors" or overlooked and dismissed.

- **Social stereotypes and stigma about neurodivergent conditions** can lead to bias and misunderstanding. They can also lead to reluctance from caregivers in seeking a diagnosis or services and reluctance from teachers in suggesting that a student be evaluated. Some families might worry that their child will be "labeled" and therefore resist pursuing evaluation.

- **Cultural perceptions of neurodivergence** vary, and some of your students may belong to cultures that either interpret neurodivergent behaviors differently than you do or don't talk about disability. This can lead to underidentification of neurodivergence in certain student populations (Bolding, Rapa, and Mulholland 2022).

- **Economic barriers to diagnostic evaluation** exist. Even though the school evaluation process is provided at no cost to families, the goal is to look at eligibility for educational identification, not medical diagnosis. Families with limited financial resources may struggle to access diagnostic services to make sure their children have the support they need outside of school as well.

- **Overlapping symptoms** can make clear identification more challenging. Many neurodivergent conditions share symptoms or can co-occur. For instance, ADHD and autism can co-occur and share certain traits, making it harder to identify what accommodations and services would best support a student.

- **Age-related challenges,** since some neurodivergent conditions may not be clearly apparent until a student is older, are another barrier. Early identification can be especially challenging when symptoms are mild or if a student has developed coping mechanisms and masking skills. For instance, many students who eventually receive an autism diagnosis are first identified as having delayed speech or attention challenges.

- **Gender biases and gendered expectations** of how a certain type of neurodivergence "should" look are another barrier to identification. Research has shown that certain neurodivergent conditions—most specifically autism—may manifest differently based on a student's gender identity. Historically, autism has been underdiagnosed in female students because of biases and expectations around gender (Cumin, Pelaez, and Mottron 2021).

- **Systemic barriers in educational systems,** such as a shortage of evaluators or other resources, can lead to a resistance to referring neurodivergent students for evaluation. While this isn't a legally valid barrier, it happens in some schools despite teachers' best efforts to get students the support they need.

- **Overreliance on standardized testing,** which might not capture the full range of a student's abilities or challenges, can result in misidentification or nonidentification. In addition, some of the evaluation tools used to identify neurodivergence aren't culturally or linguistically appropriate for all students.

Addressing these barriers to identification is essential. Schools and systems need to adopt a more inclusive approach to identifying neurodivergent students that considers biases and stereotypes, as well as students' cultural and linguistic identities. It's also key that parents feel supported and comfortable that neurodivergence won't cause their children to be labeled or held apart from peers. (See pages 182–186 in chapter 7 for more on understanding family concerns.)

Learner Variability and Neurodiversity-Affirming Schools

All students, whether neurodivergent or not, have unique combinations of cognitive, emotional, social, and physical traits and skills that can influence how they process and acquire knowledge. *Learner variability* is a term used to describe how all students come to the classroom with these unique sets of strengths, needs, and experiences. It acknowledges that all the realms of a student's life are interconnected and that their skills vary according to context. Understanding learner variability is very well aligned with creating neurodiversity-affirming schools.

The concept of learner variability is based on Todd Rose's book *The End of Average*. It aims to dispute the myth that there is an "average learner" and to provide educators with evidence-based factors and strategies that can be easily incorporated into their practices. Recognizing learner variability includes considering the various factors that may affect a student's ability to learn and using learning science research to understand *how* these factors impact their learning.

Digital Promise's Learner Variability Project (LVP) initiative seeks to "build on emerging research on learner variability and uncover strategies to meet learners where they are across varied contexts and needs" (Digital Promise, n.d.). The LVP has identified four pillars into which the factors that affect students' abilities to learn can be divided: content, cognition, social and emotional learning, and student background. Let's take a closer look at what those pillars mean and what's included in each (Pape 2018):

- **Content** factors (or literacies) are the skills a student possesses in a certain academic domain, such as math or reading, that develop over time and are often associated with specific ages and developmental stages. A student's content skills are expected to improve over time, and education has traditionally expected them to develop in a linear fashion. Learner variability, however, recognizes that many students have a jagged or asynchronous pattern of skill-building. *(Example factors include literacy skills, such as decoding, fluency, spelling, writing, and vocabulary, and mathematical skills, such as pattern recognition, fact retrieval, and mental math processes.)*

- **Cognition** factors are the skills that help students manage, store, and process their thoughts and knowledge and self-regulate their behavior. *(Example factors include attention, concentration, cognitive flexibility, and working memory.)*

- **Social and emotional learning** factors, which we go into in depth in chapter 7, are the skills that students use to navigate social situations and understand emotions. These skills can have a big impact on students' motivation to learn. *(Examples factors include emotion and feelings, motivation, and stereotype threat.)*

- **Student background** factors consider more than the student as an individual—they include bigger things like societal and home factors that impact a student's learning. *(Example factors include home and neighborhood, sleep, socioeconomic status, cultural expectations, and connection to social and racial justice issues.)*

Recognizing learner variability is critical to building a truly neurodiversity-affirming school. By acknowledging and addressing individual differences, you can create more effective learning environments that meet the diverse needs of your students and help them feel safe enough to build emotional competence and self-regulation. These are some common tenets of learner variability to keep in mind:

- Students vary in their cognitive abilities, such as memory, attention, problem-solving, critical thinking, and information processing.
- Students prefer and benefit from various learning modalities, such as visual, auditory, and kinesthetic approaches.
- Students' motivation levels and interests impact their engagement and willingness to learn.
- Students understand and connect with new information based on their preexisting knowledge and experiences.
- Students' cultures and languages can influence their communication styles, language abilities, and perspectives.
- Students' socioeconomic statuses, access to resources, and support systems impact their abilities to learn.
- Students who are neurodivergent may require specialized instructional approaches.

Digital Promise's Learner Variability Project has a framework for looking at the four pillars that starts by asking questions about each of them (2023). Their Learning Navigator tool guides you in answering questions with a specific student in mind (see figure 1.3) and builds a profile of the student that can help you figure out the factors that may need to be addressed to support their learning. With the tool, you can explore how factors like stereotype threat may play a bigger role for one student, which can provide insight into the responsive teaching they need.

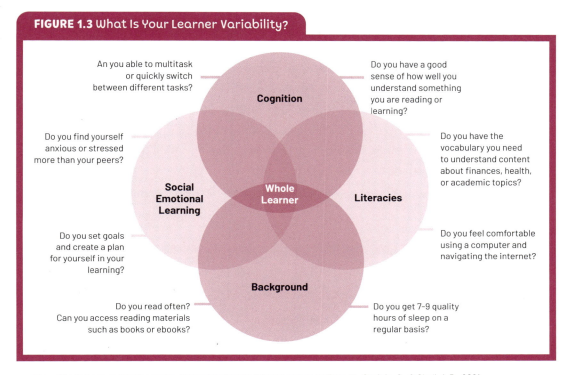

FIGURE 1.3 What Is Your Learner Variability?

From *The Science of Adult Learning: Understanding the Whole Learner,* by Tare, M., Cacicio, S., & Shell, A.R., 2021, p. 4. Copyright 2021 by Digital Promise. Reprinted with permission.

Stereotype Threat and Learner Variability

First introduced by psychologists Claude Steele and Joshua Aronson, stereotype threat is when individuals experience anxiety or fear of confirming negative stereotypes about their race, ethnicity, sexual orientation, gender identity, social status, disability status, or psychological or neurodevelopmental diagnosis (1995). Internalized ableism is an example of stereotype threat that your neurodivergent students may experience, and it can be a significant contributing factor in their learner variability profile. Anxiety around a stereotype threat can have a deleterious impact on performance and behavior in situations that relate to the stereotype (Aronson et al. 2013). Here's how the cycle of stereotype threat might work for a neurodivergent student:

1. **Activation of stereotypes:** When a student is exposed to a situation that triggers a stereotype, such as an ADHDer being in a busy environment, they become hyperaware of the fact that people may expect them to be very distractible.

2. **Anxiety and pressure:** Because the student is hyperaware, they may feel anxious or under pressure to be extremely focused in order to disprove the stereotype.

3. **Cognitive overload:** The anxiety and fear of confirming the stereotype uses mental resources, leading to cognitive overload, which reduces the capacity of the student to focus on the task they need to complete in the situation.

4. **Decreased performance:** Both the cognitive overload and the anxiety caused by stereotype threat can lead to underperformance that doesn't match the student's true skills and abilities.

The good news is that you can help mitigate stereotype threat for neurodivergent students.

Five Ways to Mitigate Stereotype Threat for Neurodivergent Learners

1. Create an environment where neurodiversity is expected, recognized, and celebrated.
2. Provide positive neurodivergent role models.
3. Emphasize students' effort, improvement, and growth.
4. Offer unbiased feedback on student performance.
5. Raise awareness about stereotype threat and its effects.

Learner Variability vs. Neurodivergence

Both learner variability and neurodivergence normalize that all people experience the world in different ways. Both concepts view learners' struggles and strengths as valuable and consider the whole person. There are, however, some important distinctions that make it difficult to use them interchangeably in schools. Neurodivergence still acknowledges the value of a diagnosis. And that matters tremendously as you have conversations about students with others, particularly parents, as there may be stigma and shame attached to a diagnosis. With learner variability, however, there's little stigma or shame involved. The idea is simply that everyone has variable ways of learning, support needs, and strengths.

Destigmatizing Neurodivergence

When working to destigmatize neurodivergence, you can implement several principles. Each of these principles (outlined below) not only creates a school environment that is neurodiversity-affirming but also works to impact the wider world by growing a community of people who have a greater understanding of neurodivergence.

Stop Fearing Labels

The first step toward destigmatizing neurodivergence is to call things what they are. We all need to stop using euphemism to avoid naming something what it is. Let's stop calling kids "a bit different," "quirky," "odd ducks," or "Sheldon." The message that these terms send is that being neurodivergent is something to be ashamed of and something to hide. Every time adults *don't* give a child a label, they are internalizing one anyway—probably "lazy," "dumb," or "unworthy." So, we ask: *Isn't it better to call something what it is?*

If a child is autistic, ask them whether they refer to themself as *autistic* or as *having autism*, and then use their preference. If a student is struggling to learn to read and is dyslexic, don't let them continue to struggle without giving them a label to help them understand why this skill is so hard. Educate them about dyslexia and help them understand that the neurological differences in their brain are what is making it hard to learn to read. Then assure them that there are specific tools that can help brains just like theirs.

Normalize Accommodations

A major barrier to obtaining accommodations is the fact that they aren't readily available or accessible in many situations. Because of this, self-advocacy is an important skill for neurodivergent students to learn. Even so, they aren't often given opportunities to successfully self-advocate when they are young. School is the perfect setting for students to learn what accommodations work for them, how and where they can access them, and what to expect when they request an accommodation. If a neurodivergent student needs an accommodation that you're unable to meet, it's important to find an alternative. If students are shut down when they ask for accommodations, they learn not to ask. Every time an accommodation is denied, a neurodivergent child learns it is better to hide their needs than meet them.

Accommodations, when normalized and made available, are good for all students. For example, a student grieving the loss of a pet might appreciate an opportunity to work in a quiet environment; a student feeling worried and stressed about family difficulties might find using fidgets calming. And many students would benefit from the availability of speech-to-text apps when completing a writing task.

Provide Community Education

In addition to normalizing labels and accommodations for neurodivergent students, the school must work to get the broader community on board. When principals, teachers, counselors, and school staff have an understanding of what neurodivergent students need, they can work together to create an environment where those students can thrive, from PE to the lunchroom to the bus and beyond. When neuro-normative students have opportunities to learn about neurodiversity, they can become advocates. Shedding light on neurodiversity brings it out of the shadows. Talking about it openly in the community transforms it into something that is valued and understood, instead of cloaked in shame.

Community education about neurodiversity must equitably reach all families in your school. This may mean providing information in students' home languages, offering free child care during in-person events, and providing an option to watch events virtually or view recordings. Consider the barriers that may prevent families from accessing information about neurodiversity and work to remove them.

Question the Status Quo

People do a lot of things in education simply because it is the way they've always been done. Timed tests, group projects, and discipline systems have been part of the school ecosystem since before most educators were in school. Some things change; fads come and go. But when creating a neurodiversity-affirming school, all educators need to ask themselves why they do certain things the way they do them. Becoming neurodiversity-affirming often requires a change in thinking.

In a neurodiversity-affirming school, when you see a student struggling, you ask what might be causing the struggle. Then, once you've identified a possible source for the difficulty, you take it a step further by asking: *Is this activity/practice necessary? What is my goal with it? Does it align with this student's needs or are there ways to make accommodations or adjustments?* For example, imagine a student with slow processing speed combined with sensory needs that impact their fine-motor skills. If they are given a timed math test and must complete a certain number of math problems within a two-minute window, what is really being graded? The teacher is looking for math fluency and automaticity, yes. However, the student is also being graded on processing speed and fine-motor skills. Is there a better way this teacher can measure progress toward a goal of math fluency and automaticity than a two-minute timed test?

When you stop to question the way things have always been done, you open a world of opportunities to find new ways to help the students within our neurodiverse schools.

Benjamin

Benjamin is autistic and has ADHD. He calls himself an AuDHDer, so we will too. Since the time Benjamin was a baby, he's done what clinicians refer to as "stimming": when he's excited, he flaps his hands and jumps up and down. He doesn't hurt himself or others, and to him, this movement an expression of pure joy—of happiness. In fact, as soon as he was able to put words to it, he called his movement "flappiness" or being "flappy." It's the perfect descriptor for Benjamin, and any time someone asks why he does it, he says, "My body can't hold in all the excitement, so I have flappiness."

Over time, the neighborhood kids and Benjamin's friends have joined him in being "flappy" when something exciting happens. And in school, any teacher who asks why he's so jumpy will quickly be corrected by Benjamin or his friends. "It's flappiness," they say. "You should ask him why he's so excited."

Neurodiversity-Affirming Language

If we're going to talk about how to create neurodiversity-affirming schools—and we are—we need to do some level-setting about language. One thing people often do in education is use deficit-based language: what students can't do, what skills they're lacking, what the problem is, what's wrong, what's missing. It's a model that has made it easier to find ways to fix what's broken. After all, if you know that a student is easily distracted and has difficulty following directions, then isn't it easy to say that the fix is to find interventions to teach them to stay on task so they can more easily follow along?

A neurodiversity-affirming approach asks you to consider that it's not something about the student that needs to be fixed. What if you spoke differently about the struggles you see? What if you used neurodiversity-affirming language to acknowledge the ways your students experience the world?

Neurodiversity-affirming language sees and honors the whole child. It gives students a level of comfort that allows them to unmask, encourages acceptance of who they are, and provides ways to reduce struggles. Neurodiversity-affirming language presents neutral information, acknowledges strengths, takes away the idea that there's a "right" and a "wrong" way to do things, and, most importantly, presumes competence. (For a list of ten ways you can show your neurodivergent students that you presume their competence, see page 80 in chapter 3.)

When we presume competence, here's what we're saying:

- We assume every student is able to learn.
- We know all students are intelligent in their own way.
- We see difference as different, not less.
- We respect students' independence and their right to be communicated with directly in age-appropriate ways, and we use language and examples they understand.
- We recognize there are multiple ways for students to show what they know.

Using neurodiversity-affirming language helps create spaces that welcome acceptance and understanding. It stops educators from centering neuro-normative ways of experiencing the world when they talk about student success, and it recognizes that neurodivergent students have valuable ways of approaching and interacting with the world that deserve to be acknowledged and described in terms that reflect their experiences. For an elaboration on what neurodiversity-affirming language looks like in academic and social goals, see page 266 in chapter 11.

One of the big debates in education (and in the neurodiversity movement) is whether to use person-first or identity-first language when referring to neurodivergent students. (You may hear these abbreviated as PFL and IFL.) Like other professionals in education and psychology, we were taught to use person-first language: a student with autism, a child with ADHD, a learner with dyslexia. However, neurodivergent self-advocates often prefer identity-first language, referring to themselves as dyslexic, autistic, ADHDers, or AuDHDers.

When people use identity-first language, it's because they believe the way their neuro-variation makes them show up in and experience the world helped shaped them into becoming who they are. In many cases, it's what helped them become self-advocates, find community, and embrace the neurodiversity movement. We recognize that, as neurodivergent people ourselves, a person can't be separated from their neurodivergence. It is part of who they are—their personality, community, and culture. Using identity-first language recognizes this. There isn't a way to separate a person from their neurodivergence, because without it, they'd be a totally different person.

Language matters. Identity matters. Eliminating stigma matters. And because of that, we're squarely in favor of identity-first language, when it's possible to use it.

Our Perspectives on IFL vs. PFL

Amanda: When it comes down to it, I always defer to the individual's preference for what they use and want others to use to refer to them. But generally, you'll hear me use identity-first language because it's *my* preference and that of my family. One of my sons is autistic and the other is an AuDHDer. I am neurodivergent too. It's a part of who I am, and if I were to say, "I'm a person with OCD and sensory processing issues," there'd be an implication that my OCD and sensory processing issues are something that could or should be left behind, let go of, or "cured." But being neurodivergent has shaped who I am, and I don't know what it's like to be any other version of myself. I don't know what it's like to be a person without neurodivergent traits.

I have a fundamental problem with the reasoning of person-first language asking us to remember that I am a person first. In fact, it concerns me that we must consciously keep in mind that someone is a person (first).

Emily: I think a lot about the language we use and the messages it conveys about our values. I also believe that the language we use influences how we think and feel about things. This is why I gravitate toward using identity-first language.

At the risk of being hyperbolic, I give the following examples of person-first language: a person with cancer, a child with anxiety, or a student with a nut allergy. In each of these examples, it makes sense that we would separate the person from the label. We want to get rid of the cancer, help the child overcome their anxiety, or protect the student from their nut allergy. Neurodivergent diagnoses are different. For most types of neurodivergence, separating the person from the label doesn't make much sense. Neurodivergence isn't something that we should aim to get rid of, overcome, or protect from. "Curing" a neurodivergent diagnosis essentially means changing the way a person is.

Here's another example of how language conveys our values and influences our emotions: I work in the field of twice-exceptionality (people/students who both are cognitively gifted and have a disability). If you pay attention, most people have no problem using the term *gifted* when it comes to describing that type of neurodivergence. People almost always use the terms *gifted kids* and *gifted students* (rather than *students with gifts and talents*).

Why is it okay to refer to a *gifted child* but insist that the correct term is a *child with autism*? Because language conveys values, and society embraces intelligence and stigmatizes neurodivergence.

What to Remember

- A neurodiversity-affirming school welcomes neurodivergent students to be authentically themselves. The neurodiversity movement is working to depathologize neurodivergence and move toward a framework that recognizes the normal variation within human development.
- Identity-first language is generally used within the neurodiversity community because many neurodivergent people see their identity as intertwined with their neurodivergence.
- Schools can work to destigmatize neurodivergence throughout their community by accepting labels/diagnoses (instead of shying away from them), normalizing the use of accommodations, involving and educating the stakeholders in the school community, and questioning the status quo when things don't seem to be working for a neurodivergent student.

Chapter 2

Understanding Your Neurodivergent Learners

Points to Ponder

- How can being neurodivergent influence a student's school experience?
- Why is it important to understand the difference between a medical diagnosis and an educational identification?
- How have you seen the concept of neurodiversity expand over time?

Every day, we encounter students whose neurodivergent experiences shape how they communicate, engage, and learn. Sometimes, these differences might be apparent, while at other times, they might quietly influence a student's daily school life. Throughout this chapter, we'll explore various neurodivergent diagnoses, reflecting on their implications in educational settings. This chapter also emphasizes the importance of recognizing how neurodivergence impacts students' identities, challenges, strengths, and—most importantly—learning. By understanding these neurodivergences and who they impact, you become better equipped to meet your students where they are, facilitate effective, inclusive learning environments, and recognize and value the diverse ways in which they experience the world.

A Linear Spectrum Is Too Shallow

Autism has traditionally been understood as a linear spectrum, with individuals placed along a scale ranging from "less autistic" to "more autistic." Since the concept of the spectrum has become more widely understood, many have begun to use it beyond autism to think of other neurodivergent diagnoses, like ADHD, in a similar way. However, the idea of a linear spectrum minimizes and oversimplifies the highly complex nature of neurodivergence. It has led to confusion about the incredible variation among neurodivergent people and has kept some people from being identified. Since their presentation doesn't align with what is expected, they aren't referred for assessment.

Viewing autism (and other neurodivergent diagnoses) as a web instead of a linear scale provides a much more nuanced framework for understanding the diverse range of student experiences. In a web, the innermost part indicates "lower support needs," meaning the individual is least impacted in this area. As the web progresses outward, the level of support needed in each area is higher, meaning these are areas that provide more difficulty for the individual, who would likely benefit from additional support and accommodations.

Figures 2.1 and 2.2 show an autistic student's neurodivergence conceptualized as a linear scale versus a web. In the web, you can see that this particular student has high support needs with social interactions and displays very intense focus on special interests. At the same time, they have much lower support needs around routines and are not as reliant on repetition. The web, compared to the linear scale, provides a much fuller picture of the student.

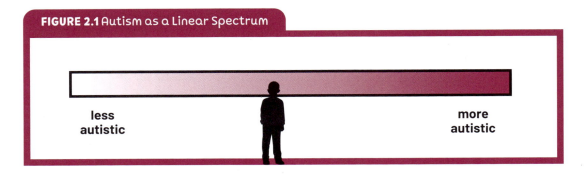

FIGURE 2.1 Autism as a Linear Spectrum

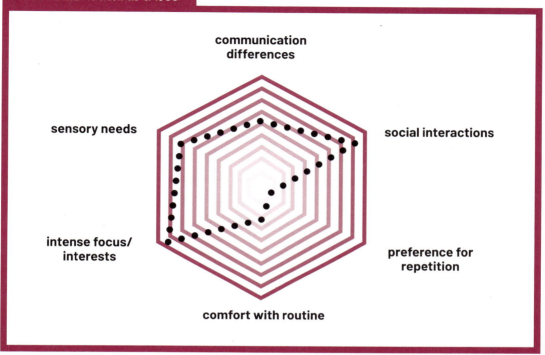

FIGURE 2.2 Autism as a Web

The idea of conceptualizing neurodivergence as web can be used with most diagnoses. This perspective is helpful when you meet a student who doesn't "look like" the other autistic, or ADHD, or gifted students you've met, because it emphasizes the uniqueness of each neurodivergent learner. Take figure 2.3 for example.

There is one final factor in understanding these webs of characteristics and needs: the point where each characteristic falls is moveable, depending on the situation. For example, the amount of support this ADHDer requires for sensory needs might vary based on an accumulation of other factors, such as what the student's stress level is on a particular day or in a particular setting. A need that is evident one day might be less evident the next. As we progress through the various neurodivergences described in this chapter, try to consider each of the characteristics and how they might be influenced or supported by the environments and situations your students encounter.

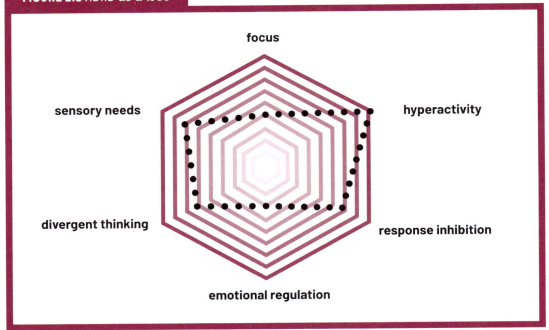

FIGURE 2.3 ADHD as a Web

Diagnoses, Identification, and Labels

Emily: There's a lot of stigma surrounding many of the diagnoses that form part of the neurodiversity paradigm. In the past, there seemed to be pressure to avoid labeling kids. However, I think the approach to diagnosis and identification may be shifting.

Amanda: First, I would say that it's important to understand the distinction between diagnosis and educational identification that was discussed in chapter 1. Having a diagnosis doesn't mean a student automatically receives an educational identification and services. So, if a student's diagnosis doesn't result in them receiving support or services in school through legal means, that label may not have much of an impact on them in school.

If a student has an educational identification, however, this signifies that they need specialized instruction or accommodations based on their diagnosis and traits, and it's legally documented. For this reason, I think an educational identification can be very useful. But there are also some risks, such as people applying their own assumptions or stereotypes about a "label" to expectations of what a student can do or how they might interact in the classroom. I'm curious about your opinion on the difference between an actual diagnosis and using the term *neurodivergent*.

Emily: I find the term *neurodivergent* useful when discussing a group of diagnoses that fit under it. Additionally, there might be individuals who exhibit many neurodivergent traits but don't qualify for an official medical diagnosis for various reasons. The label can be helpful for those people to recognize these traits in themselves or use it to explain their needs. However, possibly due to my clinical background, I lean more toward the benefits of an official diagnosis such as autism, ADHD, or OCD, if possible.

In an ideal world, we wouldn't need labels. We would just give kids what they need. But we aren't there yet. Labels are often the key that opens up supports for children. I wish that weren't the case, but it is what it is right now.

Understanding Neurodivergent Labels

Because we don't live in an ideal world where neurodivergent kids can easily get the supports they need in school without identification, the more we talk about neurodivergent diagnoses, the more we can promote understanding. Students whose neurodivergent traits impact their learning would benefit from a diagnosis or identification so they can get support. To match supports to neurodivergent students, it is helpful to know what diagnoses fit under the umbrella of neurodivergence.

The following sections share more about the diagnoses we identified in chapter 1, including neurodivergent diagnoses and those diagnoses that straddle the space between neurodivergent and psychological. As you read about these diagnoses, always remember that a diagnosis doesn't define a student—it helps you understand them a bit better.

Autism

Autism is characterized by differences in social relationships and communication preferences, as well as comfort with routine and repetition. The varying strengths and needs of autistic individuals can have a wide range of presentations. However, autism is typically identified based on two main categories of needs: communication differences and comfort with routine (American Psychological Association (APA) 2013).

Communication Differences

The first area of difference recognized in autistic students is related to social communication and social interaction. There are three main characteristics in this area. For a formal autism diagnosis, someone must exhibit each of these three characteristics:

- **Social and emotional reciprocity:** Autistic students frequently have their own ways of engaging in conversation or responding to social cues. These are some examples of what this might look like:

    - An autistic student may repeat phrases from their favorite shows during conversations, using these quotes to express their emotions or thoughts. (See chapter 9 for more information on echolalia.)

- Instead of engaging in a group conversation, a student might prefer one-on-one interactions and respond more openly in intimate settings.
- A student might not respond to praise or excitement in expected ways. They may give a thumbs-up instead of verbally acknowledging a compliment, or they may choose not to respond at all.

Nonverbal communication: Autistic students may communicate through alternative means, such as using specific gestures, avoiding eye contact, or relying on body language. You might see this expressed in ways such as these:

- An autistic student may avoid eye contact while listening intently to instructions because focusing on the words without the distraction or discomfort of making eye contact is a more effective way for them to receive the information.
- A student's facial expressions may not align with typical expectations during communicating. For example, an autistic student may maintain a neutral face even when discussing something they are excited about.

Social relationships: Autistic students may have differences in developing and maintaining typical social relationships or have preferences for these relationships that are different from peers. This might appear in the following ways:

- Some autistic students prefer to spend time alone and don't feel driven to socialize in the same way other students do. A student may form deep connections with only one or two peers, relying on those friendships instead of engaging with the larger group.
- Autistic students' social interactions might be most successful when centered around specific interests, and they might prefer to engage in conversations only about favorite subjects.
- An autistic student may prefer to work alone on a group project or to contribute in a specific area where they feel most comfortable and capable.

Amina

Amina, an autistic ten-year-old, was deeply passionate about ancient civilizations, particularly the Egyptians. She communicated in a way that worked for her, often repeating phrases from documentaries she watched and avoiding eye contact while listening intently. Group projects could be challenging for her, so she usually worked alone, but would at times contribute her vast knowledge of ancient cultures to the other groups. Her classmates typically responded to praise from the teacher with smiles and cheers, but Amina became known for her preferred response of a quiet thumbs-up. Her teacher, Mrs. Johnson, tapped into Amina's specialized interest, weaving it into lessons and allowing her to express her thoughts through detailed drawings of pyramids and hieroglyphs. Amina's passion for ancient Egypt not only enriched her and classmates' learning experiences but also fostered empathy, curiosity, and appreciation for neurodivergence among her peers.

Comfort with Repetition, Routine, and Consistency

Autistic individuals typically prefer repetition, routine, and consistency and rely on them as coping skills. For a medical identification of autism, at least two of the following characteristics must be present (APA 2013).

Different styles of movement or communication: Autistic students may express themselves through unique movement patterns or display focused engagement with particular subjects, phrases, or words. Here's what this could potentially look like:

- An autistic student may have a particular rhythm or pattern in walking or moving, expressing a sense of comfort or security in this repeated motion.
- During a conversation, a student might use a unique combination of words or phrases that makes sense to them but may need clarification for others. They might find using these exact phrases comforting or expressive of their emotions.
- Autistic play may involve sorting and categorizing items.

Preference for consistency and established routines: Autistic students may find stability and reassurance in familiar routines and may need support during unexpected transitions. For instance, this might appear in these ways:

- An autistic student may feel most comfortable sitting in the same seat every day and might become distressed or disoriented if asked to change locations without warning.
- A change in the daily schedule without advance notice or a clear explanation might lead to anxiety or confusion for an autistic student.
- An autistic student might have a specific routine for packing up at the end of the day. Rushing them or changing the process could cause them to become upset or overwhelmed.

Specialized interests and focused passion: Some autistic students may have passionate interests in specific topics, demonstrating a depth of focus and expertise. Following are some examples of what this might look like:

- An autistic student might have an intense interest in a specific subject, such as dinosaurs, vacuum cleaners, or social justice. They become highly engaged in classroom activities or projects related to that topic.
- A student may seek to connect unrelated classroom topics to their specialized interest, finding surprising ways to relate history, literature, or mathematics to their passion.
- An autistic student might dedicate significant personal time to exploring their interests, creating elaborate projects or presentations and eagerly sharing them with classmates and teachers; it may also be difficult for them to regulate their focus on topics that aren't connected to this interest.

Different responses to sensory input: Autistic learners may experience and react to sensory experiences, such as sounds or textures, in their own ways. These reactions may be more or less intense than typically expected. Here are some possible manifestations of this:

- An autistic student may be hypersensitive to certain sounds, like the bell or loud talking, and react to them with discomfort or anxiety.

- A student might seek specific textures or avoid others, such as preferring to write with a particular type of pencil or avoiding certain fabrics.
- Certain visual stimuli, like bright lights or busy wall decorations, might be distracting or overwhelming for an autistic student.

Pathological (Pervasive) Demand Avoidance

Pathological (or pervasive) demand avoidance (PDA) is an area of growing awareness and is frequently discussed in the neurodiversity community. Advocates for the label describe PDA as a subtype or profile of autism, driven by a persistent need for control and autonomy. When this need for autonomy is threatened, advocates say, it triggers a fight/flight/freeze/fawn response in students, resulting in intense emotional dysregulation and difficulty in managing "ordinary" daily tasks and requests (O'Nions et al. 2018). Other people express concerns about the PDA label. For example, the idea that PDA is some sort of subtype or unique profile separate from autism can muddle the diagnostic process and can cause confusion around whether individuals who do not meet general criteria for an autism diagnosis might still be PDA (Green et al. 2018). They also worry about the vagueness of the concept of demand avoidance, which could lead to inconsistent or subjective diagnoses (Kildahl et al. 2021). PDA is also not recognized in diagnostic manuals, further fueling the debate. While some believe that official recognition of PDA could lead to more tailored support, others urge caution, emphasizing the need for robust scientific evidence before adding new categories.

A significant concern related to the PDA diagnosis is the potential for pathologizing normal autistic traits or adaptive behaviors (Moore 2020). All of us can display avoidance behaviors, particularly when feeling stressed. The tricky part is distinguishing between what's a natural response to stress and what's potentially harmful. It's important to tread carefully here, so as not to wrongly label or stigmatize autistic individuals. More information about PDA and other types of demand avoidance, as well as strategies for it, is included in chapter 6 because of this. But ultimately, the strategies that can benefit students who exhibit characteristics of PDA can benefit many students who show demand avoidance, regardless of an identification or label.

Hyperlexia

Hyperlexia is often seen in autistic children and is characterized by an early and intense fascination with letters and numbers and an ability to read words well above age level (Ostrolenk et al. 2017). Hyperlexia is not merely advanced reading ability. While these students may read fluently and recognize words that are beyond their peers' comprehension, they might still struggle to understand the underlying meaning or context of what they're reading. Whereas dyslexic students may have difficulty tying the visual cue of a letter to a sound, the pattern-recognition skills of hyperlexic students allow them to easily learn to identify letters, words, and their sounds.

In early childhood, signs of hyperlexia might manifest as a toddler's keen interest in letters, spelling, or numbers, sometimes before they can speak in full sentences. They may be drawn to books, signs, or logos and can even begin to read words without anyone teaching them. Children with hyperlexia may memorize the alphabet at an unusually young age or be captivated by license plates and signs during car rides.

Although both hyperlexia and early reading in a gifted child are characterized by an ability to read at a young age, there are distinct differences between the two. Children with hyperlexia may begin reading without formal instruction, but their reading ability is often accompanied by challenges in comprehension, understanding metaphors, and engaging in abstract thinking. On the other hand, early reading in gifted children is typically part of a broader set of advanced cognitive abilities. These children often demonstrate not only the ability to decode words but also a deep understanding of a text. They are likely to grasp nuances, engage in critical thinking about what they've read, and connect it to other knowledge and experiences. In essence, while hyperlexia emphasizes the mechanical decoding of words, early reading in a gifted child involves a more comprehensive linguistic and cognitive engagement with the text.

Autism and Intellectual Disabilities

One criticism of the neurodiversity movement is that by not using "functioning" labels for autistic individuals, it's perpetuating a skewed and stereotypical view of autism, leaving out many people who also have intellectual disabilities (Waizbard-Bartov et al. 2023). This stereotype is common in movies, television, and other types of media that highlight autistic characters and stories of autistic people who have remarkable abilities or talents. However, the conversation about autism can't be had without acknowledging that while autism and intellectual disability are distinct conditions, they can co-occur.

A Brief History of Autism and Functioning Labels

Leo Kanner is recognized as being the first to identify autism in 1943. Hans Asperger made similar observations around the same time, identifying what later came to be known as Asperger's syndrome (Silberman 2015). In the *DSM-III*, introduced in 1980, infantile autism was a diagnosis focusing on a narrow set of criteria. (The diagnosis was later renamed *autistic disorder* in the *DSM-III-R* in 1987.) A diagnosis at this time required that a child showed signs of autism prior to thirty months of age. The label focused specifically on a lack of responsiveness to people, language deficits, and a resistance to change in routines. Many autistic children who did not exactly fit those restrictive criteria went undiagnosed.

It wasn't until 1994 that the *DSM-IV* introduced the category of pervasive developmental disorders (PDD). These diagnoses encompassed autistic disorder and the newly added Asperger's syndrome. The main difference between autistic disorder and Asperger's syndrome at this time was that an individual diagnosed with Asperger's syndrome did not exhibit a general delay in language.

In 2013, the *DSM-5* merged all subcategories into one umbrella diagnosis of autism spectrum disorder (ASD), focusing on a spectrum approach. This change was somewhat controversial, as it eliminated distinct diagnoses like Asperger's syndrome. But once the language differences among autistic individuals were better understood, the differentiation between autism and Asperger's was no longer as clear; individuals with an Asperger's diagnosis typically also have differences and difficulties with communication and language. In addition to combining these diagnoses, the *DSM-5* was also first version of the manual to include sensory differences in the criteria for diagnosis.

Many people ask what is causing the uptick in diagnoses of autism. First, because the diagnosis of Asperger's wasn't created until 1994, any individual who didn't experience a significant language delay before age three didn't meet the criteria for an autism diagnosis (Silberman 2015). It has only been thirty years since the diagnosis of Asperger's was officially created, and until a diagnosis "exists," it is difficult for researchers to study it, and professionals aren't able to diagnose it. The children who were among the first to be diagnosed with autism and Asperger's under these greater diagnostic criteria are now adults and are among those leading the charge for a more neurodiversity-affirming world.

Another major change in diagnosis of autism and Asperger's is related to the increased awareness and understanding of the diversity within the autism spectrum. The label of "high-functioning" autism (which has fallen out of favor) has its roots in the desire to differentiate individuals on the autism spectrum based on observed abilities, especially in terms of language skills and cognitive ability. The term was intended to help professionals, educators, and parents identify specific needs and strengths, guiding them in providing the appropriate support and interventions. However, the perception and use of functioning labels in autism have faced considerable criticism for oversimplifying a complex condition, leading to potential misunderstandings and stigmatization. Neurodiversity advocates argue that these labels frequently do not capture the full range of an individual's experiences and can inadvertently pigeonhole them into broad categories. As the diagnostic criteria have evolved, so too have the perceptions surrounding the functioning labels and levels within the current autism diagnosis. The *DSM-5*, for instance, introduced levels of support (1, 2, or 3) to indicate the amount of assistance required by an individual. While the aim of this is a more nuanced and individualized approach to understanding and treating autism, it is viewed by many as imperfect.

The shift toward a spectrum approach has opened doors for many individuals who might have been overlooked or misdiagnosed under previous diagnostic criteria. Though the spectrum approach is still imperfect, the focus on a broader range of symptoms and the acknowledgment of the individual variations within the autism community allows for recognition and support of a wider array of individuals. This change in perception and the continuous refinement of diagnostic criteria are part of an ongoing effort to move away from a one-size-fits-all approach to autism, embracing the complexity and individuality that defines the condition. It reflects a growing commitment to viewing autism not as a disorder to be treated but as a diverse and multifaceted aspect of human neurology that must be understood in its full context.

At the time of this writing, there is debate about separating the labels in some way, such as by designating a diagnosis of "profound autism" for autistic individuals with intellectual disabilities or other more disabling impacts (Kapp 2023; Wachtel et al. 2024). Since the *DSM-5* was published in 2013, we anticipate the release of the *DSM-6* within the next few years, which could provide yet another shift in diagnostic understanding and identification.

Talking about both autism and intellectual disability can introduce complexity when simplicity is preferred. But omitting intellectual disability from the conversation results in a narrower representation and understanding of autism.

It's essential to recognize the importance of including all autistic people in conversations and advocacy efforts, including those with co-occurring intellectual disabilities. Doing so ensures a holistic understanding of the autism spectrum and promotes inclusive practices and policies. From a school-based perspective, it's also essential for providing interventions and supports that address the entire breadth of students' needs.

ADHD (Attention Deficit/Hyperactivity Disorder)

Note: Although the neurodiversity movement tries to move away from pathologizing language, such as the word disorder, *the acronym ADHD is commonly known, and no alternative has been agreed upon. In this book, we use* ADHDer *as an identity-first term.*

ADHD is characterized by specific diagnostic criteria related to attention regulation, hyperactivity, and impulsiveness. Emotional regulation difficulties and executive functioning struggles are also often associated with ADHD, although they are not part of the formal diagnostic criteria. The diagnosis is typically based on two main areas of need: attention and hyperactivity/impulsiveness. To qualify for a medical diagnosis of ADHD, a student may show only signs of inattention (ADHD—predominantly inattentive type), only signs of hyperactivity (ADHD—predominantly hyperactive type), or a mix of both (ADHD—combined type) (APA 2013).

Attention Regulation and Executive Functioning

The first area of diagnosis for ADHD includes challenges in attention regulation and is often associated with difficulties in executive functioning.

Inattention: Many ADHDers struggle with sustaining attention in tasks or play activities, often leading to distraction or loss of focus and difficulties in organizing tasks and following through. Many ADHDers are able to direct and sustain attention when focusing on a task that is interesting to them or in an area of strength. Ability to sustain attention to those types of tasks does not exclude someone from being an ADHDer. Inattention may manifest in several ways:

- An ADHDer may struggle with staying on task during a classroom discussion because their mind is frequently going on various tangents.
- Instead of following traditional organizational methods, a student might have trouble organizing their tasks, resulting in incomplete homework or the appearance of carelessness.
- A student may lack organizational skills, leading them to frequently lose necessary items.

Hyperactivity and Impulsiveness

Along with challenges in attention regulation, students with ADHD might exhibit hyperactivity, restlessness, and/or impulsiveness.

Physical hyperactivity: Students with ADHD may display an active engagement style that reflects their unique need for physical stimulation and kinetic connection to their environment. Physical hyperactivity might look like this:

- ADHD students may express a need to tap, fidget, or otherwise move during seated lessons, highlighting a sensory connection to learning.
- A student might struggle to remain seated for an extended amount of time and may prefer to stand or move around during class.
- ADHDers may prefer active and engaging methods for learning, reflecting a need for stimulating and hands-on approaches rather than traditional quiet reading or individual work.

Impulsiveness: ADHDers may respond quickly and spontaneously, reflecting a unique processing style that emphasizes immediate reaction. You might see this in the classroom in this way:

- An ADHDer may share answers or ideas enthusiastically before a question is fully asked, displaying a rapid connection to the subject.
- A student might make decisions quickly during group activities. They may be frustrated with the pacing of other group members, who may seem to move too slowly. Alternatively, while the student's ideas may be creative and relevant, their

group members may express their own frustration when the student struggles to wait for others' responses.

- ADHD students might shift from one activity to another without completing tasks, reflecting a need for diverse and engaging stimuli and strategies for guided focus and collaboration.

Emotional Regulation Difficulties

Emotional regulation difficulties are not formally part of the diagnostic criteria for ADHD, but they are often observed in ADHDers (Soler-Gutiérrez, Pérez-González, and Mayas 2023). Frequent swift and intense mood changes can be characteristic of some students, manifesting as unpredictable emotional responses and difficulties in coping with frustration. Emotional regulation difficulties may appear like this:

- A student might express intense frustration with a challenging task, showing a low frustration tolerance.
- ADHDers might temporarily withdraw from an activity when feeling overwhelmed, signaling a need for space or a particular support structure.
- ADHD students might react with intense emotional outbursts or withdrawal after perceived criticism or exclusion, reflecting a sensitivity to rejection that is often described as rejection sensitivity dysphoria (see page 161).

Specific Learning Disabilities (Dyslexia, Dyscalculia, Dysgraphia)

Specific learning disabilities (SLDs) include a range of challenges that can affect how an individual learns, writes, reads, or manages numbers. Three common SLDs are dyslexia, dyscalculia, and dysgraphia. SLDs manifest uniquely in individuals and often require specialized support or interventions.

Important Note: Many educators have frequently been told that their schools are unable to identify and provide services for dyslexia or dyscalculia. This is untrue. In fact, the Individuals with Disabilities Education Act (IDEA) (the federal law that governs special education) names dyslexia as a type of specific learning disability, and in 2015, the Office of

Special Education and Rehabilitative Services (OSEP) released guidance reminding schools that there is no reason they should not being using the words dyslexia, dyscalculia, *and* dysgraphia *in IEPs (Yudin 2015). Some of the confusion is due to the different language that is used in the medical model for diagnosis versus the educational term* specific learning disability. *The* DSM-5 *uses the term* specific learning disability *and includes the terms* dyslexia, dyscalculia, *and* dysgraphia *as qualifiers. For example, a student with an IEP for "specific learning disability in the areas of reading fluency and phonological processing" is almost certainly dyslexic.*

Dyslexia: Reading and Language Processing

Dyslexia is characterized by difficulties in phonological processing, which affects reading, spelling, and writing. It is not a reflection of intelligence or effort but rather a unique way the brain processes written and spoken language (Shaywitz and Shaywitz 2020).

Reading difficulties: Dyslexic students may struggle with decoding words, leading to slow or inaccurate reading. This may manifest in several ways:

- A student might have difficulty reading aloud, often mispronouncing words or pausing frequently.
- A dyslexic student may need more time to complete reading assignments and might struggle with comprehension due to their focus on decoding.
- A student may avoid reading or show increased frustration with reading tasks.

Spelling and writing challenges: In addition to reading, dyslexia can affect spelling and writing, causing struggles with these tasks. Examples might include the following:

- A student might consistently misspell common words, despite repeated instruction and practice.
- A dyslexic student may have difficulties putting their thoughts into writing, reflecting a disconnect between oral and written language.
- A student's written work may be disorganized or lack clarity, despite clear oral expression of the same ideas.

Sophie

Sophie was diagnosed with dyslexia in second grade. She had always found reading and writing to be her biggest challenges in school. She would often mispronounce words while reading aloud and needed extra time to complete reading assignments. Her struggles with decoding affected her comprehension, and she became increasingly frustrated with reading tasks. Writing was equally challenging for Sophie, with misspelled words and disorganized thoughts despite her clear oral expression. Her teacher, Mr. Thompson, recognized Sophie's strengths and her unique way of processing language. He introduced specialized support, such as one-on-one reading sessions and multisensory learning techniques, and he allowed her to express her understanding through oral presentations rather than written reports. With these supports, Sophie's confidence began to grow, and she became more engaged in the classroom.

Dyscalculia: Mathematical Understanding and Processing

Dyscalculia involves difficulties in understanding numeracy, number symbols, and mathematical concepts, leading to struggles in learning and applying mathematical principles (Price and Ansari 2013).

Number sense and calculation: Students with dyscalculia may find it challenging to grasp numerical concepts. Here are a few ways this may look:

- A dyscalculic student may struggle to understand the value of numbers, often confusing their relationships or orders.
- A student might have difficulty performing simple calculations, even with the use of visual aids or calculators.
- A dyscalculic student may avoid or express anxiety about math-related tasks, reflecting a deep struggle with the subject.
- A dyscalculic student may struggle to understand that the numeral 6 is the same as the word *six* and that these both mean six items.

Spatial awareness and measurement: These areas can also be problematic for students with dyscalculia. Examples might include the following:

- A student might struggle with understanding geometric shapes or spatial relationships.
- A student may find measuring objects or distances particularly challenging, even with hands-on practice.
- A dyscalculic student might have difficulty interpreting graphs, charts, or visual representations of mathematical information.

Dysgraphia: Writing and Fine Motor Skills

Dysgraphia is characterized by difficulties in the physical act of writing, including handwriting, spelling, and organizing thoughts on paper (McCloskey and Rapp 2017).

Organization and expression: Dysgraphia can affect a student's organization and expression of thoughts in writing. This might look like this:

- A dysgraphic student might struggle to organize their thoughts on paper, resulting in disjointed or unclear writing.
- A student may have difficulty with spelling and grammar, reflecting a struggle to connect spoken language with written language.
- A dysgraphic student may require additional time or support for writing assignments, including the use of technology or one-on-one support.

Handwriting challenges: Dysgraphic students may struggle with handwriting, leading to issues like these:

- A dysgraphic student may have slow, laborious handwriting that is difficult to read.
- A student might experience physical discomfort or fatigue while writing, affecting their ability to complete written tasks.
- A student may prefer typing or other means of recording information, reflecting a need for alternative methods.

Developmental Coordination Disorder (Dyspraxia)

Developmental coordination disorder (DCD), or dyspraxia, is characterized by difficulties related to coordination and motor planning and may also include problems with speech (verbal dyspraxia). The diagnosis often highlights struggles with fine and gross motor skills and organization, and sometimes sensory sensitivities (Wilson et al. 2012).

Coordination and Motor Planning

The first area of diagnosis for DCD includes challenges in coordination and motor planning.

Coordination: Individuals with DCD often struggle with both fine and gross motor skills, leading to difficulties in performing tasks that require balance, agility, and precision. This may manifest in these ways:

- A student may find it challenging to participate in physical education activities, often struggling with balance and coordination.
- Handwriting might be a struggle for a dyspraxic student because of difficulties in holding a pen correctly and forming letters with precision.
- A student might often bump into objects or drop things, reflecting difficulties with spatial awareness and hand-eye coordination.

Motor planning: Dyspraxia also impacts a student's ability to plan and sequence motor tasks. Here's what this might look like:

- A student may have trouble getting dressed, struggling with the sequence of putting on clothes and manipulating buttons or zippers.
- A student might struggle with tasks that require multiple steps, such as cooking or crafting, often becoming confused with the order or execution of actions.
- The effort required to plan and coordinate the movements needed for writing might lead to a student having a slow writing pace, messy or inconsistent handwriting, or frustration during timed writing tasks.

Speech: Verbal dyspraxia affects the ability to form sounds and words accurately. This might manifest like this:

- A student may have difficulty articulating words clearly, struggling with specific sounds or the rhythm and flow of speech.
- Early language development may be delayed, reflecting a student's struggle to coordinate the muscle movements required for speech.

Carlos

Carlos had always loved art class, but scissors and brushes felt strangely uncooperative in his hands. His teachers initially mistook his struggles for carelessness or lack of effort, but after his diagnosis of developmental coordination disorder, they came to understand his unique challenges. They replaced the physical education activities that left Carlos feeling left out with personalized exercises to help him build coordination and balance. In art class, they introduced adaptive tools and extra time, allowing Carlos to express himself creatively. Additionally, Carlos began to self-advocate, understanding the needs he had and asking for support before getting frustrated and wanting to quit.

Cognitive Giftedness

Cognitive giftedness is characterized by specific traits related to advanced intellectual abilities, creative thinking, and intense curiosity. Gifted individuals may show exceptional abilities in areas such as logic, mathematics, language, and the arts. A student might demonstrate giftedness in a specific area (mathematically gifted), a broad range of abilities (global giftedness), or a combination of giftedness with a disability (twice-exceptionality).

Broadly speaking, a student is identified as gifted after taking a cognitive assessment (IQ test); generally, a score above the 95th percentile compared to their same-age peers is a common benchmark for identifying cognitive giftedness. However, because there are no official diagnostic criteria established by the American Psychiatric Association and published in the *DSM-5*, there is not a true consensus on exactly what score identifies someone who is cognitively gifted.

How a student is identified for gifted education services varies widely depending on your state's laws and district's policies. Some schools rely on nationally normed ability tests, like the Weschler Intelligence Scale for Children (WISC-V), Naglieri Nonverbal Ability Test (NNAT3), or Cognitive Ability Test (CogAT). Others look to achievement scores in specific academic areas, like reading and math, measured by state tests or the Iowa Test of Basic Skills (ITBS). Many districts have moved to using local norms to identify students for gifted education services, meaning that rather than using nationally normed data, they look to their own student population to determine the top percentage of students who receive services. Additionally, how services are provided varies as well. Some states include gifted education under special education services, while others do not have specific criteria as to how—or if—districts must provide gifted education to students (Rinn, Mun, and Hodges 2022).

Processing Differences

Cognitively gifted students process information differently than other students. These differences in how they process both internal and external stimuli influence how they learn and how they interact with the world around them.

Information processing: Gifted individuals process the information they receive in unique ways. They may excel in complex problem-solving, abstract thinking, and creativity. This may manifest in several ways:

- A gifted student may grasp new concepts rapidly, seeking more in-depth knowledge and engaging with advanced materials beyond their grade level.
- Instead of following standard learning paths, a student might explore creative solutions to problems, reflecting an unconventional thinking style.
- A student may show intense curiosity in specific subjects, leading them to invest time and energy in personal projects or research.

Processing differences: Cognitively gifted students often display unique patterns of thinking and learning. These might manifest like this:

- A gifted student may have a mild to moderately heightened sensitivity to sensory experiences. They may be more aware of, in tune to, or distracted by external stimuli.

- A student may struggle with domain-specific perfectionism, displaying a strong desire to excel in every task that falls within a narrow area of ability. (For example, a highly skilled and talented basketball player may show perfectionistic tendencies related to their basketball skills.)
- A student might feel out of sync with peers due to their unique interests or intensity, requiring supportive strategies for social interaction.

Twice-Exceptionality

Twice-exceptionality refers to the coexistence of giftedness with a disability, such as ADHD, autism, or SLDs. Twice-exceptional (2e) learners can slip through the cracks in our educational system because they are frequently able to compensate for their areas of weakness with their overall cognitive ability. Twice-exceptional learners are also often difficult to identify and support. The complex layering of their ability and disability makes it more difficult to notice their struggles because they frequently manage academic requirements sufficiently. Twice-exceptional learners are often identified or diagnosed with a neurodivergent diagnosis such as autism, ADHD, or SLD when they are much older because the areas of concern go unnoticed longer due to their cognitive ability or background knowledge.

For example, a twice-exceptional gifted/dyslexic student may have a depth of background knowledge and ability to memorize words that hides their struggles with phonological processing. A gifted/autistic learner may fly beneath the radar because they appear "quirky" but are able to compensate for their difficulties, at least for a while. The *DSM-5* (2013) notes that concerns related to social communication, specifically, "may not become fully manifest until social demands exceed limited capabilities." In fact, research shows that autistic individuals are one-and-a-half times more likely to have cognitive ability that measures in the superior (gifted) range, meaning a higher proportion of autistic students are cognitively gifted than allistic students (Billeiter and Froiland 2022). Gifted/ADHDers may slip through the cracks in a similar fashion. Their high intelligence and ability to quickly grasp new concepts can mask their challenges with attention and impulse control. It is only when the complexity of the material or the organizational demands exceed their coping strategies that their difficulties become apparent. ADHDers are often creative and can have advanced problem-solving skills, but these strengths can overshadow underlying issues related to focus and executive function.

Twice-exceptional learners' giftedness can also sometimes be obscured by their disabilities. In these cases, the focus may shift entirely to the disability, leading to a failure to recognize the underlying cognitive abilities that also need nurturing and support. This lack of recognition can stifle the student's intellectual growth and lead to frustration and underachievement. Universal screening tools (processes where schools assess every student in a single grade level for gifted identification, rather than relying on teacher recommendation) have been an asset in helping identify 2e learners who, in the past, wouldn't have been identified by their teachers as possibly gifted.

Twice-exceptional learners may have both intellectual strengths and challenges and social and emotional differences.

Intellectual strengths and challenges: Twice-exceptional students may display advanced cognitive abilities alongside specific challenges. Here's how this might look:

- A 2e student may excel in mathematics while struggling with reading or writing due to a coexisting disability.
- A 2e student may experience frustration or confusion in traditional learning environments, reflecting a need for tailored support and understanding.

Social and emotional aspects: The complex nature of twice-exceptionality often involves nuanced social and emotional aspects, such as these:

- A 2e student might feel pressure to conform to labels or struggle to understand their unique capabilities. The contrasting areas of strength and challenge might create confusion in self-identity, leading to frustration or a lack of self-confidence.
- A 2e student may find it difficult to connect with peers because they may not fit stereotypes of "gifted" or "disabled," leading to feelings of isolation or rejection.

Amari

Amari's remarkable talent in solving complex mathematical problems was apparent from an early age. While Amari quickly absorbed advanced material beyond their grade level, they often felt disconnected from classmates due to their unconventional thinking and intense focus on personal interests. Amari's teachers identified their cognitive giftedness and discovered that Amari was twice-exceptional, excelling in logic and mathematics but struggling with a coexisting disability in reading. By tailoring support to meet Amari's unique needs, educators were able to nurture Amari's mathematical genius while addressing their challenges.

Encouraged to embrace both their strengths and weaknesses, Amari flourished academically without losing sight of their individuality. Amari's teachers' understanding of Amari's cognitive giftedness and twice-exceptionality allowed Amari to thrive in an environment that appreciated their brilliance and provided support where needed.

Intellectual Disabilities

Note: At the time of writing, people in a neurodiversity-affirming environment typically use the phrase intellectually disabled. *We acknowledge that language around intellectual disabilities is lagging behind the language around other neurodivergent labels due to the stigma that surrounds them.*

Intellectual disabilities are characterized by unique variations in cognitive functioning and adaptive behavior that might include diverse strengths and challenges in areas such as reasoning, learning, and problem-solving. These differences create specific needs and opportunities for personalized support and growth. A diagnosis of intellectual disability is typically based on two main areas of needs: cognitive functioning and adaptive behavior.

Cognitive Functioning and Unique Learning Styles

The first area of diagnosis for intellectual disabilities includes individualized cognitive functioning and learning styles that may differ from traditional expectations. Since intellectually disabled students process information and learn at their unique pace and style, they require tailored learning experiences. This may manifest in ways like this:

- A student may require more time to understand complex concepts, supported by increased frequency of practice with and exposure to a new skill or a thorough step-by-step approach.
- A student may thrive on repetition and consistency and prefer structured and supportive learning environments.

Adaptive Behavior and Personal Growth

Along with variations in cognitive functioning, intellectually disabled individuals might also experience differences in adaptive behavior, including socialization preferences, daily living skills, and personal independence. They may need tailored support in adaptive skills that reflects their distinct developmental paths and personal growth needs. Here's how this might look:

- A student may more actively engage with peers and participate in group activities when provided with explicit information and intentional opportunities to practice social interactions.
- A student may benefit from support with daily living skills as they move toward independence and self-reliance.
- Reflecting a preference for clarity and stability, a student may display increased comfort and focus when following predictable routines and clear expectations.

Obsessive-Compulsive Thinking

Obsessive-compulsive thinking (listed in the *DSM-5* as obsessive-compulsive disorder, or OCD) is characterized by the presence of obsessions (recurring, unwanted thoughts) and compulsions (repetitive behaviors or mental acts). These experiences can be both time-consuming and distressing, but they are also a manifestation of a unique pattern of thinking and behaving.

Cycle of obsessive thinking and compulsive behaviors: Obsessions are persistent, unwanted, and distressing intrusive thoughts or images that can create discomfort. Compulsions are repetitive behaviors that people with OCD feel driven to perform. For a student with obsessive-compulsive thinking, these obsessive thoughts and accompanying compulsive behaviors may manifest in these ways:

- A student's need for things to feel "just right" may lead them to repetitively redo their work until they achieve a sense of completeness or correctness.
- A student's intrusive thoughts around symmetry or order may cause them to arrange classroom materials in a particular pattern.
- A student's unwanted thoughts about harm may prompt them to seek verbal reassurance from teachers or peers about safety.
- A student may experience obsessive thinking as an overwhelming sense that something bad might happen. The compulsive behavior, however, may be entirely internal, such as skip counting to a certain number in their mind. If they are interrupted, they may need to start again to get rid of the obsessive thought.
- A student may experience a "primarily-O" manifestation of obsessive-compulsive thinking, with few or no compulsive behaviors but significant, repetitive, and cyclical intrusive thoughts that are difficult to eliminate.

Tourette Syndrome

Tourette syndrome is characterized by both vocal and motor tics, which are unexpected and rapid movements or sounds (APA 2013). It's essential to recognize these tics as neurological phenomena that are not within an individual's control. Tourette syndrome has many similarities with ADHD and is often co-occurring with it. The similarities between Tourette and ADHD may include challenges in impulse control and attention regulation.

Motor and vocal tics: Vocal tics are exhibited as unexpected vocalizations; motor tics typically manifest as physical expressions. These tics can range from simple and subtle to complex and more noticeable:

- A student may exhibit simple motor tics as sudden, brief movements like blinking, head-jerking, or shrugging. Simple verbal tics might include coughing, clearing the throat, or whistling.
- A student with more complex motor tics might perform movements such as touching or tapping objects, reflecting a distinctive way of physically engaging with their environment. Complex verbal tics can include repeating others' words or phrases, speaking in a different rhythm or tone, or using seemingly random words. *Note: Using socially inappropriate or taboo words is a relatively rare manifestation of complex vocal tics and is not present in all individuals with Tourette.*

Bipolar

Bipolar is characterized by specific diagnostic criteria related to dramatic mood changes, including episodes of mania (elevated mood) and depression (low mood). These mood swings can significantly impact energy, activity levels, concentration, and decision-making. The diagnosis is typically based on two main areas of needs: mania and depression (APA 2013).

It is extremely rare for young children to be diagnosed as bipolar. The average age of onset and diagnosis of most individuals falls between the ages of fifteen and twenty-five. Fewer than 5 percent of individuals diagnosed with bipolar have an onset age younger than twelve (Baldessarini et al. 2012). Bipolar is a diagnosis that fits within the neurodiversity paradigm because it is lifelong and influences how a person thinks, learns, and interacts; however, symptoms can be dangerous and may be mitigated with medication.

Mania: The first area of diagnosis for bipolar includes challenges in regulating manic episodes, which are often characterized by increased energy, enthusiasm, and creativity. These periods of heightened mood and energy may manifest like this:

- A student may exhibit elevated energy and enthusiasm, engaging in multiple activities or taking on ambitious projects, which reflects a unique need for stimulation and creative expression.
- A student might show rapid speech or racing thoughts, reflecting a heightened connection to ideas and creativity, which invites strategies for guided focus and structured task management.

Depression: Bipolar students may also display periods of low mood and decreased energy, interest, concentration, and decision-making, reflecting their unique need for support and understanding during these phases. Here's how that might look:

- A student may show decreased interest in activities, requiring encouragement, support, and alternative approaches to learning and engagement—highlighting a need for personalized connection strategies.
- A student might struggle with concentration and decision-making, reflecting a unique pace and method of processing information and requiring strategies for paced learning and supportive decision-making guidance.

Disruptive Mood Dysregulation Disorder and Oppositional Defiant Disorder

Two comparable diagnoses that you may see students with are disruptive mood dysregulation disorder (DMDD) and oppositional defiant disorder (ODD).

DMDD was added to the *DSM-5* in 2013. The main goal of this diagnosis is to provide a label for behaviors that appear similar to bipolar behaviors, such as heightened, mania-like moods and intense impulsive outbursts. One concern that led to DMDD's inclusion was that children were being given a misdiagnosis of bipolar (Baweja et al. 2016). The thought was that DMDD could be a kind of "placeholder" diagnosis for kids struggling with this type of dysregulation, in place of a diagnosis of bipolar, which carries significant lifelong implications and which may be inaccurate since the typical age of onset of bipolar is late-teens and early twenties (Coryell et al. 2013). Bipolar is also frequently treated with medications that can have significant side effects.

ODD is another diagnosis that focuses specifically on how a child interacts with others—specifically, the adults in their life. A child diagnosed with ODD likely has patterns of defiant, angry, or vindictive behavior (APA 2013). Additionally, ODD is a diagnosis that can only be given to children, since the behaviors are specifically related to the power hierarchy within adult-child relationships.

The problem with both of these diagnoses is that they describe behaviors—what people see from the outside—and ignore what is causing the dysregulation in the first place. What are the accommodations for a child who is defiant? Well, it depends on what is causing the defiance. What are the supports for a child who is emotionally dysregulated? Again, it depends on the underlying cause of the dysregulation.

The purpose of a diagnosis should be to identify the best way to support the individual, whether through therapeutic approaches, medical interventions, or accommodations. Focusing solely on the outward appearance of what a behavior looks like and how it impacts other people ignores the most important part of bringing kids into the process and supporting them.

What to Remember

- Neurodivergent students may exhibit differences in socialization preferences, learning, attention, mood, and other cognitive skills that are distinctly unlike current societal standards. How you respond to and provide support for those variations can drastically impact a student's experience in school.
- Diagnosis and educational identification are not the same thing and serve different purposes. A medical diagnosis seeks to categorize and understand a neurodevelopmental or psychological difference, while an educational identification seeks to understand how a student's unique needs impact their learning, with an eye toward tailoring education to meet those needs.
- Students with neurodevelopmental diagnoses, including conditions like autism, ADHD, and learning disabilities, are generally considered neurodivergent, although the label is less important than recognizing that being neurodivergent means having a brain that operates a bit differently from what's considered typical.

Chapter 3

Dismantling Ableism and Creating a Neurodiversity-Affirming Culture

 Points to Ponder

- How do inclusion and neurodiversity-affirming classrooms differ?
- What are the impacts of ableism and internalized ableism?
- How can co-teaching help you support neurodivergent students?

Let's think about inclusion for a minute. It's a concept that has come a long way in education. With the reauthorization of IDEA in 2004, mainstreaming—placing students with disabilities into general education classrooms for some or all of the school day, rather than segregating them into separate, specialized settings—became common practice (US Department of Education 2024). However, mainstreaming as a practice didn't always consider how to educate students once they were in the classroom. There was a much bigger focus on having students be around their peers than on learning alongside them. Today, the majority of schools have moved away from talking about and practicing mainstreaming to talking about being inclusive of disabled students. While this difference in wording may not seem like a big change, it reflects bigger shifts in the way people think about including students with disabilities in educational settings.

Research suggests that neurodivergent students benefit from spending time in classrooms with peers who aren't neurodivergent. They have lower rates of absenteeism and higher graduation rates with this model than with a pull-out special education one (Hehir, Pascucci, and Pascucci 2016). The same research also shows that neuro-normative students gain benefits from time with neurodivergent peers, not the least of which is being more comfortable with differences. Your school may even have inclusion classrooms, which, by deliberate design, are made up of a balance of students with a wide range of abilities, including students with disabilities and those without. Inclusion is a worthwhile goal, and having inclusive classrooms is a good start to creating a neurodiversity-affirming school. But we challenge you to think about inclusion differently.

When people talk about inclusion, something is often missing in the conversation: the fact that inclusion wouldn't exist without exclusion. It's important to recognize the uncomfortable truth that inclusion means that somebody has the power to decide who gets to be included. That's not belonging.

True belonging isn't about being included in spaces you'd otherwise be excluded from. It's about feeling welcome from the start. And neurodiversity-affirming schools start from the place of assuming all students belong. They ask you to believe that there is no true neuro-normative student and that disability—whether it's neurodivergence or another type—is a social construct.

Until society and education systems recognize, respect, and protect neurodivergence as a social identity, similar to ethnicity, sexual orientation, or gender, neurodivergent people are protected under disability laws. The current education world is one full of labels and diagnoses, and those labels entitle neurodivergent students to accommodations. Disability laws put everyone in the position of having to treat neurodivergence as a disability instead of an identity. And though neurodivergent students may not consider themselves legally disabled, the education system does.

This chapter shares ways to confront and dismantle ableism and other strategies to create a neurodiversity-affirming culture in your school or classroom. It also explores the impact of ableism on kids and how to avoid burnout in neurodivergent students and shares our Neurodivergent Learners' Bill of Rights and Neurodiversity-Affirming Teachers' Compact of Shared Beliefs.

Conceptual Models of Disability

There are two ways to look at what is typically called *disability*, including neurodivergence and the labels and diagnoses that accompany it: the medical model and the social model. These two models don't always align.

Education systems have been built in a way that mirrors the medical model of disability. For instance, person-first language originated with the medical model, which views "disorders" as defects or deficits that the field of medicine and health care professionals should aim to fix. There's value to the medical model in that it helps provide protections and support under laws like the Americans with Disabilities Act (ADA), the Individuals with Disabilities Education Act (IDEA), and Section 504 of the Rehabilitation Act, which we'll get into more in chapter 11. That said, the medical model also sets educators up to view any characteristics, behaviors, or patterns of learning that don't fit the idea of a "typical" student through a deficit lens, which means they spend a lot of time trying to change or fix them.

On the other hand, the social model of disability looks at disability not as an inherent defect in a person but as the consequences a person experiences based on how their differences affect them in their environment and how these consequences get in the way of their ability to function (Wehmeyer 2013). From this perspective, it's not neurodivergence that is disabling—it's systemic barriers, negative attitudes, societal views, and exclusion that create the *concept* of disability. In other words, it is not the students who are disabled, but the environment—the school—that is disabling.

Sometimes these barriers are apparent, like staircases that don't have accompanying ramps, while other times they are less apparent, like not having written text to accompany verbal directions. Those barriers that are more apparent are often easier to address. Barriers that are less visible affect all students with disabilities, whether the disability is apparent (such as a physical disability) or nonapparent (such as neurodivergence). These less-obvious barriers can be harder to identify, and therefore more difficult to address. For instance, the attitudes of nondisabled people toward disability and stereotypes of disability are less-visible barriers.

Understanding and Confronting Ableism

Viewing disability through a social model is crucial to creating neurodiversity-affirming schools. And it requires you to understand and confront ableism, which is a huge barrier to making sure all students feel as though they belong. The simplest explanation of ableism is that it's rooted in the idea that disabled people need "fixing." It defines people both by their disability and by comparison to nondisabled people.

But ableism isn't simple, so a more in-depth explanation is also necessary. Ableism is a form of prejudice against disabled individuals, whether conscious or not. It's based in the belief that nondisabled is the preferred and superior state of being. This results in marginalization and exclusion, unequal treatment, limited opportunities, increased stigma, and lower expectations for disabled students, including those who are neurodivergent. Like other "-isms," it classifies a group of people as "less than" and contains comparison, stereotype, misconception, and generalization.

Ableism shows up in ways that include the following:

- **making assumptions or generalizations** about disabled students based on their diagnoses, without considering or getting to know their strengths, talents, and abilities
- **feeling pity** for disabled students based on your assumptions of what limitations they have or challenges they face
- **viewing disabled students as inspirational** because of what they're able to do "despite" their disability and without considering how the same thing wouldn't be seen as inspirational if a nondisabled student did it
- **believing and acting on misconceptions** without taking time to check the facts
- **excluding disabled students** from educational and social opportunities due to assumptions about what they can, can't, or would want to do, which denies students agency and choice
- **engaging in microaggressions,** even if they're unintentional, including using language that compares something undesirable to disability (see figure 3.1)

Ableism is such a deeply ingrained societal attitude that many disabled people are ableist too. This leads to something known as internalized ableism. That's when disabled people accept and believe negative stereotypes, beliefs, and attitudes about disability. Internalized ableism can cause neurodivergent students to feel embarrassed about

FIGURE 3.1 Ableist vs. Non-Ableist Language

Ableist Phrasing	Non-Ableist Phrasing
That's so crazy!	That's unbelievable/surprising!
They're blind to the facts.	They're unaware of the facts.
She's wheelchair bound.	She's a wheelchair-user/uses a wheelchair.
He's suffering from anxiety.	He lives with anxiety.
That argument is so lame.	That argument is weak.
She's handicapped/handicapable/specially or differently abled.	She's disabled/has a disability.
I work with special needs students.	I work with disabled students.
That's stupid/'r-word.'	That is less than impressive.
The plane was crippled by the storm.	The plane was damaged by the storm.

or blame themselves for being neurodivergent. It can also cause a desire to hide their neurodivergence, reject support or not seek it out, or try to meet society's standards of "normal." In doing so, many neurodivergent students essentially reject aspects of themselves and their life experiences that impact their sense of identity (Manalili 2021). Strategies to create safe environments and encourage student authenticity can help combat internalized ableism (see pages 76 and 133).

Talking about ableism can be uncomfortable. None of us wants to think that we hold beliefs that could harm our students. But for most people, ableism is unconscious, because it's embedded into society as a whole, not just education systems. It's essential to challenge and confront ableism—whether it be in yourself or in others—to promote a more equitable environment for all students.

We say this knowing that it's not easy and that you won't always get it right. The best you can do is be aware, think carefully about *why* you think or believe something about a neurodivergent student, and correct yourself when you get it wrong. It's also important to be mindful of your language and avoid using demeaning terms or ones that perpetuate stereotypes. Instead, aim for respectful and inclusive language that helps promote understanding.

The Impact of Ableism on Neurodivergent Kids

Emily: I was diagnosed with ADHD when I was in the fifth grade. This was at a time when ADHD was really starting to be understood and diagnosed, but girls were often missed. When I was in high school, my junior year to be exact, I wrote a term paper titled "ADHD, the Excuse of the '90s." Looking back, I realize how much internalized ableism I had about what I should be able to do and what I could accomplish if I tried harder and weren't so lazy. It probably took me at least a decade and a half, if not longer, to really understand myself, how my brain worked, and what ADHD truly meant. I've been working on moving beyond some of that internalized ableism, but it's an ongoing process.

Amanda: I love that you tell that story, because I am neurodivergent and have all these different diagnoses that could add up to anything. When I talk to people, they often say to me, "It's so amazing what you've overcome." For a long time, I agreed with that. I thought, "Yeah, I've overcome. I've come so far." But then I realized that wasn't right. It was a mistake to think that I had to overcome anything. Now, I say, "I didn't overcome. I've become." To me, that's been a big step in realizing how huge ableism is in society. I felt like I had to assert that I wasn't disabled. Now, I can say, "I've become this person because I've learned how to interact with my environment in ways that make me feel less disabled."

Emily: I find it interesting that schools for so long have been a place where we really try to get kids to act, behave, and perform in certain ways, regardless of their personality, interests, skills, or abilities. It's kind of a cookie-cutter program. I feel like it contributes to that internalized ableism, which has a long-term effect on so many kids.

Amanda: It does have a long-term effect on kids. One of the things we need to think about when we discuss neurodiversity is being able to comfortably have conversations about ableism. It feels personal when you suggest to a teacher, parent, or whomever, that we should talk about what ableism is. They feel like you're saying that they're doing something wrong. But I think we need to normalize the fact that this is just a part of our society. If we start acknowledging and recognizing ableism, start saying things differently, and start expecting different norms, then it's not anybody's fault. It's just the way the systems have been built. Recognizing that our systems have flaws, and talking about what those flaws are and how we can change them, is the only way we can even begin to discuss internalized ableism. If we can't even acknowledge that ableism exists, how are we going to discuss the fact that kids internalize it and make judgments and comparisons about themselves based on it over the course of their lives?

Emily: In school, everyone is expected to do all the things. I feel like we need to make our schools more adaptable because, in many ways, that's what empowers kids to find their strengths, break free of internalized ableism, and ultimately live lives that are aligned with who they are and with *their* strengths and struggles.

Amanda: What you have just described is the fact that the environment in school is disabling. Right? Environments are disabling. When that student gets to college or enters the workplace, they're still autistic or an ADHDer, but maybe they have found environments where they don't feel disabled because ableism isn't showing up. That's what we want to get to across the board—a place where a person can walk in and say, "I have this diagnosis. I have these traits, but I don't feel disabled because I can make adaptations. It's available to me. I can do what I need to do to be me and make things work for me without feeling ashamed."

Intersecting Identities

Ableism

Ableism might look different across cultures, and it should be considered a factor that can prevent access to diagnosis and accommodations. Cultures that place a high level of importance on conformity may have greater stigma around the differences in behavior or interests that neurodivergent people have when compared to cultures that place higher value on individuality. Families whose cultures expect academic achievement may be hesitant to acknowledge that their children are struggling and that accommodations could be beneficial. Seeking diagnosis and support for neurodivergent people has primarily been driven in the United States by the majority White, middle-class population. Considering the barriers that families may experience to understanding and supporting their neurodivergent children can help you contextualize families' perception of their children's needs.

It is important to remember that some students' cultures value neurodiversity as well. The Māori, for example, believe that autistic children have strong spirits and are closer to a higher realm. Keri Opai, a linguist and educator, coined the term *takiwātanga* for autistic children. It means "in their own time and space" (*Education Gazette* 2023).

Where to Start When Creating a Neurodiversity-Affirming Culture

How *do* you create a culture in your classroom and school that is neurodiversity-affirming? You've picked up this book, so it's likely that you're already off to a good start!

If you've already taken steps to address barriers to belonging in your classroom or school, you likely also see areas for improvement. Take a moment to *really* think about your school or your classroom. Ask yourself:

- What do I/we already say or do that lets all students know they belong?
- What do I/we already do with my/our physical spaces that supports neurodivergent learners?

Think about your answers to these questions as you read our Neurodivergent Learners' Bill of Rights on page 78 and the following sections about where to start in creating a neurodiversity-affirming culture in your classroom and wider school.

Use Neurodiversity-Affirming Language

The words we use are powerful! We already talked a bit about confronting ableism through using non-ableist language, but that's not the only way to use language to build spaces of belonging. You can also begin using neurodiversity-affirming language. Here are some examples of neurodiversity-affirming language and what it can do:

- It presents information in a neutral way, acknowledging strengths and presuming competence.
- It avoids using the medicalized term *disorder* (unless necessary for legal reasons) and instead uses the term *condition*.
- It uses the more neutral phrase *co-occurring* instead of *co-morbidity* when a student has more than one condition that impacts their learning.
- It describes specific support needs and strengths instead of using functioning labels (for example, "low support needs in [situation/environment]" rather than "high functioning").
- It avoids using phrases like *suffers from* to make it clear that being neurodivergent isn't a tragic condition.

Provide Choice

Studies show that it can be difficult to accommodate everyone's needs, but the one commonality is providing choice. We'll talk more about the power of choice when it comes to learning in chapter 4, when we go into depth about Universal Design for Learning.

Neurodivergent Learners' Bill of Rights

1. **Right to Inclusivity:** All neurodivergent learners have the right to be educated in an inclusive environment that values and respects their neurodivergence.

2. **Right to Accommodations:** Neurodivergent learners have the right to accommodations that respect their unique learning styles and needs and promote their personal and academic growth. This may include appropriate assistive technology and adaptive tools that can support their learning and independence, or comprehensive, respectful, and timely assessments to identify their specific strengths, needs, and optimal learning strategies.

3. **Right to Be Understood:** Neurodivergent learners have the right to be understood, accepted, and valued for their unique neurological wiring. This includes educators understanding that certain traits, such as fidgeting, stimming, or tapping, may be a form of communication or coping mechanisms, and not something to change.

4. **Right to Participation:** Neurodivergent learners have the right to actively participate in decisions that affect their education, including IEP or 504 meetings, accommodations discussions, and other relevant forums.

5. **Right to Autonomy and Personal Preference:** All neurodivergent learners have the right to express and exercise their personal preferences in relation to their learning and social experiences. This includes the choice to work independently when appropriate, select their preferred method of learning and engagement, and decide on their participation in recess or social activities. This ensures that each learner's individual needs and preferences are respected and accommodated, fostering their autonomy and self-confidence.

6. **Right to Respect:** All neurodivergent learners have the right to be free from harassment, bullying, and discrimination based on their neurodivergence. This includes the right to confidentiality and privacy regarding being neurodivergent. It also means that all students in the building are educated about neurodiversity so the expectation to adapt doesn't fall solely on neurodivergent students.

7. **Right to Advocacy:** All neurodivergent learners have the right to learn about, understand, and exercise their rights and advocate for their unique needs. This includes the right to have opportunities to self-advocate in a range of situations. This advocacy should be aimed at empowering neurodivergent learners, fostering their self-determination, and promoting their full participation in their education and broader life experiences.

Understand How Design Affects Students

Understanding how design elements affect your neurodivergent students is key when creating spaces to accommodate them. The colors of the walls, the use of carpeting in certain spaces, and even the way the lighting is set up can be neurodiversity-affirming choices.

Here's how two schools are thinking about designing spaces for learning (Stanley 2023).

Katy ISD: When building a new school, Katy ISD in Texas took the opportunity to think about how to create a multitude of learning spaces that allowed for both group and individual work, while also considering that movement, texture, and color can impact students' moods and creativity. They created an open-concept school, which still has traditional closed-door classrooms, but also uses every square foot of the building in an open-concept, modular design. The hallways are wider than usual, allowing for a variety of breakout spaces. The middle of the hallways have traditional flooring, but each side is carpeted, with various types of seating, tables, standing desks, and whiteboards on the walls. This design allows for individual work, group work, and even in-the-moment brainstorming sessions for both students and educators.

Stevenson High School: For Stevenson High School in Lincolnshire, Illinois, the impact of sound and noise on learners was a concern. So when they redesigned, instead of using traditional tile, they chose to install modular carpet tiles throughout the whole school to help absorb sound. Thinking about stress reduction, they also chose to paint certain walls a calming green.

Presume Competence

How you interact with and think about your students' agency also makes a big difference in creating a neurodiversity-affirming culture. Neurodivergent students should expect a certain level of respect and support in your classroom. It's not enough for you to presume competence and believe in inclusion and belonging; your students need to know your beliefs and feel they're true.

You can start by talking to your whole class about the idea of presuming competence, what it looks like when you do it, and what it can look like when they expect it. Sharing the statements below with students provides them with language they can use to express their expectations. It's also a springboard for discussion, giving them a chance to share their own expectations and wants.

Ways Neurodivergent Students Say Educators Can Presume Their Competence

1. Believe that I have important thoughts, feelings, opinions, and things to contribute to a conversation.
2. Ask me if I need help before giving it and let me tell you what type of help I would like.
3. Speak to me directly and not to my support person, parent, caregiver, or friend. (Please ask others to speak directly to me as well.)
4. Talk to me in the same tone of voice you would use when speaking to anyone else my age.
5. Do not assume that I can't understand what you're saying to or about me.
6. Allow me to answer questions for myself and let me make my own decisions.
7. Change the words, not the meaning, if I ask you to rephrase something.
8. Be mindful of your body language, tone of voice, and other nonverbal cues. They communicate whether you presume my competence as much as your words do.
9. Recognize that there may be a difference between what I understand and what I can show you I know.
10. Remember that my behavior serves a purpose. When I don't look you in the eye, or when I tap, spin, fidget, or other something else, I am self-regulating.

Engaging Families

Family engagement is also needed to create a neurodiversity-affirming school culture. It's sometimes easy to forget that students have families or caregivers who are part of the equation. That's a lot of people who want to be engaged, who want information, and who can provide perspective on what a student's neurodivergence looks like in action at home.

Sometimes families may seem reluctant to participate, but that doesn't mean they don't want to be engaged. They may be worried about being judged. They may have had their own negative experiences with school, or they, too, may be neurodivergent and not communicate in ways you'd expect. Engaging families also means considering, anticipating, and mitigating any barriers that they might be facing. A few common barriers and ways to mitigate them are outlined below.

Barrier: Feeling Unwelcome

Families of neurodivergent students may feel isolated and excluded from school communities for a variety of reasons. Many families have had uncomfortable experiences with schools in the past and are wary of feeling blamed or shamed for or about their children's difficulty at school. There could also be cultural differences at play that cause a family to feel unwelcome at school. In some cultures, it's disrespectful to question a teacher's approach or ask about classroom practices. And in other cultures, disabilities and trouble with learning are simply not talked about.

Explicitly asking families what they need to feel welcome is the most important way of including them. It shows them that school is a safe and supportive space you're creating where their children belong. And it means you're not making assumptions about why they're not engaging.

Barrier: Difficulty or Reluctance in Communicating

Families of neurodivergent students don't always know the most effective ways to communicate with their children's school. When a student has a learning plan, there are usually multiple contacts and touchpoints—from teachers to case managers—and it can be exhausting and overwhelming for families to sort out who to talk to about what. They may also not trust that their input is welcome or will be heard or acted upon.

Raising a neurodivergent child means that a family probably spends a lot of time talking about their child. They may not want to be asked questions they've answered many times before, and they may come off as irritated, frustrated, or argumentative because they've been advocating for and answering questions about their child for years. Communicating effectively can begin by simply acknowledging that you don't know what to ask, but that you want to listen. It also helps when families know that you will be speaking up and looking out for all your students. Being a voice of support and setting the standard as someone who will speak up for students' needs goes a long way in establishing trust, especially with families who have had negative experiences with school systems.

Barrier: Power Imbalances

Keep in mind that neurodivergent conditions can be genetic. This means that some students' families likely have generations of experience feeling misunderstood and less-than. That's a power imbalance that's hard to shift. Sharing your thoughts around presuming competence and the Neurodivergent Learners' Bill of Rights (page 78) can help families know that you not only believe in their children's potential but you're also creating a space that will allow their children to be themselves.

Changing power imbalances also requires openness to being wrong and being able to live with the discomfort of being corrected. There are always things to learn from families, your students, and the neurodiversity movement at large. Don't be afraid to admit what you don't know, and assure families that you're willing to learn from people who are united by the experience of being neurodivergent.

Trauma-Informed and Neurodiversity-Affirming Practices

The adverse childhood experiences (ACE) study released in the late 1990s changed the landscape of schools in significant ways (Chafouleas, Pickens, and Gherardi 2021). Trauma-informed practices have been brought into educational settings, providing educators with an understanding of the impact of trauma on how students learn. In many ways, trauma-informed and neurodiversity-affirming practices align and integrate well.

The hard truth is that for many neurodivergent learners, school is an environment where trauma occurs. Neurodivergent students may feel as if they're the square peg being forced into the round hole, day after day, at school. They are disciplined for being different and excluded from social interactions. They are bombarded with uncomfortable sensory stimuli, yet prevented from accessing sensory strategies that can help them regulate emotions and focus. They're accused of being "weird," or they work so hard not to be seen as different that they end up burning themselves out by the time high school is over.

Schools ask neurodivergent students daily to adapt in ways that aren't natural for them. In a world where fitting in can seem like the ultimate goal, many kids twist and turn themselves to meet expectations. Some find their own rhythm, while others get called out for being themselves. Continually facing these high-stress situations is like a slow drip of "little-t" trauma. Over time, this doesn't just fade away; it leads these students to dodge challenges, doubt their worth, and struggle with self-esteem (van der Kolk 2015; Cloitre et al. 2009).

You might be thinking that it sounds dramatic to say that being neurodivergent in school can feel traumatic, but many adults who've been down that road will tell you about the deep-seated stress they remember. Their stories (see the vignettes about Lisabeth and Judah on the next page) show just how real and lingering these experiences can be, reminding us all of the need for understanding and compassion.

Because trauma-informed and neurodiversity-affirming practices work to remove stress from the school environment, they naturally complement each other. Both focus on seeing students as individuals, with their own experiences and points of view. They challenge the harmful stereotypes and discrimination that too often limit students' potential. They recognize that consistency and predictability play a huge part in making students feel safe and understood at school, and they both provide clear rules and routines. Taking what you've learned from trauma-informed practices that are already in place in schools and overlaying the concept of the neurodiversity-affirming school is a powerful way to create an environment where all students thrive.

Lisabeth

Lisabeth was a bright student who went through school as an undiagnosed AuDHDer. Lisabeth managed through elementary and middle school, but the pressure of high school courses was overwhelming. Pushing through burnout to meet the expectations put on her, plus constant efforts to camouflage her difficulties without the opportunity for accommodations, led to intense feelings of inefficacy and fear. The transition to college was difficult, and without the structure of home and the high school setting, she ended up dropping out after two consecutive incomplete semesters. Several years later, the residual trauma of being unsupported in the academic setting continues to be a major barrier to Lisabeth's pursuit of the higher education that she desires.

Judah

Judah is a neurodivergent young adult who is also dealing with the residual effects of "little-t" trauma from the educational setting. He was diagnosed as an ADHDer in first grade but wasn't identified as autistic until he was in high school. Although Judah had an IEP to help with emotional regulation and executive functioning during the last few years of his high school experience, he continues to be extremely distrustful of educators, who assumed his difficulties were due to a lack of motivation. Though he is enrolled part-time at a local community college, he has intense emotional reactions to relatively typical expectations in those classes and vacillates between hypervigilance to manage the expectations of his professors and a complete avoidance of the steps necessary to be successful—both common trauma reactions.

Burnout in Neurodivergent Students

The issue of burnout in neurodivergent children deserves our attention as we create neurodiversity-affirming schools. Burnout is a psychological syndrome that arises due to ongoing exposure to stressors that are unable (or seem unable) to be changed. Although it is commonly associated with compassion fatigue resulting from emotionally draining careers, burnout can be experienced by anyone, regardless of age or occupation. It manifests in three principal areas (World Health Organization 2022):

1. **Overwhelming exhaustion:** The exhaustion from burnout goes beyond mere tiredness. Individuals grappling with this facet of burnout feel profound fatigue, experience a significant drop in their energy levels, and find it challenging to muster the motivation to complete even the most basic tasks.
2. **Cynicism:** This dimension of burnout isn't just about feeling jaded. Burnout cynicism dives deeper, fostering feelings of helplessness and negativity. An individual experiencing it may grow skeptical of others' intentions, even if people are reaching out with genuine offers of support or connection.
3. **Ineffectiveness:** A profound feeling of lack of accomplishment characterizes this area of burnout. Such individuals often harbor thoughts like "Everything I attempt fails" and "Things never seem to get better."

The intersection of burnout and neurodivergence paints a vivid picture: being in unsupportive environments is stressful and creates a need for neurodivergent individuals to hide their neurodivergent traits. The act of constantly portraying an inauthentic version of themselves then becomes a chronic stressor, leading to burnout. The continued stress of having to show up and be in the unsupportive environment every day further exacerbates the burnout.

School is often a major stressor that neurodivergent students experience. Too often, the approach is to just push kids through each school day. While this approach works for some students, this relentless drive can induce a trauma response in neurodivergent children, making even the thought of school an emotional burden. The physiological response they experience can take the form of a panic attacks. Eventually, they may no longer be able to push past the stress and anxiety, leading to school avoidance or refusal.

The perpetual demands of school routines, coupled with the lurking fear of disciplinary actions for underdeveloped executive functioning skills or emotional regulation challenges, pile on even more stress. Add to this the very real challenges of exclusion or bullying by peers, and the stress can become nearly insurmountable. When these stressors pile up, neurodivergent students start associating feelings of ineffectiveness with school, and may begin to believe that they'll never achieve success (Spaeth and Pearson 2023).

The road to recovery from burnout is long and is built on a foundation of trust and safety. The best solution is to be proactive and avoid burnout in the first place by creating a neurodiversity-affirming classroom and school culture. In addition to creating this nurturing environment, you can teach neurodivergent students about the signs of burnout and help them recognize when self-care is appropriate to prevent it from occurring.

Can You "Grow Out" of Neurodivergence?

One thing we commonly hear when leading trainings and in conversations is people describing how they or someone they know "used to be" neurodivergent but "grew out of" their autism or ADHD as an adult. They may describe an experience of struggling with issues related to their diagnosis when young and in school, yet no longer having the same difficulties once they reached adulthood. Is it more likely that these folks "grew out of" their diagnoses, or that they were finally able to have the autonomy and agency to make decisions about their lives that make sense to them?

Rather than having "grown out of" their neurodivergence, it is more probable that they graduated and entered a program of study they're passionate about or found a job that allows (or requires) them to utilize their strengths. Hyperactivity, for example, melts away if you have a job that keeps you active throughout the day. Social communication difficulties become irrelevant when you are able to communicate about a passion with colleagues who share it. Learning differences don't matter so much if you aren't forced to sit through a class in your area of weakness every single day.

> This freedom to choose the type of environment that fits one's neurodivergence may make it appear as if a person outgrew a diagnosis they had in their school years. But instead of being stuck in the one-size-fits-all education system that was exacerbating their areas of difficulty, their chosen environments leverage the strengths they have that mitigate those areas of difficulty.

Collaboration Between Staff and Co-Teaching

Though you can work to create a neurodiversity-affirming culture in your classroom, you can't create an overall neurodiversity-affirming school that mitigates neurodivergent burnout, makes students feel safe, and reduces the stressors of an education system by yourself. This work requires close collaboration and a shared commitment amongst school staff. To go back to the idea of inclusion as a starting point, having a shared belief in the benefits of inclusive classrooms is a good beginning.

The concept of neurodiversity is built on the idea that difference is natural. It doesn't just apply to students whose neurological wiring gets in the way of their learning. When you reframe inclusive schools as neurodiversity-affirming ones, it's not hard to build collaborative relationships and a shared belief system with colleagues. Our Neurodiversity-Affirming Teachers' Compact of Shared Beliefs (page 88) is a good place to start. We created this compact as a complementary piece to the Neurodivergent Learners' Bill of Rights, identifying the educator's role in guaranteeing that those rights are provided to their students.

One way to ensure that teachers are working together to create neurodiversity-affirming classrooms in a school and getting the support they need to educate diverse learners in those classrooms is to leverage the use of integrated collaborative team-teaching (also known as co-teaching).

True collaborative co-teaching requires you to put aside the trepidation you may have about opening your classroom to another teacher—trepidation about not having full "control" over your classroom and what happens in it. It also requires you to believe

The Neurodiversity-Affirming Teachers' Compact of Shared Beliefs

1. **We believe difference is different, not less.** Every learner has unique strengths, challenges, and experiences. Those differences make our classrooms stronger and more diverse. We try our best to understand, accept, and value all learners' unique neurological wiring.

2. **We believe all students learn differently.** Not all students will gain and retain knowledge in the same way. It is our responsibility as teachers not only to try to meet and understand the needs of all our students but also to provide information in multiple ways to meet those needs.

3. **We believe in showing respect to all students.** Every learner deserves to be respected and feel a sense of belonging in the classroom. We show respect to all students and protect them from harassment, bullying, and discrimination based on their neurodivergence. This includes understanding that behavior is not personally directed and may be a form of communication or a coping mechanism.

4. **We believe all students deserve accommodation and differentiation.** Regardless of whether a neurodivergent student has a specialized learning plan, we will design instruction and provide accommodations and support that can help them make progress. When appropriate and possible, we will advocate for a "push-in" model, so that neurodivergent students don't have to leave the classroom for services like occupational therapy or reading instruction.

5. **We believe all students should have agency.** All learners deserve to make and express choices about how they wish to interact in learning and social settings. Whenever possible, we will allow all students to select their preferred method of learning and engagement and decide on their participation in social activities to support their right to agency and autonomy.

6. **We believe in honoring advocacy.** Every neurodivergent learner has the right to understand and speak up for their unique needs. It is our responsibility to educate ourselves about the types of things our students may self-advocate for and understand what this may look or sound like. When our students self-advocate, we will remain open to hearing them express their need and to honor and accommodate those needs as much as it is in our power to do so.

7. **We believe all students can—and should—participate.** All learners are capable of actively participating in decisions that affect their education. We encourage and will support neurodivergent students in participating in the classroom, IEP or 504 meetings, accommodations discussions, and other relevant situations.

8. **We believe in holding all students to high expectations.** All students' learning goals should be based on the expectation that they will be able to meet the academic standards set out by the school and state. It is our responsibility to provide or seek out support in providing differentiated instruction so that neurodivergent students can meet those standards and learn the same materials and content as the rest of the class.

that this kind of collaboration benefits your students. It can be hard to do, but studies show that when co-teachers take the time to build trusting relationships, and respect and tap into each teacher's expertise, collaborative team-teaching can successfully meet the diverse learning needs of students (Cook et al. 2017).

In the best circumstances, collaborative team-teaching pairs general education teachers with special education teachers in a general education classroom. This is one of the most effective ways of providing instruction to support the academic and social and emotional needs of all learners—not just neurodivergent students.

Fostering Effective Collaboration When Co-Teaching

Collaborative teaching offers valuable benefits, yet implementation can pose challenges—particularly when there's a perceived power imbalance between newer teachers and more experienced ones. It can also be difficult for co-teachers to work together when they hold differing teaching philosophies. Nevertheless, there are strategies co-teachers can use to facilitate success. One of the easiest of these is to reinforce your status as a team by displaying both your names on your classroom door, assignments, and other materials. This helps students recognize your collaborative efforts and discourages them from seeking out divides or inconsistencies in your approaches.

Other ways to foster collaboration include the following:

- **Establish shared expectations.** Before the year begins, have a conversation with your co-teacher about expectations for how you'll handle things such as behavior management, homework, and so forth. If you've already worked together, this is a time to revisit any challenges that arose and find ways to avoid them this school year. Resolving any differences and reaching a consensus on how to run your shared class is beneficial to you and your students. It also can ward off any good-cop/bad-cop dynamics. At the beginning of the year, trimester, or quarter, you can share with your students that you had this conversation to help create a more trusting and positive classroom culture.

- **Create regular collaborative planning time.** It's critical to keep open lines of communication with your co-teacher and to be able to raise concerns respectfully—and not in front of students. Dedicating time to collaborate, especially when planning and reflecting on jointly taught lessons, gives you that opportunity. It's also a good idea to try to keep your planning time aligned with other teachers' and administrators' time (as possible) so you can seek their advice, support, and ideas.

- **Coordinate and agree upon responsibilities.** Regardless of the model of teaching you're using, it's essential to know which responsibilities belong to who. It allows lessons to go more smoothly and gives you a starting place when you need to debrief together.

Types of Co-Teaching

There are several co-teaching models, each of which has use cases, unique strengths, and challenges, and all of which look a little different from each other in the classroom. Here is a closer look at some common co-teaching models.

Team-Teaching

In this fully collaborative model, both teachers are actively engaged in delivering instruction to the whole class. Co-teachers are both in the classroom and share equal responsibility for planning, teaching, and assessing student learning, but they haven't necessarily planned who is going to take which part of the lesson. If one teacher makes a point and the other wants to elaborate, they can and will. And if a student needs something explained in a different way, co-teachers can ask each other for support.

Why use it:

- It helps neurodivergent students build flexible thinking skills by introducing them to different ways of teaching the same material.
- It provides opportunities for students to ask questions and engage with the material without being seen as disruptive or taking the class off course.
- It shows students what it can look like when people work together collaboratively, even when they don't think the same way.
- It allows for presenting material in multiple ways.

What can be hard about it:

- It makes some teachers feel vulnerable to have someone else watch and potentially critique their approach.

- It requires shared understanding of grading and definition of success, not just between co-teachers but among students as well.
- It asks students to trust both teachers equally, which can be hard for students who have had difficult experiences with other teachers.

Parallel Teaching

In this approach, the class is split into two groups, and co-teachers deliver the same content simultaneously to each group. This allows for smaller group instruction, increased opportunities for student interaction, and a way to more easily reach learners who need differentiated instruction.

Why use it:

- It allows for a more manageable student-teacher ratio, which can make neurodivergent students feel less on the spot and more able to participate.
- It gives students the chance to engage with the material and their teachers in more depth.
- It provides the opportunity to teach to data-driven groups, either of varying abilities or of similar needs.

What can be hard about it:

- It requires careful planning to make sure all students walk away with the same content and understanding of it.
- It can be difficult to control for sensory overload, factors of distractibility, and, to some degree, hurt feelings if a student feels like they've been placed in the "wrong" group.
- It requires some mechanism to track time to make sure the lesson ends on time for both groups.

Alternative or "Big Group/Small Group" Teaching

In this approach, one teacher works with the majority of the students, while the other works with a smaller group who may benefit from additional support or more enriching content. This approach is highly data driven, as this type of teaching works well when co-teachers know which students have skill gaps that need to be addressed and which are ready to move on to more advanced skills.

Why use it:
- It allows for more manageable student-teacher ratios, which can make neurodivergent students feel less on the spot and more able to participate.
- It gives students the chance to engage with the material and the teachers in more depth.
- It reinforces that all students sometimes need additional support without singling out students who struggle.
- It accounts for the need for enrichment as much as the need for intervention.

What can be hard about it:
- It can be overwhelming or cause emotional dysregulation for students who feel self-conscious in small groups.
- It doesn't account for some students needing or preferring to work on their own.
- It requires significant pre-teaching and understanding around expectations for large and small group work.
- It requires careful planning to make sure all students understand the material the large group was taught.

Station Teaching

In the station-teaching approach, the class is divided into small groups, and each teacher leads one group in a specific learning activity or station. Students rotate through the stations, receiving differentiated instruction from each teacher—learning the same material but in different ways.

Why use it:
- It provides students the chance to work with and get to know both teachers.
- It allows for independent workstations where students can practice taking charge of their own learning in a low-stakes situation.

- It provides an opportunity for deliberate flexible grouping to differentiate learning.
- It allows neurodivergent students who struggle with focus and concentration a natural mechanism to move around and reengage when stations switch.
- It supports UDL.

What can be hard about it:
- It can be frustrating for students who don't work or process information as quickly as others—they may not get to or through all the stations.
- It can be overwhelming for students who struggle with sensory regulation.
- It requires significant pre-teaching and understanding around expectations for independent work.

One Teach, One Assist

In this approach, either co-teacher assumes the role of the primary instructor, while the other provides support by circulating through the classroom to assist individual students or manage behavior. This model is particularly helpful for classrooms with diverse learning needs.

Why use it:
- It provides students who need extra support a discrete way to ask for and get it.
- It allows teachers to see where, when, and which learners are struggling.
- It helps teachers begin to understand what behavior is truly off track and what behavior supports learning for neurodivergent students.

What can be hard about it:
- It can make it difficult for some students to see co-teachers as "equal" if only one is teaching.
- It may stifle learner agency if help is instantly available, as not all students will want to engage in productive struggle.

One Teach, One Observe

In this approach, one teacher takes the lead in delivering instruction while the other observes and gathers data on student engagement, understanding, and behavior. The observer can provide valuable feedback and insights not only to improve teaching practice but also to improve learner agency. When one teacher is available to observe how students are engaging, it helps both teachers track learning needs and use of accommodations.

Why use it:

- It allows for observation and data collection by a teacher already known to students.
- It provides little disruption to the classroom culture.
- It helps gather data that can inform future co-teaching approaches.

What can be hard about it:

- It is difficult for students to know if they can ask for help from the observing teacher, especially if that teacher is typically available for support.

What to Remember

- Ableism must be confronted to create a neurodiversity-affirming school. Questioning the beliefs that one has surrounding ability and disability is a starting point. Students can also be impacted by internalized ableism.
- Students benefit when all stakeholders involved in supporting them are engaged in the development and implementation of the plan to support them. This includes not only teachers and school professionals but also involvement from families, which may require invitation and intention from the educator.
- There are a variety of models of collaborative teaching that allow educators to work together to meet the needs of their students.

CHAPTER 4

Universal Design for Learning as a Neurodiversity-Affirming Practice

 Points to Ponder

- Which learners does Universal Design for Learning support?
- What does Universal Design for Learning look like in practice?
- How can you reduce barriers to learning before they arise?

When you hear the phrase *Universal Design for Learning*, what is your first thought? Do you wonder why we're talking about yet another way of designing education? Do you want to know how you're supposed to implement this practice into your teaching on top of everything else you're doing? Do you ask how you can create neurodiversity-affirming classrooms if you're supposed to teach students in a universal way?

These are common questions that come up in the conversations we've had with educators about Universal Design for Learning. The phrase itself can be confusing to parse. If we're talking about design-based learning, we're limiting ourselves to a pedagogy mostly used in STEM, which not only doesn't meet the unique needs of neurodivergent learners but also doesn't include the breadth of topics we teach our students. And if we're using the word *universal* to mean "one way of learning," that's at cross-purposes with recognizing, respecting, and responding to the needs of neurodivergent students.

Defining Universal Design for Learning

Defining Universal Design for Learning, more commonly known as UDL, is easier when you start by understanding what it's not. Let's look at that first:

- **UDL is not finding one universal way to teach all students.** Students don't all learn in one way, whether they're neurodivergent or not.
- **UDL is not asking you to use design-based learning for all subjects.** Not everything can be taught in a way that asks students to build, develop, or create a product or system that solves a real-life problem.
- **UDL is not designing a new educational system or curriculum.** It's unreasonable—and just plain silly—to expect that all classroom teachers are also policymakers and curriculum designers.
- **UDL is not replacing the need for differentiated instruction.** All students will continue to have individual needs that educators must support to help them achieve. Students will continue to need help in accessing the material and meeting their goals. UDL doesn't replace differentiation, but it can reduce it.

So, what *is* UDL? UDL is an approach to teaching that proactively removes barriers to learning to give all students a chance to succeed and become expert learners. Right about now, you might be thinking, "Well, that's not much clearer." Stay with us.

Universal Design's Influence on UDL

Universal Design for Learning leans into the idea of universal design, a concept that architects, engineers, software developers, and environmental designers use when creating buildings, spaces, and products. Universal design follows a set of principles (see figure 4.1) to guide the design of environments and products to ensure they are accessible to and usable by as many people as possible, regardless of age, size, or disability (NC State University 1997).

FIGURE 4.1 The Seven Principles of Universal Design

Equitable Use
The design is useful and marketable to people with diverse abilities.

Flexibility in Use
The design accommodates a wide range of individual preferences and abilities.

Simple and Intuitive Use
Use of the design is easy to understand, regardless of the user's experience, knowledge, language skills, or current concentration level.

Perceptible Information
The design communicates necessary information effectively to the user, regardless of ambient conditions or the user's sensory abilities.

Tolerance for Error
The design minimizes hazards and adverse consequences of accidental or unintended actions.

Low Physical Effort
The design can be used efficiently and comfortably with minimal fatigue.

Size and Space for Appropriate Use
Appropriate size and space are provided for approach, reach, manipulation, and use, regardless of the user's body size, posture, or mobility.

Universal design is part of your everyday life, whether or not you notice it. Take, for example, the automatic doors at a store. You may not need them to open for you, but it's certainly convenient when you're pushing a shopping cart or have your hands full. But for someone with mobility issues, automatic doors are more than just convenient, they're necessary.

Universal design is also the reason you can watch a video on your phone without the sound on. The captioning feature makes it easy for you to avoid disturbing other people, and it makes that same video accessible to people with hearing impairments. Universal design doesn't just make the world more accessible for people with disabilities; it makes the world easier for *all* people. Something usable by, accessible to, and helpful to most people is just good design.

UDL makes learning more accessible to neurodivergent students by giving them varied ways to gain information and show what they know. But it also makes learning more accessible for all students. And learning being accessible to most students is just good teaching.

The Principles of UDL

UDL is important as you aim to create classrooms that not only are inclusive but that affirm neurodivergence and other identities. Just as the goal of universal design is to remove barriers to access for everyday spaces and experiences, the goal of UDL is to remove barriers to learning at school. It's about building classroom spaces and learning experiences that provide engaging and accessible ways to learn that flex to the strengths and needs of each student.

Just like universal design uses a set of principles to help guide the creation of environments and products, UDL uses a set of principles as a framework for creating lesson plans, assessments, and classroom environments. The principles provide a framework for educators to create equitable access to learning: each student has access to the appropriate resources and support *they* need to be a thriving learner. The principles of UDL look at the *why*, *what*, and *how* of learning.

Principle 1: Provide Multiple Means of Engagement

Engagement is all about motivation, or the *why* of learning.

Think for a minute about your day: *What motivated you to teach the material you taught today?* Maybe it was because you felt pressured to get that much further along in the curriculum. Maybe it's because a teachable moment presented itself and you were inspired to put it to good use. No matter what it was, that was your *why*.

Now take a minute to think about your students. You probably had some who were really engaged, some who were somewhat engaged, and some who weren't engaged at all. What do you think motivated the students who were engaged? What kept them intellectually present and curious? No matter what it was, that was their *why*.

Each learner's *why* is going to be different. It's important for you to remember that your students' motivation for learning what you're teaching is not always the same as your motivation for teaching it. Finding out what motivates your neurodivergent students to learn and how they feel about what you're teaching, and then using that information in your presentation of the content as often as you can, is a good way to engage them. Building strong relationships and getting to know students is a first step to understanding who they are and what they enjoy. Taking the extra step to know what piques their curiosity and makes them eager to learn is what this first principle is all about.

Some students are really into learning new things. But some, especially those who have anxiety, are routine oriented, or experience demand avoidance, may not only be less interested in learning something new but also actively resistant to it. Giving students a choice of how to engage with the content and showing them how it relates to their real lives goes a long way toward increasing intrinsic motivation, interest, and willingness to learn.

While providing multiple means of engagement sounds great theoretically, it's important to know what it looks like in action. At its simplest, it means that when you plan lessons, you should be thinking about all the different ways for students to access and interact with the content you're teaching and looking for ways to engage and hold their interest. If you're teaching about dinosaurs, for example, you don't have to just talk about dinosaurs. You can find books of varying levels of difficulty to explore. You could provide pictures with information, audiobooks, videos about dinosaurs, educational websites to explore, or even a virtual field trip to a natural history museum. And if you have a student who has encyclopedic knowledge of dinosaurs, you can let that student teach some of what they know. In this one example, you've provided students with several things:

- the ability to make choices about how they learn
- an assignment that feels relevant to their lives, talents, and interests
- some ways to make learning feel gamified
- a chance for them to get up and move around

In other words, you've given them ways to find their *why* and helped them become self-motivated learners.

Principle 2: Provide Multiple Means of Representation

Representation is all about how you convey information and how your students make sense of it—or the *what* of learning.

Providing multiple means of representation is key for teaching neurodivergent students. Their unique strengths and challenges mean they don't always take in information in a conventional way. This principle ensures that all your students have multiple ways to understand and use information.

Making sense of information isn't as simple as it sounds. It's a multifaceted process that starts with the perception of the information, then moves to the processing and making sense of it, and finally to being able to do something with what's been perceived and processed. That's hard enough for any learner, but for neurodivergent learners, it's even harder, because not all those systems function as smoothly as you'd expect.

Here's an example: Think about the last book you read. What was it about? Who were the main characters? Where did it take place? Most importantly, what did you need to be able to do to answer these questions? It took a lot more than just reading. Let's break it down:

- **You needed to read fluently enough to understand the meaning of the text.** For learners who have language-based learning disabilities, their understanding of a text is not something you can take for granted. These students may struggle to read the words, let alone glean meaning from the sentences and paragraphs.
- **You needed to be able to make sense of the vocabulary.** Whether it's through context clues or prior knowledge, making enough sense of the information you

read to answer questions about a book means you understood any vocabulary that was specific to the text. How confusing it would be to read the Harry Potter series if you didn't know that a lot of its words don't exist elsewhere! There's no prior knowledge that can be accessed to make sense of what a muggle or a dementor is.

- **You needed to be able to focus your attention on the book.** ADHDers and those with other neurodivergent traits can find it hard to sustain their attention, especially in a classroom, where there are always things competing for students' attention. They may be distracted by sensory input you don't notice, such as fluorescent lights, birds outside the window, or the smell of lunch wafting in from the cafeteria. If a book isn't interesting to them, then it may not keep their attention even when they're trying their best to concentrate on it.

- **You needed an understanding of the characters' experiences.** Students who are very concrete thinkers may have difficulty imagining themselves in situations or places they've never been or seen. They may also have trouble connecting emotionally with a character if the character's emotion is not one they've experienced or can easily identify.

The bottom line is that learning isn't always as easy as you might assume it will be since there's no one way that's best to convey information to everyone in a class. Neurodivergent—and all—students benefit from access to a variety of ways to get the *what* of your content. Some will do better with visual representations of information, such as picture menus or directions or graphic organizers showing key concepts. Others may prefer audio options, like audiobooks or verbal directions in addition to written ones. Some students need to see or do something to understand it, which might mean viewing video about how to solve a math problem or using manipulatives to try it in action. In giving options to learn by text, audio, video, or hands-on learning, you give all students agency over how to access the material in whatever way best suits *their* needs, complements *their* strengths, and allows them to make connections in *their* way.

Principle 3: Provide Multiple Means of Action and Expression

Action and expression are all about the *how* of learning—students showing what they know, whether it be in the form of a quiz, an essay, or even just telling you what they learned.

But this part of learning can be really frustrating for some students. We've heard more than one neurodivergent student say things like "Why do I have to prove I've learned it? You saw me do it!" and "How come I have to show my work? I got the answer right." And honestly, you can probably empathize. After all, when you took your driver's test, you weren't expected to show how you got to knowing how to drive. Nobody asks you to prove you know how to use the complex formula chart when you do your taxes.

Part of this frustration comes from how teachers ask students to show what they know. Teachers tend to default to asking them to do this in writing or verbally. But when neurodivergent learners struggle with writing, organizing thoughts, or speech, requiring them to use these methods of sharing doesn't give them a fair chance to accurately express their knowledge. The action and expression principle of UDL won't entirely take away the frustration that comes with having to show how you know something, but it can help manage it by changing the *how* of the sharing.

"Multiple means of action and expression" has options beyond writing and speaking built into the principle itself—namely action and expression. Instead of a written book report, what if you gave students the option to do a series of short informational videos? Or to bake something delicious to show they've learned measurement or about a culture's foods? What if you asked them to create a digital arts project, design a web tool, or build something physically to show what they know? Best of all—*What if you told students exactly what they needed to be able to show you they'd learned, then gave them the choice of how to express it?*

Giving students multiple ways to demonstrate that they've gained knowledge and mastered skills can not only help them take charge of their own learning; it can also help them feel successful. It affirms that the way they create meaning and share information is valuable, which in turn continues to create spaces where neurodivergent thinking is valued.

How UDL Supports Neurodivergent Learners

The enhanced flexibility and customization that is core to UDL effectively supports the needs of neurodivergent learners and recognizes diverse neurocognitive styles. Here are some specific ways you can apply UDL to help learning environments be adaptable and responsive to the unique ways neurodivergent students learn and engage with the world:

- **Customize the level of challenge.** Using UDL helps you create lessons with varying levels of challenge to help maintain engagement in neurodivergent learners who might seek constant stimulation, either for focus or sensory regulation.

- **Provide choice and autonomy.** Some neurodivergent students have specific interests or preferences around how they engage with learning and may have trouble with other approaches and teachers who don't take that into mind. Allowing choice in learning activities can be empowering for them.

- **Create predictable routines and clear expectations.** While predictable routines and explicit expectations benefit all learners, they significantly and specifically benefit students who prefer and thrive in structured environments.

- **Give visual support.** Utilizing visual aids, such as charts, diagrams, and graphic organizers, can help neurodivergent students with auditory processing challenges. It also gives nonspeaking students ways to communicate what they know.

- **Use audio and visual materials.** Providing audiobooks and video content levels the playing field for students with language-based learning disorders like dyslexia and other students who struggle with traditional text-based materials.

- **Simplify and segment instructions.** Breaking down instructions into smaller, manageable steps is good practice to support all students, but it can be particularly beneficial to ADHDers and other neurodivergent learners who have difficulty with complex directions.

- **Use technology-aided expression.** Having speech-to-text software or other assistive technologies available can be a game-changer for neurodivergent students with motor challenges and those whose thoughts are faster than their fingers.

- **Provide structured task management.** Using step-by-step guides and organizational tools can support students' executive functioning by giving them ways to manage tasks and maintain focus.

- **Allow students to work at their own pace.** Personalized pacing, with options for acceleration or additional time, accommodates the varied processing speeds common in neurodivergent learners. It also gives all learners the opportunity to work at different paces in different subjects instead of putting them on a single track.

- **Use tailored evaluation.** Providing varied assessment methods, like project-based evaluations or verbal quizzes, can more accurately measure what neurodivergent students understand. This ensures that your assessments reflect students' true capabilities and knowledge, not how skilled they are at taking traditional tests.
- **Emphasize strengths and interests.** UDL encourages teachers to incorporate students' areas of strength as a way of enhancing engagement and learning outcomes.
- **Foster optional opportunities for social connections.** Creating opportunities for social interaction during learning can help neurodivergent students practice interpreting and reacting to social situations. But the choice element of UDL also allows them to decide for themselves if they want to engage socially without that choice being stigmatized.

Most of all, UDL provides the framework to create an environment where all types of learners are valued, promoting a growth mindset and resilience. By designing learning experiences that consider all learner profiles from the start, applying UDL may help reduce the stigma and isolation that can come with needing different or additional support.

Adaptable and Responsive Learning Environments

The situation: In a group project, students are brainstorming ideas for their assignment. Everyone is encouraged to share their thoughts and contribute to the discussion. The conversation is fast paced, with students frequently interjecting and building upon each other's ideas.

Perspective of others: Most students see this as a lively and productive activity. They enjoy the rapid exchange of ideas and feel that the energetic discussion helps generate creative solutions. They view interruptions and overlapping conversations as a normal part of a dynamic brainstorming process. When they notice the neurodivergent student's silence or hesitation, they might perceive it as disinterest, lack of preparation, shyness, or even aloofness. They are unaware of the internal struggle the neurodivergent student is facing.

Perspective of the neurodivergent student: A neurodivergent student may find the fast-paced and overlapping conversations overwhelming and disorienting. They struggle to process rapidly changing topics and find it difficult to identify the right moment to contribute without interrupting. The student feels anxious about not being able to keep up with the flow of ideas and worries that their voice might not be heard or valued. They perceive the environment as chaotic and stressful, making it hard for them to participate effectively. Though they are deeply engaged in the conversation internally, their external silence or delayed responses might be misinterpreted by others.

Possible follow-up: The teacher may observe the behavior of the neurodivergent student and work to understand why it appears that they are less engaged. Applying the UDL principles of multiple means of representation and multiple means of action and expression, the teacher and neurodivergent student come up with some ideas that will help the student be more in charge of their own learning process. For example, the teacher may change the structure of the brainstorming activity, giving students the option to individually brainstorm a list of questions and opt out of a group discussion, then providing an organized full-group session where each group member is invited to share. The teacher can also provide education for neuro-normative students about the different ways people process information and the need to give each person in the group a chance to contribute.

UDL in the Classroom

Right about now you might be thinking, *But I do all this anyway. You're just describing my classroom.*

You're right—many teachers naturally use UDL in the classroom because it just makes sense. In early elementary classrooms, it's not unusual to see learning stations that students rotate through over the course of a day or week to learn about a topic through multiple modalities and practice different skills. For instance, when Amanda was a kindergarten teacher, her unit about apples included the following:

- a station at which students did a taste test of different kinds of apples, took a poll in their small group, and then created a visual representation of the apples in order from least popular to most popular (*skill and modalities:* math; hands-on and sensory learning)
- a reading and listening station filled with books about apples—including paper books and audiobooks (*skill and modalities:* reading readiness; text and audio)
- a full-group activity in which she read a nonfiction picture book about the life cycle of an apple tree and the parts of an apple, followed by an individual activity in which students cut out the different parts of an apple, colored them, and glued them to posterboard (*skills and modalities:* listening comprehension, reading, fine motor; text with audio support and arts project)
- a teacher-monitored anchor chart station during which students matched the newly learned parts of an apple to the picture they had previously made (*skill and modalities:* vocabulary; arts project)

But some classrooms aren't designed in a way that supports UDL. If you want to get started using UDL in your classroom but aren't sure where to begin or want some additional ideas, following are a few practices that you can use to apply the UDL principles in your classroom without a lot of effort. Figure 4.2 also shares some key ways that the UDL classroom is different. Keep these in mind as you begin implementing UDL in your practice.

FIGURE 4.2 Typical Classrooms vs. UDL Classrooms

The "Typical" General Education Classroom	The UDL Classroom
Students are taught in a one-size-fits-all way that is focused mostly on content.	Students are taught in ways that meet the needs of varied learners and are focused on both the content and how it needs to be taught to be understood by all.
Accommodations are available to students who have them listed in an IEP or a 504 plan.	Accommodations are available for all students.
The classroom setup is more traditional, with rows of desks or groups of tables facing the teacher.	The classroom setup has many workspaces, such as quiet reading corners and space for groupwork, and the tables, desks, and chairs can be easily reorganized.
Assignments are the same for all students, giving them one way to show their knowledge and skills.	Assignments vary, giving students options for how to express their knowledge and skills.

Share the Goal of the Lesson

There's no doubt you think through the goal of a lesson before you teach it. But do you explicitly share that goal with students? Even if you think students know what the goal is, saying "The goal of today's lesson is to be able to explain the steps in the water cycle" or "Today we're focusing on how we can figure out how to move twenty-five bricks in only five steps" isn't something we all do automatically.

Talking through and posting the lesson goal helps students know what they're working to do. It's a good way to support students who have trouble with concentration or sustained focus and to help the whole class stay on task. Plus, the lesson goal is right there and accessible in situations like a student coming to class late and trying to catch up while you're teaching.

Sharing the lesson goal also tells students what you're *not* worrying about. If you want them to be able to explain the steps in the water cycle, you're hopefully not going to be grading them on their spelling or artistic ability. If you want them to figure out how to move twenty-five bricks in five steps, you're not going to be grading them on whether they used multiplication or addition or if they showed their work on paper.

Suggest Ways to Complete the Assignment

Choice is at the heart of UDL. But some of your neurodivergent students will be overwhelmed by making decisions or figuring out how to get started. Give students some suggestions of what the end product could be, tailoring your suggestions to what you know about them. With UDL, there are many creative ways to complete an assignment and still meet the goal.

For instance, depending on a student's interests and strengths, you might suggest they draw a labeled diagram of the water cycle, write an essay, tell the story through the perspective of a water droplet, create a comic strip, or find some other way that fits their interests and talents.

Have Flexible Workspaces Available

UDL is all about being flexible around where and how your students work, which, for some teachers, can be a little nerve-wracking. When students are working in all different ways and areas of the classroom, it can look like chaos—or at least that's how it might appear to someone walking past your classroom door. And when things *look* like chaos, it can *feel* like you don't have control.

Flexible workspaces aren't just about physical space, though. They're also about making room for groups of different sizes to work together, while also ensuring that students who need less stimulation to focus can have either a quiet space or resources to tune out distractions. That might mean having noise-muffling headphones and desk dividers available for any student to use.

Give Regular Feedback

It's easy to get caught in a cycle of providing feedback only when something goes wrong. That's typical of anyone, not just educators. Neurodivergent students, however, often get more negative feedback than positive. Research shows that by the time ADHDers are twelve years old, they have received close to 20,000 more negative messages about their behavior than non-ADHDers have (Jellinek 2010). That's a lot of negative feedback.

Providing daily feedback—both positive and constructive—gives all students a chance to hear what they're doing well and a chance to reflect on how they can improve. That way, if they didn't meet the day's lesson goal, they have some understanding of what they might be able to do differently next time.

Five Ways All Students Benefit from UDL

Even though UDL doesn't mean providing a singular (universal) way of teaching all students, it does show that what benefits neurodivergent students is good for all students.

1. All students benefit from having flexible options for how to show what they know and engage with material and from having reasons to be motivated to learn.
2. All students benefit from knowing the goal of a lesson up front.
3. All students benefit from having access to resources and "informal accommodations" (accommodations not specified in a learning plan).
4. All students benefit from having some agency for how they learn.
5. All students benefit from regular feedback.

Accommodations for All

Accommodations can benefit all students in a variety of ways, and they are part of UDL. Here are some reasons why providing informal classroom accommodations can be advantageous for all, not just those identified with specific learning needs:

- **It promotes an inclusive environment where all students feel valued and supported.** This helps create a diverse and accepting classroom community.
- **It encourages you to implement differentiated instruction strategies.** This provides a classroom in which teaching methods, content, and assessments are tailored to meet the unique needs and learning preferences of all students.
- **It reminds you to keep in mind and address the diverse learning preferences of all students.** This means making learning experiences more engaging and effective for all learners by adding visual, auditory, kinesthetic, or tactile elements.
- **It can reduce anxiety and stress for all students, allowing them to perform to the best of their abilities.** Providing things like extended time on tests and assignments is beneficial for all students to have as an option, even if they choose not to use it.
- **It can teach important life skills.** For instance, embracing the use of assistive technology or alternative methods of communication can enhance the technology and communication skills of all your students. And these skills are both valuable and necessary in today's ever-changing technological landscape.
- **It levels the playing field** and reduces the risk that neurodivergent students will feel unfairly disadvantaged. It ensures that all students have equitable access to educational opportunities.
- **It builds more opportunities for students to collaborate and work together in diverse teams.** This mirrors real-world situations in which everyone has different strengths and backgrounds and people need to adapt, problem-solve, and communicate effectively with one another.
- **It builds a culture of compassion, empathy, and respect.** When all students are using accommodations, they are more aware that everyone has areas of need.

Most of all, incorporating classroom accommodations for all students shows that diversity in learning is a strength to be embraced, rather than a challenge to be overcome.

Javier

Javier, an ADHDer, was known for his lively enthusiasm in the classroom. His mind frequently wandered to various tangents, and he struggled with organization, often losing essential items like pencils and textbooks. He exhibited a lot of physical hyperactivity and preferred active engagement methods, such as moving around during class. Traditional seated tasks were challenging for him, and he would often answer questions before they were fully asked. His teacher, Ms. Lee, embraced Javier's unique learning style by providing accommodations, including tools for focusing and ways to support his need for physical movement. By recognizing the needs of all her students, she also supported Javier's ADHD, turning what could have been perceived as disruption into a dynamic, engaging learning environment. His fellow students began to appreciate his creative problem-solving, and the classroom became a space where differences were celebrated, fostering a richer, more inclusive educational experience.

Unpacking Neurodivergence

The Impact of Providing Accommodations for All

Emily: When we talk about creating a neurodiversity-affirming school, I think we need to be much more adaptable. I often hear from teachers and parents that they hesitate to provide accommodations when kids are struggling with something. They use the logic that kids need to be prepared for the "real world."

I always question this, because school is not like the "real world." In the real world, if my strength is in visual-spatial abilities and not in writing, I'm not going to become a journalist. Or if my strength is in reading and writing, but I have dyscalculia, I'm not going to be an actuary. I have that autonomy and independence to make those choices. Also, if I'm struggling with something, I can ask my boss or a coworker for help or an accommodation. In school, though, everyone is expected to do all the things.

Amanda: I agree that in the "real world," you can make choices and adaptations and ask for the things you need. I absolutely think that should be happening in schools. What I wonder about is whether kids, who spend so much time in school, feel that the world of school is more their real world than their outside-of-school world. I don't know that I have an answer to that.

Emily: I think another part of it is access to accommodations, regardless of a certain diagnosis. I'm always amazed at the number of kids who struggle immensely just to get through school. Many of these kids are neurodivergent and may have 504 plans, but probably don't have IEPs. In many cases, they don't qualify for additional services, but they can get some accommodations.

Amanda: And that's like the "real world," right? There aren't necessarily services in the workplace, but there are accommodations. There are accommodations made at home, because when people live together, they lean into each other's strengths. One of my neurodivergent traits is the need to have things organized so that I know the plan. That makes me the perfect household member to oversee travel plans, and my entire family knows that.

I do think that kids internalize what they see in school. So if what they are seeing is that they don't get accommodations without a diagnosis, we need to change that. We need to help them realize that school is a place that should support them and be safe for them. We need to create these safe places at school that match what they have outside of school to help them feel most like their authentic selves.

Examining Barriers to Learning Through a UDL Lens

Allison Posey, a UDL expert and curriculum and design specialist at CAST, the Center for Applied Special Technology, compares classrooms to road trips:

> When you plan a road trip, you know you might run into detours or roadblocks that get in the way of reaching your destination. Some of those barriers are predictable, like traffic, road work, or bad weather. Knowing and anticipating those barriers can help you plan your trip so you can still get to your destination.
>
> Classroom lessons are no different. There will be barriers that prevent students from reaching the intended learning goals. Just like with a road trip, some of those barriers are predictable and can be reduced by careful planning and design. (Posey, n.d.)

When you're able to identify those barriers, Posey explains, you start looking at the *learning environment* as "abled" or "dis-abled," instead of thinking of students as such (Posey, n.d.). And that perspective is very much aligned with UDL and a neurodiversity-affirming mindset.

To keep Posey's analogy going, not every trip you take is going to be a road trip. So how and where you get stuck varies depending on how you're traveling and where you're going. On a car trip, you might get stuck in traffic. When you're flying, your flight might be delayed. And sometimes, the trains just aren't running on time.

When your students get stuck on the learning journey, the reason may vary from subject to subject (type of transportation) and even from lesson to lesson within the same subject (leg of the trip). The reasons students get stuck are as unique as they are, but there are some common barriers for neurodivergent students. A fundamental part of implementing UDL is predicting where these barriers might come up and planning around them, just in case. Here are some of those common barriers:

- Students don't have the background knowledge or the prerequisite skills.
- Students don't know or remember the steps to an activity.
- Students aren't given specific feedback on how to improve or about their progress.
- Students don't know how to attempt to do something a different way.

- Students don't know key vocabulary, formulas, or other types of assumed knowledge.
- Students don't have the social and emotional skills needed to participate in an activity.
- Students don't find relevance in a lesson.

If you're wondering if reducing barriers makes learning "too easy" for students, you wouldn't be the first teacher to have that concern. We've heard more than a few educators say they worry that providing strategies or scaffolds up front gives students a shortcut on their journey, so to speak, and could lead some students to take the "easy" route.

We ask you to take a moment to consider your own travels and answer this question: *If you knew how to get to your destination with less difficulty, would you?* If someone gave you the directions or shared tricks and tips they'd learned when they took the same trip, you'd likely follow their advice. Why wouldn't you? In your students' journey to learning, you're that seasoned guide.

Sometimes, however, the journey itself is the point. Ditching the travel analogy, there are times when it's important for students to experience productive struggle. The key is to make sure it is productive in a way that leads to better learning. Productive struggle builds a student's brain capacity by providing the right level of difficulty, unlike struggles you know they can't get past (Sriram 2020).

There are other times when scaffolds are what a student needs to gain the skills to move past being stuck. You're not *always* going to give them the shortcut, though, because once they don't need it anymore, it can be phased out. Here are some other things to consider:

- Something that may be easy for one person may not be easy for another. (This is true for all people.)
- When a goal or expectation is challenging enough, there isn't going to be an easy way. It's going to provide the right amount of challenge for each student.
- Flexibility in resources and choice in how to approach a goal provide an opportunity to talk about what worked and what didn't work in learning. This not only gives you space to talk about diversity in learning but it also helps students reflect on how they learn best.

Identifying Barriers to Learning

If you're going to reduce barriers, you need to know how to recognize them. The first step is being sure of your primary goal with a lesson. When you're planning a lesson that you'll be teaching for the first time, ask yourself: *What is most important for my students to know, be able to do, or understand?* The answer is your primary goal. If you have more than one answer, try answering the question again. You may be trying to teach too much at once.

Once you know your primary goal, you can start anticipating barriers. Review your lesson plan and ask yourself where your students might get stuck or where they might need support or accommodation. If you're having trouble with this, take a moment to think about one student instead of the whole class. Your answers to these questions identify the potential barriers. Then you can plan scaffolds to have at the ready, just in case.

For instance, if you are going to teach how to create a mathematical equation from a word problem, you may anticipate that some students will struggle to remember the process for translating certain words to mathematical symbols. The barrier you identify is that students must process and work with a lot of information all at once, including how to match signal words to their symbols. To navigate around this, you might provide a graphic organizer that matches math signal words with their symbols and/or use a video showing the process in action.

Looking Back to Look Forward

If you've been teaching for more than a couple years, you've probably taught your lessons before, which means you can identify barriers in a specific lesson by thinking about what happened in the past. These are some questions to consider:

- What directions did I need to repeat and when?
- What did I have to review or reteach?
- Did I have students who weren't fully included in the lesson?

Your answers identify the barriers, and how you solved them in the past is a good way to reduce them in the future.

Another way to look forward by looking back is to ask your students for feedback. Students are usually pretty good at telling teachers what they think and often do so without any prompting. For example, in addition to outright asking, you can listen to their words for clues. When a student says, "Do I have to . . .?" or "Should I . . .?" they're often telling you that they're stuck and don't know what to do next.

Why Use UDL

Now that you know more about UDL, what do you think?

We wouldn't be surprised if you're feeling a little overwhelmed. Many teachers are when they're first introduced to the concept. It seems like so much *work*, and you already have more than enough work to do. So why use it?

Here are our *whys*:

- **The intended outcome of UDL is to make expert learners** of all your students, which is worth investing time in. Expert learners take on a lot of the work themselves. They're informed, strategic, goal-oriented, and motivated to learn.
- **You don't need new tools, software, technology, or curriculum** to follow the principles of UDL. You just use the resources you already have—in new ways.
- **UDL is a neurodiversity-affirming practice that reduces stigma** since it includes providing accommodations for all students. Imagine how empowering it could be for your neurodivergent students to know that you're thinking about how the learning environment needs to change instead of how *they* need to change.

What to Remember

- UDL is an approach to teaching that proactively removes barriers to learning to give all students a chance to succeed and become expert learners.
- The principles of UDL guide you in recognizing and accommodating students' individual motivations and learning needs, providing various methods for students to interact with content, and allowing choices that connect to students' interests.
- Identifying and strategizing around potential barriers in the learning environment, such as lack of background knowledge or specific skills, enables educators to facilitate effective learning by viewing challenges in the context of the environment rather than the characteristics of individual students.

Chapter 5

Camouflaging, Masking, and Authenticity

Points to Ponder

- What negative effects might suppressing their neurodivergent traits have on students?
- How can you create a classroom environment that provides opportunities for your students to be their authentic selves?
- How do you create a culture where all students accept and understand neurodivergent traits?

Have you ever sat through a parent-teacher conference with a family and explained to your student's caregivers how well their child is doing in your class—how they're well-behaved, conscientious, and respectful—only to have them look at you, shocked, and ask if you are talking about the right kid? They go on to explain that their child is nothing like that at home; they are overwhelmed, anxious, withdrawn, or angry from the moment they get in the door after school until they go to bed.

What is causing this huge difference in mood and behavior? Most likely, the child is expending immense amounts of energy hiding their needs and "white knuckling" through the school day. When they get home from school, they have no energy left to continue regulating their emotions and behavior and they fall to pieces. This chapter helps you understand camouflaging and masking in neurodivergent students and shares ways you can support students in unmasking and being authentic.

Understanding Camouflaging

Many animals have evolved to use camouflage as a tool for survival. Likewise, neurodivergent people have developed strategies (or been explicitly taught) to hide their differences. Many neurodivergent people are taught from a young age to act like someone without a disability. This is known as camouflaging or masking (see Unpacking Neurodivergence below for a discussion of these terms).

The problem with camouflaging for humans is that it is exhausting. It's like running video conferencing, streaming, and thirty-six different tabs in your internet browser all at once, and then wondering why your connection is so slow. Camouflaging requires a lot of a student's bandwidth. If that bandwidth weren't being spent on hiding in plain sight, it would be available to help the student run all the other processes of learning and navigating social interactions more smoothly.

Reasons Students Camouflage

The reasons people camouflage can be broken into two broad categories: to avoid negative attention and to gain positive attention (Cage and Troxell-Whitman 2019). Avoiding attention allows neurodivergent kids to find safety or avoid embarrassment for being different. Gaining attention allows them to seek out relationships and connections they may not otherwise have. Both types of camouflaging come at the expense of a student's authenticity.

Avoiding Negative Attention

Negative attention may come in the form of teasing or bullying from peers, disciplinary action from an adult, or embarrassment and shame after making a mistake. For example, students who stim (like rocking, hand flapping, or pacing) to help regulate their emotions may be confronted with name-calling or excluded when this coping skill is not understood by peers. Many adults encourage children to reduce stimming behaviors, not realizing the benefits of those behaviors or how they might be vital to a child's ability to cope. When students internalize messages about how stimming behaviors are "wrong" or "abnormal," it can lead to a sense of shame when they're not able to suppress them.

Students with specific learning disabilities may desperately attempt to hide their difficulty with a subject. Reading aloud or completing a math problem on the board can be terrifying, especially for students whose learning needs have not been formally identified. Finding multiple excuses to avoid being put on the spot and embarrassed by their mistakes is often the only solution they can think of using. Camouflaging for these students might look like pretending not to care about academic performance or using noncompliant behavior to distract from their struggles with academic tasks. Gifted/talented students may suppress their abilities to fit in with peers and be "normal" at the expense of developing their talents and living authentically.

Neurodivergent kids may also try to mask executive functioning difficulties. Many bright students who struggle with executive functioning come to rely on their anxiety as a driver to help them compensate for their executive functioning difficulties. In attempting to avoid negative attention, they become hypervigilant perfectionists who are frequently overwhelmed and stressed out.

Additionally, neurodivergent students may hide special interests or talents that others perceive as "weird" to avoid ostracization. Though the knowledge and passion that many neurodivergent people have for their preferred topics of interest is one of the best ways for them to connect with peers who have similar interests, they frequently receive the message that sharks, or Elvis, or *Magic: The Gathering* are not topics that others are interested in discussing. Masking this integral part of their personality can make neurodivergent students feel lonely and isolated.

Gaining Positive Attention

Camouflaging may also be used to gain positive attention. Students who do this are often looking for acceptance from their peers or approval from adults. The reverse of some of the examples we provided for avoiding negative attention may fit here. The student who becomes a perfectionist to compensate for the difficulty with executive functioning may not only be working to avoid getting in trouble but also to gain the positive reinforcement from their teacher for a job well done.

Some students who struggle with interpreting the meaning of verbal communication might find themselves mimicking what others are saying without really knowing what it means. In their effort to fit in and be accepted, they may end up embarrassed if they use a phrase in a context that doesn't make sense or, worse, get in trouble because they repeated something that was hurtful or inappropriate. In these ways, mimicking might have the opposite effect from what the student intends.

Twice-exceptional students frequently use their cognitive abilities to compensate for their areas of difficulty, though they may not always realize they are doing so. Whether conscious or not, this is still a form of camouflaging. The gifted student who is also dyslexic may hide their difficulty with reading with a broad background knowledge and strong inferencing skills, for example. This allows them to perform well enough that their phonological struggles go unnoticed or unsupported and they receive positive feedback from their teachers.

Camouflaging and Masking in Neurodivergent Kids

Amanda: We talk quite a lot about masking in the context of neurodivergent students. I'd love for you to tell me a bit about what masking means to you. Often, we focus on the negative impacts, but do you think it carries any benefits?

Emily: When I think about masking and camouflaging, I see them as tools that most people use on some occasions. When we think about supporting neurodivergent kids, helping them understand what camouflaging is, what masking is, when they are masking and camouflaging, and how they feel when they do can give them the autonomy to decide when and if they want to use these actions.

Amanda: You differentiated between camouflaging and masking. I've never thought of them as separate things. Would you explain how they differ?

Emily: *Camouflaging* is the umbrella term. It's about adopting various traits or behaviors to fit in. *Masking*, on the other hand, is about suppressing or hiding certain traits or behaviors. There are also times when we mimic or imitate what other people do. They're two sides of the same coin in many ways, but I use the term *camouflaging* to encompass both aspects.

Amanda: That's helpful. I've often seen students put on others' traits or diminish some of their own, but I never thought of them as separate things. I appreciate the distinction. There's a difference between picking up on what others are doing that's socially appropriate versus noticing what I'm doing that doesn't seem socially appropriate.

Emily: Right. But for too long, we've just focused on making neurodivergent kids appear neuro-normative. We've actively taught them to hide some of their authentic characteristics. For example, a child who flaps their hands when they get excited—I know parents and teachers who have instructed kids not to do that. They'll remind them to use "quiet hands." My question is, if flapping hands is an authentic way for the child to communicate excitement and regulate emotions, and it's not harmful, why are we teaching them not to do it?

Amanda: I'd say there's no purpose, except to make us feel more comfortable or ease our worry that a child's peers might respond unkindly to them. But we should be focused on making our kids feel more comfortable. It's hard for kids to feel connected to who they are when we're asking them to be different from who they feel like on the inside. I think this makes it really hard for neurodivergent kids to grow up understanding who they are, knowing what they want from the world, and figuring out where they fit into it.

Emily: The best way to get to a point where kids don't have to mask or camouflage, in my opinion, involves two things. First, we need to teach everyone that some people look, act, or communicate differently, and that's okay. The other part is helping kids understand that they can make choices about what they're doing depending on their environment. They may want to mimic the neuro-normative trait of making eye contact when they're communicating with someone, for instance. We can teach them that there might be certain situations where they will want to do this, and if that's the case, then these are some strategies they can use. Alternatively, they can advocate for themselves and say, "I feel more comfortable looking at the floor when I'm listening to you" or "I feel more comfortable looking out the window when I'm speaking."

Amanda: I think part of this involves teaching kids that it's okay not to show up as your full self in places where you don't feel safe doing that. That's something all kids need to learn, not just neurodivergent kids. There are lots of discussions about always being your full self, but sometimes you don't want to. That's okay too.

Types of Camouflaging

Let's take a look at the variety of ways neurodivergent people may choose to camouflage.

Hiding in Plain Sight

Some neurodivergent students may try to blend in and make themselves unnoticeable. This generally requires some level of masking (suppressing certain behaviors or traits). These are two types of students who hide in plain sight:

- **The Rule Follower:** This student follows all the rules, all the time—because that's the rule. They've learned that hypervigilance around knowing and following what's expected is the best method for staying out of the way and out of trouble.
- **The Silent Student:** Fearful of saying or doing the wrong thing, this student tends to be very quiet and may struggle to self-advocate in even small ways.

Disrupting the Sight Line

Some neurodivergent students may try to disrupt situations in which they may be found out. They may attempt to make their differences come in and out of focus, so there's less threat of being noticed. These might be some students who disrupt the sight line:

- **The Frequent Flyer:** This student, who lacks confidence in their academic abilities or classroom performance, may become a frequent flyer to the bathroom, the nurse's office, or their locker to avoid the possibility of being discovered.
- **The Distractor:** Although not always intentional, this neurodivergent student becomes a master at sleight of hand. They take the focus off themselves with strategically placed tangential topics or jokes.
- **The Apathetic Academic:** For this student, it is often easier to take the stance that they don't care about a task or grades rather than admit that they care and are unable to meet expectations. Beneath the surface, this student likely feels hopeless about changing their circumstances, so they adopt the mask of ambivalence.

Camo Here, Camo There

Using different personas for different environments allows neurodivergent people to blend in in a variety of groups and situations. These students might try to blend in:

- **The Chameleon:** In creative writing they act one way, at recess another, and at home a third. Shifting in and out of camouflage for various environments helps this student feel accepted and known in multiple settings.
- **The Shapeshifter:** Adept at altering their interests, opinions, and even their manner of speaking to match those around them, this student tries to blend with the crowd. Their adaptability is driven by a desire to connect and to keep others from noticing their neurodivergence.

Following the Leader

Imitating or miming others' behaviors is a frequent strategy neurodivergent students may use to find acceptance in various social groups. Whereas masking is the suppression of certain traits, mimicking is the addition of them. These types of students mimic:

- **The Mirror:** This student may carefully monitor and mirror their peers, sometimes even when they don't understand the purpose behind the behavior. This mirroring may be of mannerisms, gestures, or body language, with the goal of gaining acceptance.
- **The Voice Memo:** Rather than mimicking behaviors, this neurodivergent student picks up and repeats phrases from their peers, even if they don't

understand the meaning. In some cases, especially if the student struggles to self-advocate and ask for clarification, they may find themselves in trouble for using the wording in a different social setting.

- **The Actor:** This student uses scripting to hide their differences by planning, rehearsing, and reciting their "lines," especially when faced with situations that cause them anxiety.

Scripting Conversations

The situation: In a classroom setting, a neurodivergent student is interacting with peers during a group project. To fit in and camouflage their neurodivergent traits, the student relies heavily on scripting and mimicking.

Perspective of others: Classmates perceive the neurodivergent student as somewhat formal and rehearsed in their interactions, but they attribute this to the student being well-prepared or particularly serious about the project. They notice the student often uses phrases or expressions that are common among the group, which they interpret as the student being attentive and a good listener. The classmates are unaware of the extensive mental preparation and effort behind this behavior.

Perspective of the neurodivergent student: The neurodivergent student experiences significant anxiety and stress in these interactions. They constantly monitor their peers to pick up cues for how to behave and speak. Using scripted phrases and responses helps them participate in conversations, but it also makes them feel as if they're performing a role rather than engaging authentically. The effort to mimic the subtle nuances of social interaction, like matching tone of voice or facial expressions, is mentally exhausting. While this strategy helps them avoid standing out, it also leads to feelings of inauthenticity and heightened anxiety, as they fear being discovered or making a mistake in their performance. This ongoing effort to mask their neurodivergent traits can be draining and isolating, impacting their overall sense of well-being.

Possible follow-up: As the teacher builds a culture of understanding and acceptance in their classroom throughout the year, the neurodivergent student begins to relax and allow themselves to be more authentic. The teacher continually opens the door for all students to self-advocate and to get more comfortable with asking the teacher about the meanings behind certain words and phrases. That allows the neurodivergent student to eventually feel comfortable to do this with groupmates. With coaching from the teacher, the neurodivergent student and their peers learn to accept requests for clarification at face value and do not condescend to classmates who ask for them. This helps the neurodivergent student ultimately choose language they are more comfortable using without feeling the need to script their conversations.

Short- and Long-Term Effects of Camouflaging

Camouflaging, by whatever means a student uses, has both short- and long-term effects on their well-being. Understanding the impact of these behaviors can help you talk to students about their experiences, coach them to self-advocate as needed, and improve your relationships with them.

The following list of the impacts of camouflaging is not exhaustive, since every child is unique. But it can help you understand how the actions you take to support neurodivergent kids as they develop their own authentic ways of being can impact their long-term well-being. Camouflaging can be a tool for navigating a world that prioritizes neuro-norms, but continuously using it can lead to a number of negative effects (Bernardin et al. 2021):

- **Students feel a loss of identity, like they don't know who they really are.** This can contribute to low self-esteem, feelings of isolation, and depression.
- **Students' diagnosis or identification is delayed, resulting in a lack of support.** When students are effective at camouflaging, they might not get the diagnosis or support they need early on. Research shows that students who receive early intervention have significant gains and improvement in social and emotional, cognitive, and adaptive and/or behavioral functioning (McManus et al. 2019).
- **Students' actions inadvertently reinforce stereotypes and stigmatization.** When neurodivergent students feel the need to camouflage, it can perpetuate ideas around there being "normal" or "correct" ways to act or be.
- **Students have difficulty building authentic connections.** While masking might seem to help make social interactions easier, it can make it hard for neurodivergent students to connect with others based on who they are behind the mask.

Camouflaging can also lead to imposter syndrome because the individual may be putting in a lot more effort beneath the surface than what is visible to others.

You can educate your students about camouflaging and give them opportunities to self-evaluate situations where they may be using it. By bringing camouflaging to their awareness, educators empower students to make decisions about when and where they choose to use it and where they feel safe to take off their masks.

Simone

Simone was diagnosed with ADHD in eighth grade when her parents were concerned about the amount of time it was taking her to complete her homework and an increase in irritability and tearfulness that seemed like anxiety. When they spoke to her doctor about their concerns, Simone's parents were surprised when the doctor referred them for an

ADHD assessment. Simone was diagnosed with ADHD—predominantly inattentive type.

How had the signs of her inattention gone unnoticed for so long? Simone was a bright student who, although always a bit disorganized, had excellent grades. Throughout elementary school, she compensated for her difficulty with executive functioning with her intelligence, supported by elementary teachers who followed up on her assignments and other work. She generally worked quickly, so even though she was often distracted, she was still able to get her work finished in the same amount of time as peers.

Once Simone got to middle school, the cognitive load necessary for her to succeed began to exceed the level of effort she was used to putting into her schoolwork. After several experiences of teachers admonishing her for missing work or careless errors on her assignments, Simone became hypervigilant about her schoolwork. She started carrying all her materials in her backpack throughout the entire school day to avoid showing up to class without everything she might need. She repeatedly checked the online portal for assignments and went over her work multiple times so she could ensure that it was perfect before turning it in. Her fear of and anxiety around being embarrassed in front of her peers or disappointing her teachers drove her into a cycle of perfectionism that eventually led to burnout. It was this burnout that finally prompted Simone's parents to seek outside help.

Simone had been spending immense time and energy camouflaging her executive functioning difficulties to avoid negative attention. Building the skill of self-advocacy and offering some basic, reasonable accommodations helped her build confidence and gradually reduced the habit of hypervigilance she had created.

Authenticity as the Antidote

The antidote to the negative impacts of camouflaging for neurodivergent students is often finding methods and approaches that encourage them to regulate their attention, develop peer relationships, and process their emotions in ways that are beneficial to and preferred by them. Allowing this authenticity avoids the stress that comes when neurodivergent students constantly adopt unnatural behaviors and traits.

You don't know exactly what beliefs and messages your neurodivergent students have picked up from their earlier experiences at school and out in the world, but it is fair to assume that for many of them, the expectation to hide aspects of their neurodivergence has been internalized to some extent. When educators create neurodiversity-affirming environments in schools, they provide spaces where students can explore what it means for them to be authentic. Educators explicitly encourage students to develop strategies that work for them and offer opportunities to learn about how their brains differ from peers'. Open discussion of neurodiversity and different types of brains is needed for students to begin to unravel internalized ableist messages.

The Role of Privilege in Being Authentic

Authenticity is a privilege not all people have. Those from marginalized communities are too often expected to camouflage and assimilate to the majority culture every day—this can take the form of code switching, changing hair and clothing, or hiding their background, religion, relationships, and so on. Though authenticity can be life-affirming, the social impacts of choosing authenticity over assimilation can also negatively affect a person's opportunities for employment, relationships, and influence (Fawzy 2015).

Neurodivergent people have much to consider when unmasking. They are often pressured to mask and keep their neurodivergent traits under wraps in public. Part of this is due to safety concerns. People in positions of power, such as law enforcement professionals, may misinterpret an individual's neurodivergent communication style. The difficulty with social language pragmatics and interpreting unfamiliar situations and the intent of unfamiliar individuals leaves neurodivergent individuals at risk, as can behaviors like sensory stimming.

Another factor that can influence one's privilege to unmask involves the potential lack of safety in a home environment. Neurodivergent children and teens who live in abusive, neglectful, or otherwise traumatic environments may be at risk if they choose not to camouflage. Sensory stims may be seen as "weird" and put a child in danger if they bother or disturb an emotionally or physically abusive caretaker; saying the "wrong thing" due to an inaccurate interpretation of a situation or responding impulsively can lead to danger in some environments.

Neurodivergent individuals who are also part of another marginalized community have even more to consider. For example, Black girls are frequently overdisciplined, in part due to manifestations and expectations of White femininity that are unaligned with cultural expectations of Black femininity (Hines-Datiri and Carter Andrews 2017). Many autistic individuals are very direct and, at times, blunt in their communication styles. How might these two factors influence each other for a Black female autistic student and how she is disciplined in a school setting?

Though an ideal world would allow all people to lead authentic lives, free from the expectation to camouflage, we're not there yet. And while educators can value the importance of teaching self-advocacy and unmasking to neurodivergent students, they also need to recognize the realities those students may be facing—and work with children and their families to help them make informed and safe decisions about when, where, and how to unmask.

Intersecting Identities

Research shows that autistic individuals and ADHDers are more likely to be members of the LGBTQ+ community than non-autistic people or non-ADHDers are (Dewinter, De Graaf, and Begeer 2017; Goetz and Adams 2022). Just as many neurodivergent people camouflage and mask their differences, LGBTQ+ people may hide this stigmatized aspect of themselves. The intersectionality of being both a member of the LGBTQ+ community and neurodivergent adds complexity to both these identities. It also heightens the pressure to camouflage aspects of both.

Neurodivergent individuals in the LGBTQ+ community may find themselves employing more complex strategies to navigate social expectations and biases. This dual experience of camouflaging can lead to a greater sense of isolation and a heightened need for safe, accepting spaces where they can express all facets of their identity without judgment or misunderstanding. Recognizing and addressing the unique challenges faced by LGBTQ+ neurodivergent students is essential to providing appropriate support and fostering a school environment where they can thrive authentically.

Examining Educators' Role

The impact of our ableist society is something neurodiversity-affirming educators need to get comfortable exploring, examining, and challenging. How you view certain behaviors is skewed by your own expectations and by the experience you had of being allowed authenticity as a young person. For educators to understand camouflaging and create affirming environments where their students feel safe being authentic, they need to consistently ask one question: *Why?*

- Why does it matter if a student prefers to read a book at recess or lunch rather than interacting with peers?
- Why is it necessary for a child to sit still with their eyes on the speaker when listening in class?
- Why do we mind if a student paces, fidgets, or draws while learning?
- Why do we insist that every student work in a group on projects?

There may very well be multiple answers to those questions, some more valid than others. But, as you question why you do things the way you do, you must also ask these follow-up questions, with your group of students in mind:

- Where did this assumption come from?
- Is the goal of changing the child's behavior *actually* best for them, or is it what I've been taught is *expected* of them?

- If the child is pushed to comply with these requests, to what extent is it asking them to camouflage for the sake of blending in?
- What is the cost to the student of being asked to camouflage?
- Whose goal is it: the student's, mine, or society's?

The reality of being in the classroom and the logistics that go along with managing a room full of varying needs can mean it's difficult to make all the accommodations students need. But by considering traits and accommodations judiciously and challenging the status quo, you empower kids to choose to unmask and live authentically.

Neurodiversity-Affirming Supports for Unmasking and Authenticity

Just as students must unlearn the expectations of society to live with authenticity, so must educators also unlearn these expectations. We were all students at one time and likely grew up in environments that used behavioral interventions to discipline young people for neurodivergent traits. Even those of us who are strongly involved with the neurodiversity movement must constantly question our prior expectations and beliefs.

Many of the interventions and tools educators are familiar with using are *not* neurodiversity-affirming. For example, some neurodivergent people prefer not to make eye contact with others when they are listening to them speak. But what's the best way to help a student who experiences discomfort with making eye contact? Many well-meaning professionals suggest coaching the neurodivergent student to learn to look at someone's nose or ear or forehead so that they appear to be making eye contact. However, this is essentially a masking strategy, and one that does not allow the neurodivergent student authenticity in communicating.

What can you do instead of practices like this? Take steps to assess your tools and make sure you are using neurodiversity-affirming strategies and supports. Here's an example of these steps using the eye contact example described above.

Step 1: Identify the purpose of the skill/strategy. Why are you asking the neurodivergent person to modify their behavior or communication? Some people may suggest that eye contact is important because it demonstrates respect for the person speaking or because it shows attentive listening. Drilling down a little further, though, the answer is because eye contact is a social expectation.

Step 2: Question how neurodiversity-affirming the technique is. When the purpose of a skill or strategy is based in neuro-normative experiences, you need to question whether the technique allows the neurodivergent person to act in an authentic way. If the technique is ultimately to make the neurodivergent person appear as though they aren't neurodivergent, then it isn't an affirming strategy. The strategy to appear to be making eye contact is based on neuro-normative social expectations and is, therefore, not neurodiversity-affirming.

Step 3: Offer alternatives that recognize neurodivergent needs. Help neurodivergent students understand both the common societal expectations and what options might be available to help them feel more comfortable. Talk about when they might want to choose certain tools over others, emphasizing the weighing of potential benefits and drawbacks of any behavior. Often, self-advocacy is one of the best possible strategies to handle neuro-normative expectations. A neurodivergent student might say, "It is easier for me to focus on what you are saying when I look at the floor instead of your face. Just know that I am listening even if I don't make eye contact." It can also be helpful to offer suggestions for situations that are less accommodating. For example, looking at someone's ear instead of their eyes when listening to them speak isn't a bad tool, but neurodivergent students should be empowered to know they have the choice in all situations.

Step 4: Develop community awareness of neurodivergent needs. As we shared in the introduction (page 9), the pressure to understand others should not fall solely on neurodivergent people's shoulders. The lack of understanding about communication strategies and other neurodivergent needs is not a one-way street. People who think, learn, and communicate in more neuro-normative ways could do more to understand neurodivergent people (Milton 2012). For example, help school staff understand that a neurodivergent student's lack of eye contact during communication is not a sign of disrespect or inattention. In fact, in many instances it is an aid in communicating.

Education of and awareness in the community reduces the pressure for neurodivergent students to constantly be masking or self-advocating. You might share that removing the focus on maintaining eye contact has benefits for everyone, not just students. In fact, research has shown that when confronted with a challenging question, adults shift their gaze away from the face of the person who posed the question 85 percent of the time (Phelps, Doherty-Sneddon, and Warnock 2006). Here some other things you might share with your community to build awareness of how not sustaining eye contact can be beneficial (Abeles and Yuval-Greenberg 2017):

- When engaged in conversation, the brain expends energy deciphering facial cues while simultaneously processing verbal content.
- Straining to sustain eye contact can deplete cognitive resources, prompting individuals to occasionally avert their gaze to conserve mental energy.
- Research indicates that when students divert their visual attention from their teacher, they are significantly more likely to generate the correct response to posed questions.

In addition to questioning your current strategies and adopting more neurodiversity-affirming ones, you can support neurodivergent students' authenticity by building all students' awareness of camouflaging. The TRUE strategy we created gives steps that students can use to determine if they are comfortable with camouflaging in various environments. This method validates the fact that camouflaging is something all of us do occasionally and helps students base their actions on a cost-benefit analysis.

- **Trust your feelings.** The first step in the TRUE method is to trust your instincts about what feels comfortable for you. Teach students that this means honoring their feelings in social situations. Far too often, neurodivergent people are encouraged to ignore their experiences and emotions in social situations, but it is very difficult for them to learn to trust themselves if they must constantly go against what feels comfortable for them.
- **Reflect on camouflaging.** The second step is to reflect on when, why, and how you camouflage or mask. Guide students to think about the situations in which they use camouflaging. Are there certain environments in which they camouflage more often than others? Certain groups of people? Are they camouflaging by mimicking others' behaviors, hiding sensory needs, or something else?
- **Understand your needs.** Understanding the ways camouflaging affects personal well-being is the third step. How much stress does a particular behavior cause? How much benefit does it provide in certain environments? Does it ensure safety

or cause risk? Is the energy that students are using to camouflage worth the effort? How and when are they able to rest and regain that energy?

- **Experiment with expression.** The final step is to try out different levels of self-expression in safe spaces. Help students practice communicating their needs and boundaries to discover what feels authentic to them. Aid them in developing strategies to exit situations that are uncomfortable and to assess other situations before they enter them.

Helping students develop self-awareness about camouflaging and teaching them strategies for self-advocacy and authenticity are key to helping them build self-efficacy and avoid burnout.

What to Remember

- Camouflaging and masking serve as mechanisms for avoiding negative attention or gaining positive attention. Students may not know that they are doing these things, yet they suffer the negative impacts, such as mental and physical exhaustion, loneliness, and feeling unseen.
- Creating neurodiversity-affirming environments means that you need to ask yourself why you encourage students to mask and deliberately provide nonjudgmental spaces in which students feel safe being their authentic selves.
- Explicitly encouraging students to develop strategies that work for them and offering opportunities to learn about how their brains differ from peers' brains affirms that all people approach the world differently and there is no one right way to be or act.

Chapter 6

Rethinking Behavior in the Classroom

Points to Ponder

- What behavior-management systems are frequently used in your school or classroom? How do these systems impact neurodivergent learners?
- How can you help students develop the skills to regulate their emotions and behaviors?
- What strategies can help you get students invested in developing emotional regulation skills?

Neurodivergent students are frequently labeled as "difficult," "defiant," or "disrespectful." However, these labels are most often based on educators' perceptions of a student's behavior. A neurodivergent student may have behaviors that are difficult *for educators to handle*, are defiant *to educators' demands*, or *appear* disrespectful *to educators*. But when you take time to look beneath a behavior, you can learn about what is happening in the student's internal world and find ways to help them solve those problems. Perhaps it is fear, or confusion, or difficulty communicating, or a million other things that are surfacing as a particular behavior.

Of course, neurodivergent students aren't always labeled negatively; some present themselves as perfect students, compensating for their areas of difficulty because of intense underlying anxiety. Or perfectionism is driven by a survival response to fawn, to avoid conflict at all costs. While these students may not be "troublemakers," their difficulty with regulating their emotions leads to unhealthy patterns and high levels of stress.

There are many reasons why neurodivergent learners might struggle with regulating their emotions. School can be rather chaotic—schedules change, peer expectations shift, and academic tasks vary. Students' internal worlds shift, too, depending on how they slept, what stresses they're experiencing, or how kids treated them on the morning bus ride. The variability of these many factors explains why a student may be calm, cool, and collected one day and a dysregulated heap of emotion the next.

Trauma-informed practices provide insight into how educators can support neurodivergent students. The reason these practices are essential in the learning community is because they recognize that learners can't learn if they are in survival mode. Many neurodivergent learners, especially when they're struggling with emotional regulation, are often in survival mode. They are also in survival mode any time they are focused on camouflaging and masking their neurodivergent traits for acceptance or safety. The dyscalculic learner who worries about being asked to solve math problems in front of the class, the autistic student who is constantly on high alert because they don't know what wrong thing they'll say, and the ADHDer who suppresses their need to fidget are all sacrificing a large portion of their learning capability to simply get through the day.

A neurodiversity-affirming school can help students learn to regulate emotions and mitigate flight, fight, freeze, or fawn responses because school becomes an environment where students feel safe and where they can learn. A neurodiversity-affirming school encourages students to know and understand themselves and to self-advocate for their needs. It engages co-regulation before asking for self-regulation and allows students to develop those skills in a natural learning trajectory of progress followed by regression followed by more progress. Finally, a neurodiversity-affirming school doesn't use discipline or shaming to "teach" emotional-regulation skills. This chapter offers a neurodiversity-affirming approach to student behavior.

Moving Beyond Behaviors and Using Co-Regulation

Neurodivergent students often have unique ways of experiencing and expressing emotions. Some may struggle with emotional regulation, which can manifest as meltdowns, shutdowns, sensory overload, or difficulties with social interactions. Traditional approaches (such as the use of behavior charts) often emphasize suppressing or modifying these behaviors to conform to societal expectations. A neurodiversity-affirming school, however, prioritizes emotional regulation and shifts the focus toward supporting students' emotional well-being and helping them develop self-regulation skills. This involves recognizing that emotional regulation is a complex process influenced by a variety of factors, including sensory sensitivities, communication differences, executive functioning challenges, and differences in emotional processing. Most of all, a neurodiversity-affirming school operates with an assumption that behavior is a form of communication.

All Behavior Is Communication

Educators often learn to attribute "misbehavior" to a "wrong choice" that a student makes about how to act in a particular situation. They may believe that since students have been informed of the rules, any time they don't adhere to them, they are making a conscious decision not to. But reality is rarely so simple. Student behavior doesn't happen in a void without other influences and motivations. One of the best ways to avoid falling into the trap of assuming it does is to ask yourself why a student is doing something, to challenge yourself to look for the context of a behavior.

Compliance-based interpretations focus on what the student has done wrong and only provide a surface-level understanding of the situation based on what the educator observes or assumes. When they don't dig a bit deeper, their only option is to treat the situation like a discipline issue. Still, some of the most widely used models of understanding and modifying behavior are focused primarily on compliance and outward-facing manifestations of behavior. For example, the ABC Model is a fundamental concept in behavioral psychology that stands for antecedent-behavior-consequence. The antecedent is an event that triggers a specific behavior, the behavior is the response, and the consequence is whatever reinforces or discourages the behavior.

The problem with this approach is that it relies on observable behaviors and provides only a surface-level understanding of why a behavior occurred.

Working to understand the context of a neurodivergent student's behavior takes time, consistency, curiosity, and communication. Often, a student may not have the self-awareness to be able to interpret on their own why they engaged in a certain behavior. You should encourage them to build this awareness, engage with them with a sense of curiosity, and ask them to engage with you. Once you work with them to understand some of their underlying motivations and emotions, you can collaborate with them to come up with alternative ideas should a similar situation arise in the future. Figure 6.1 explores various student behaviors and how educators can interpret them as communication rather than noncompliance.

There are, of course, consequences for students' actions, but consequences are not synonymous with punishment. Similarly, discipline doesn't necessarily refer to strict, punitive measures. Instead, it should be a framework for setting boundaries, fostering self-control, and promoting personal growth. Discipline, properly understood, is a means of guiding individuals toward better choices, helping them learn from their mistakes, and empowering them to develop habits that lead to greater success and satisfaction (Gartrell 2020; Morin, n.d.). It is about teaching and learning, not retribution or revenge.

Behavior Charts Don't Work . . .

Many neurodivergent adults have a horror story about how they had some sort of "behavior chart" as a kid, and that memory is seared in their mind. They were petrified of having a "yellow" or "red" day, or they had their name scrawled on the board for everyone to see (then circled or check-marked if they messed up more than once), or they had to do the walk of shame across the classroom to "flip a card," "clip down," or turn in a token.

You're probably able to anticipate how this person might respond if you were to ask their feelings about these experiences. Did the behavior management system work? Did they learn their lesson and change their ways? Their answer to both questions is likely to be no.

Behavior-based systems take a one-size-fits-all approach and neglect the unique personalities, backgrounds, and learning styles of students, leading to ineffective or inequitable outcomes. They are often overly punitive, fostering an environment of fear

FIGURE 6.1 Interpreting Behavior as Communication

Behavior	Compliance-Based Interpretation (surface-level understanding)	Communication-Based Interpretation (contextual understanding)
A student rushes to be at the front of the line, even cutting in front of peers at times and causing a disruption.	The rule is that students walk calmly to the line and never cut in front of others. Not doing so indicates a choice to disobey this rule.	Through discussion with the student, it is discovered that they feel anxious about timeliness and cope by attempting to be the first to arrive to special area classes. The student's teacher can then develop strategies to alleviate this anxiety.
A student often fidgets and moves around in their seat during lessons.	The student is being disruptive and not adhering to classroom norms of sitting still during lessons.	When exploring the situation with the student, their teacher learns that the student has sensory or focus needs and is using movement to help manage those needs and stay engaged with the lesson.
A student rarely participates in group work and tends to work alone.	The student is not following the classroom expectations around teamwork and collaboration.	Upon further investigation, it seems the student finds social interactions challenging or overwhelming. Working independently helps them feel more comfortable and focused.
A student often interrupts their teacher or classmates during discussions.	The student is being disrespectful by not waiting their turn to speak.	After offering the student an opportunity to reflect on the situation, the teacher finds that the student's difficulty to manage impulsive responses combined with their high level of enthusiasm about the topic is what's causing them difficulty with response inhibition.
A student often refuses to engage in a certain activity or task.	The student is being defiant and not following directions.	Influenced by difficulties with cognitive flexibility and problem-solving, the student feels "stuck" when tasks are overly challenging or stressful, and they lack the coping skills to navigate the situation.

along with an emphasis on extrinsic motivation rather than genuine love for learning. They perpetuate inequity and bias, disproportionately affecting not only neurodivergent students but also students from marginalized backgrounds.

Even when teachers are generous enough to allow students to "earn back" cards, clips, or tokens, or have checkmarks or circles erased, these types of behavior systems are huge failures. They promote public shaming and "work" only for the kids who don't need them—that is the neuro-normative kids who probably need only a gentle reminder to get back on track. Even kids who get only positive feedback in these systems can become reliant on compliments and people-pleasing. So why do educators use them?

Some teachers will argue that they use these systems in an effective way and that they look for the context of a student's behaviors to help understand motivations and find solutions. Our question to those teachers is this: *What is it about these systems that you couldn't do without them?* If you are already processing the situation with the student, what is the benefit of an external, and public, measure of their success or failure?

We do recognize a couple ways educators who use these systems find value, but we're skeptical that the benefits outweigh the drawbacks. First, we understand the benefits of having a simple way to communicate a student's behavior to a parent. Behavior charts may accomplish this on the surface, but we believe there are other ways to do so. The second reason is that these systems frequently gain short-term compliance from the shame of being called out in front of peers or the embarrassment of once again disappointing adults. But this doesn't actually fix the problem. And, in many ways, it undermines the trust and relationship between teacher and child, making other problems worse.

Rethinking Behavior Charts

Emily: My very first year teaching, my mentor teacher used a behavior chart in her classroom that was a color-based card system displayed in library card catalog pockets. When students were off task, not following directions, or otherwise not behaving as expected, they were asked to "flip a card" to the next color.

I knew from my own experience as a student that I didn't enjoy this type of behavior plan, but as a newbie teacher, I followed suit because I didn't know any better. Over the years, I've come to realize that there are many other options to support students and that these types of systems are at best ineffective, and at worst harmful. I also know that many teachers still use these kinds of behavior systems. What are some of the reasons you've heard that teachers either still use these systems or are hesitant to try anything else?

Amanda: Well, firstly, like you, I did the same thing as a newbie teacher because I also didn't know better. You're far from alone there. When I talk with teachers about behavior management and behavior charts, so many of them say they know these systems aren't ideal but they don't know what else to use. They also talk about feeling pressured to use them because it's what the other teachers in their school do.

Looking back on my own training and hearing these reports from teachers makes me wonder why there aren't classes in teacher preparation programs about ways to manage behavior. What do you think teachers should know about behavior management before they have their own classrooms? And who do you think should be teaching them that?

Emily: I think one of the primary things to realize is that nobody is suggesting that there should be no boundaries, rules, or expectations. However, when we're talking about neurodivergent kids, we also have to realize that bribery and threats won't teach self-regulation.

Self-regulation is a skill that everyone needs to learn. Some students learn it intuitively; some need more direct support and instruction. Each student develops those skills on their own neurodevelopmental timeline.

I like your point about specifically teaching behavior management skills to teachers in their programs of study, because skills like that are, in my experience, infrequently explicitly taught to pre-service teachers. But it's not just about behavior management strategies; it also comes down to the culture and expectations that are already established in the school. Just like we did, new teachers tend to go with the flow of what everyone else in the building is doing. District and building initiatives are often directly focused on specific programs or incentive plans for students, so that likely is why these practices have continued.

Amanda: We both know that it's already hard to be a new teacher! There's a push-pull of wanting to bring new ideas and innovative practices into the classroom while also trying to fit into the existing culture of the school. It makes me wonder whether we ought to be thinking about how we can teach pre-service teachers and upskill existing teachers at the same time. That way everybody is learning and applying the same skills without feeling singled out, which, now that I say it out loud, is exactly what we hope for when it comes to our neurodivergent students too.

. . . Unless Kids Are in Charge

In stark contrast to behavior charts is co-regulation. Co-regulation involves students in recognizing their strengths and struggles, fostering self-reflection and strategy development. By empowering students to take charge of managing their behavior and take responsibility for their actions, co-regulation helps them become more invested in the outcomes. While it may sound unconventional or chaotic to some, co-regulation, when carefully orchestrated, is a system built on trust, respect, and understanding.

It is also a system that has the power to fundamentally transform classroom dynamics by actively engaging students in their emotional regulation. Through co-regulation, educators foster a partnership with students, guiding them in understanding their internal worlds and developing strategies for their self-reflection and growth. This approach emphasizes collaborative problem-solving, empathy, and a sense of agency and responsibility. By prioritizing co-regulation, you can create a classroom environment that values each student's unique experiences and equips them with the skills needed to navigate the complexities of the learning process and foster positive social interactions.

In this system, students acknowledge their mistakes privately and personally. They actively participate in identifying their challenges and devising strategies to overcome them. If needed, a student may maintain a private behavior chart to track their actions and outcomes. However, the student is taught to self-evaluate their progress, rather than the teacher or another person in power assessing their success or failure. This practice enables a personalized approach to discipline, tailored to individual needs and experiences. And it cultivates a sense of accountability and self-awareness in students, encouraging them to recognize their own behavioral patterns, comprehend consequences, and implement positive changes.

For instance, if a student struggles with response inhibition during classroom discussions and frequently calls out and interrupts the speaker, they could be responsible for maintaining a tally chart. Each time they notice that they've interrupted, they make a tally on one side of the chart; each time they catch themselves just *before* interrupting, they track that event on the other side. This heightened awareness alone can be a powerful catalyst for change. To ensure this process doesn't become self-punishment, teachers provide support and guidance, reinforcing the idea that the objective is understanding and improvement, not shame. Framing the tracking as a method of "gathering data" can move the goal away from success or failure to discovering what works and what doesn't. Tracking both interruptions and successfully caught interruptions also moves away from solely highlighting "bad" behavior.

To be clear, granting students agency in this way does not mean teachers relinquish their authority or role as guides. Rather, it avoids a power vacuum and empowers students to take charge of their behavior and its consequences, growing their autonomy and self-regulation. Teachers maintain the crucial role of facilitator, steering conversations, offering insights, and helping students connect actions with outcomes.

The initial implementation of co-regulation certainly presents challenges. And while it might seem easier to adopt a system that yields immediate compliance, the long-term benefits of co-regulation far outweigh the initial investment. This shift can foster an environment of respect and understanding that extends beyond the confines of your classroom, preparing students not only for school, but for life itself.

Trevor

As a first grader, Trevor was thrilled to be back in school. He loved school, his friends, and learning. His parents suspected that Trevor was an ADHDer (his two older siblings were diagnosed); however, they hadn't yet formalized the diagnosis.

Trevor's teacher used a behavior-management system that had kids "clip up" and "clip down" throughout the day. Each student was provided a clothespin with their name on it, which started each day in the middle position on a color-coded poster chart hanging on the classroom wall. If students needed reminders to stay on task or follow directions, they had to clip down. If they were "making good choices," they were awarded opportunities to clip up.

Trevor came home the first week with several yellow and orange days, after having to clip down for behaviors. He was impulsive and silly with his friends, had difficulty getting started on and finishing his morning work, and was having a hard time sitting still during circle time. By the end of the second week of school, Trevor told his parents he "hated school" and didn't want to get up in the mornings.

Trevor understood why he was getting in trouble but had no strategies to improve or change his behavior. Additionally, the range of reasons he was being asked to clip down made it difficult for him to know what he was doing "wrong." Without specific instruction and guidance, he just knew he needed to "be a better listener."

With the assistance of the guidance counselor, Trevor, his parents, and the teacher met together to develop a plan. Asking the teacher to stop utilizing the behavior chart completely was a big ask, so instead they planned to modify how the teacher would use it with Trevor. They decided to focus solely on morning work as a goal and created a laminated visual checklist for Trevor to use each morning at his desk. It allowed Trevor to self-assess how well he did each morning with building the routine of gathering his materials and completing his morning work. The teacher would take a few minutes to talk about the self-assessment and reinforce the successes he had, as well as brainstorm ideas for how to improve the areas that were difficult. The "color" for his day was determined based on this narrow goal. As Trevor progressed through the year, he and his teacher were able to gradually shift to build other routines and help Trevor build awareness and self-regulation. Once Trevor didn't feel like a "bad kid" every day, his enthusiasm for going to school returned.

Examples of Student-Tracked Behaviors

The following examples show various skills and tracking methods that could be used as part of co-regulation to help students build awareness in areas they want to improve. Students and teachers can collaborate to identify the question and set the criteria, but the student should be the one to track the information and follow up with the teacher at an agreed-upon time. Some students (especially older students) may hesitate to have a paper copy on which they are documenting these items, so a shared spreadsheet or other electronic method might provide the privacy the student needs to feel comfortable with this process. During debriefing, the teacher and student can look for ideas to help modify the systems that are in place to provide additional support, accommodations, or routines.

Staying on Task

Question: Was I able to stay on task during my independent work time?

Criteria:

1. I stayed at my workspace during work time.
2. I used fidgets as tools (not toys) to direct my focus.
3. I noticed when my mind wandered and redirected it to my work.

Task	1. Did I stay at my workspace?	2. If I needed fidgets, did I use them as a tool?	3. Did I refocus when my mind wandered?
Spelling work	Y	N	N
Math classwork	Y	Y	Y
Science questions	Y	N	N

Emotional Regulation

Question: When I'm feeling stressed or anxious, can I try a strategy to calm myself down?

Stressor (What made me feel anxious?)	On a scale of 1–5, how stressed was I when I noticed I was feeling anxious?	Which strategy did I try?	On a scale of 1–5, how stressed did I feel after trying the strategy?
Taking the math test	4	☐ Counting my breaths ☑ Reframing my thoughts ☐ Focusing on a fidget ☐ Asking to take a break	2.75

Organizing Materials

Question: Did I have/was I able to access all my materials for class today?

Criteria: Mark one tally for each item that was accessed.

1. Laptop
2. Writing utensils
3. Paper/notebook
4. Homework?

Class	Tallies	Reasons for any missing/forgotten materials
Language Arts	IIII	
Science	III	Lost my highlighter and needed it for article
Social Studies	IIII	
Math	III	Left my homework in my locker

Co-Regulation Before Self-Regulation

As discussed, co-regulation is a classroom practice that can help students develop self-regulation skills. The teacher models self-regulation and works with students who need support. By embracing this approach, you can better assist students in navigating the complex terrain of learning and emotional self-management.

Neurodivergent learners, with their unique ways of perceiving and interacting with the world, may sometimes struggle to self-regulate. By employing co-regulation strategies, teachers can meet these students on their individual paths and guide them toward successful self-regulation. Co-regulation is an essential tool for managing sensory overload and mitigating anxiety, which helps establish a more comfortable and productive learning environment.

Co-regulation moves away from telling a child what to do or not to do and toward providing supportive scaffolding that includes modeling and assistance (when needed) as they build their self-regulation skills. These are some ideas for building co-regulation into your classroom:

- Guide group breathing exercises with the whole class, and follow up by supporting individual students in utilizing the same strategies in one-on-one situations when they are working to regulate emotions.
- Give students options for how to manage intense emotions, providing information about the benefits of each strategy.
- Implement emotion check-ins at regular intervals throughout the day, where students can express how they're feeling using an emotions chart, feelings wheel, or rating scale.
- Provide consistent, predictable routines and visual schedules, which can give students a sense of security and reduce anxiety (APA 2015).
- Teach an emotion word of the day to expand students' emotional vocabularies, which in turn can enhance their ability to identify and communicate feelings.

Successful co-regulation heavily relies on a solid relationship between you and your students. This connection, built on trust, empathy, and positivity, creates a safe space for students to express their feelings and work on managing them under your guidance. Co-regulation starts with you actively guiding the student and gradually reducing your guidance as they become more capable of self-regulation. Figure 6.2 details this cycle.

Is PBIS Neurodiversity-Affirming?

Positive Behavioral Interventions and Supports (PBIS) is a widely used behaviorism-based framework for managing student behavior. Behaviorism is a psychological concept that suggests that behaviors are observable and measurable, and it posits that rewards and consequences can be utilized to modify them. PBIS frameworks often offer tokens, rewards, or praise (extrinsic reinforcers) when students follow expectations, and they attempt to deescalate "unwanted behaviors" by establishing universal expectations throughout the school setting.

The idea of proactively teaching expectations and developing routines can be useful when supporting neurodivergent learners. But the stated goal of PBIS is to "effectively teach appropriate social, emotional, and behavioral (SEB) skills" to all students. The question is: *Who is deciding what behavior is "unwanted" and what behavior is "appropriate"?* It is fair to assume that "appropriate" behavior is code for neuro-normative behavior. Universal expectations in PBIS might include expectations around how a student is supposed to sit through class, pay attention, communicate, or socialize, all of which might be areas where neurodivergent learners process and interact differently than their peers.

A common Tier 1 PBIS pre-teaching intervention is to post signs in the classroom about what a student who is actively listening and learning looks like: eyes on the speaker, feet on the floor, hands empty and placed on the desk or in the lap. For many neurodivergent learners, this expectation is not only unrealistic but also harmful to their likelihood of achieving the goal of school, which should be to learn the material being taught and not to follow a rigid set of rules for behavior. Under many PBIS programs, students who are able to meet this expectation may be given tickets to reward them for their compliance. The students who can't are subjected to constant correction until they figure out some way to camouflage their needs at the detriment of learning the material.

When a student is engaging in "unwanted behaviors," the PBIS framework encourages interventions to teach the child how to reduce them. This might include behavior tracking by a teacher and further positive reinforcement for "appropriate behavior" or reduction of rewards (essentially, punishment) for "unwanted behavior."

But at what point does a student's failure to eliminate a particular behavior mean they are moved to Tier 2, in which they are deemed "at risk for developing more serious unwanted behavior"? And how does a teacher determine that a student is "at risk for *developing* more serious unwanted behavior" if they haven't yet exhibited it?

This framework singles out neurodivergent students and students who come from cultural backgrounds in which the view of what "appropriate" behavior is varies from the norm defined by current educational settings. When a student's behavior is constantly viewed as noncompliant and defiant, it doesn't take long before they learn either that they must camouflage and mask behaviors that seem natural to them (like meeting sensory needs) or that they are a "bad kid."

It seems odd to us that schools and teachers, who tend to be big believers in the importance of intrinsic motivation to learn, rely on such tactics to gain student compliance. Additionally, especially for neurodivergent learners, the emphasis on compliance without necessarily teaching why a certain behavior is being required can put students at risk for abuse in the future (Siegel et al. 2015; Lynch 2019). The idea that one must comply with the adults or other people in power simply because they say there is a certain way things should be done undermines a student's self-trust and sense of safety; in the future, when an adult instructs them to do something, they may believe that they have no choice or voice in the situation.

It is one thing to set expectations and have routines in schools. Nobody is debating that these are helpful for all students, and often most importantly neurodivergent students. However, the presence of blanket expectations that are based on neuro-normative standards and that don't consider individual differences such as neurodivergence, trauma history, or cultural background end up causing harm for many students (Kim and Venet 2023).

We question the use of a system that relies so heavily on extrinsic manipulation to gain student compliance and believe that the PBIS framework and neurodiversity-affirming schools are not compatible.

Declarative language—using statements to share information, express emotions, or give opinions—is an integral component of co-regulation. Contrary to imperative language, which typically gives orders or makes requests, declarative language creates an atmosphere of collaboration and mutual respect (Mänty et al. 2022; Hadwin, Järvelä, and Miller 2011). For example, instead of commanding a student to "be quiet," you might remark, "I notice it's getting quite noisy in here, which could make it hard for some of us to focus." This approach is less about dictating what *should* be done and more about *fostering a shared understanding* of the situation at hand, creating a problem-solving environment.

Declarative language is particularly beneficial for neurodivergent learners, who often process information differently than neuro-normative peers. By clearly and explicitly stating your observations, feelings, and intentions, you make the expectations more accessible and understandable. This can significantly reduce students' anxiety levels, as they feel more included and aware of the situation, making it easier for them to participate in the regulation process.

Consider this scenario: A student sits in front of a blank sheet during an assignment, seemingly not having started their work. Instead of asking the student why they haven't started yet, the teacher might comment, "I see you're taking a moment before diving into your work. Sometimes it helps to gather our thoughts first or talk through what we need to do with someone." This approach includes a gentle reminder of the task and an offer of help, while respecting the possibility that the student's process might involve internal reflection or mental planning before committing to paper. It reframes what might be perceived as inaction or procrastination into a legitimate part of a learning strategy, thereby acknowledging and validating diverse approaches to tasks.

Additionally, when you use declarative language, you model a constructive way of communicating emotions and intentions. For example, if you say, "I feel overwhelmed when it's too noisy and I have a hard time focusing," you provide context for students to understand the impact of their actions, fostering empathy.

Declarative language can be incorporated into the co-regulation strategies previously mentioned. It can be used during group breathing exercises, where you might state, "As I take a deep breath in, I feel my body starting to relax." During emotion check-ins, you could share first, modeling how to identify and communicate feelings. Declarative language can also be used in establishing routines: "After we finish our math activity, we will have a quick stretch break before moving onto reading."

FIGURE 6.2 The Cycle of Co-Regulation

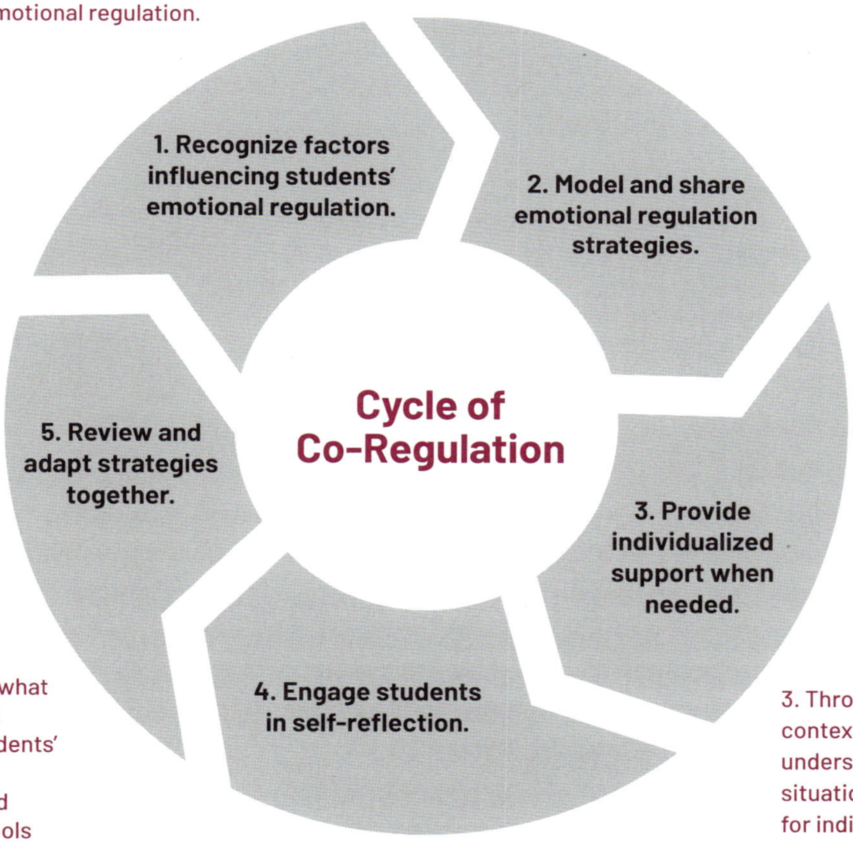

1. Factors such as sensory sensitivities, communication differences, executive function challenges, and emotional processing differences can all influence emotional regulation.

2. Integrate strategies like deep breathing and positive self-talk into your daily classroom routines to model what they look like in action. Students can practice the strategies while they are regulated.

Cycle of Co-Regulation

1. Recognize factors influencing students' emotional regulation.
2. Model and share emotional regulation strategies.
3. Provide individualized support when needed.
4. Engage students in self-reflection.
5. Review and adapt strategies together.

5. Determine what factors might influence students' emotional regulation and brainstorm tools and techniques they might try in the future.

4. Ask students about what is working and what isn't when they feel emotionally dysregulated. Allow their reflections to guide these conversations.

3. Through contextualized understanding of a situation, offer support for individual students as needed by using declarative language and offering choices for tools and techniques students can try.

Chapter 6: Rethinking Behavior in the Classroom

Another connection between declarative language and self-regulation is the parallel between declarative language and mindfulness. Mindfulness is primarily about building an awareness of the connection between what is happening in one's mind, body, and environment in the present moment. A major component of integrating mindfulness is making observations about what is happening to you mentally and physically. Saying to yourself, "Oh, there's that anxious thought about my college application," is a form of declarative language. It is a nonjudgmental statement about what is happening. Using declarative language in the classroom provides a format or model for students' own self-talk around regulating emotions. Figure 6.3 shares examples of how to rephrase common statements using declarative language.

Pascal

Mr. Lee moves between rows of desks. He pauses by Pascal, a neurodivergent student who often finds it hard to switch tasks or deal with too much noise. Today, Pascal is fidgeting, a sign that the long period of silent work is becoming overwhelming. Mr. Lee speaks in a calm, matter-of-fact tone. "It looks like some of us might be feeling a bit restless after having such a long stretch of quiet work time. I'm thinking maybe it is a good time for a brain break." The class responds positively, and Pascal's tension visibly lessens.

During a math lesson, Mr. Lee notices Pascal struggling, his paper crinkled in frustration. Mr. Lee approaches with a practical demeanor. "I notice from your body language that you're feeling frustrated with this assignment. I wonder if there's something that might help." Pascal opens up about the difficulty he's facing, and Mr. Lee offers specific, step-by-step help, along with words of encouragement. He also gently reminds the class, "When voices get loud, I worry that people will have trouble concentrating. Maybe there's something that could help us keep our volume in check." The noise level drops, helping not just Pascal but all students focus better. Mr. Lee's approach is straightforward and nurturing, implementing declarative language to support Pascal and foster a sense of community in his classroom.

FIGURE 6.3 Examples of Using Declarative Language

Topic	Typical Phrasing	Declarative Language
Focus and concentration	"You need to pay attention."	"I notice it's a bit hard to focus right now."
Preparing materials	"Get out your pencils."	"We're going to need our pencils for this activity."
Emotional dysregulation	"You need to use your coping strategies."	"It looks like things are overwhelming. I'll know you'd like some help when you lift your head off the desk."
Task completion	"Why haven't you finished this yet?"	"It seems there's a bit more to do here."
Group discussions	"You need to raise your hand to answer the question."	"I'll know someone wants to add to the conversation when I see their hand raised."

Demand Avoidance

In writing about rethinking behavior in the neurodiversity-affirming classroom, we cannot neglect to specifically mention the need to rethink demand avoidance behaviors, as these behaviors can be challenging to understand and support. Throughout this section, we'll review pathological demand avoidance (PDA) and how it shows up in the classroom, what else might be behind a neurodivergent student's demand avoidance behavior, and how you can support students with demand avoidance.

Pathological (Pervasive) Demand Avoidance

As discussed in chapter 2, PDA describes a unique profile often linked with autism. It is characterized by a strong drive for autonomy, often resulting in the person pushing back against ordinary demands to an intense degree. Advocates say it's a helpful lens for understanding a group of individuals within the broad spectrum of neurodiversity (Milton and Ryan 2022). Frequently cited PDA behaviors—such as a strong desire for control driven primarily by anxiety, mood swings, impulsiveness, and a love for role-playing—aren't typical autism traits, so this label fills in some gaps in understanding. In students with characteristics of PDA, a hypersensitive nervous system leads requests and expectations to trigger a fight/flight/freeze/fawn response to the perceived threat of a demand (O'Nions et al. 2018).

Examples of PDA behaviors include the following:

- **Resisting simple requests:** An autistic student with characteristics of PDA may resist or avoid complying with what seem like simple requests, such as putting away a book or joining a group activity.
- **Avoidant behavior:** A student might use social strategies to avoid demands, such as distracting the person making the request or making excuses.
- **Meltdowns in response to demands:** A student might have severe meltdowns in response to everyday demands and expectations.
- **Difficulty with routine transitions:** A student might find transitions between different activities or environments particularly stressful, leading to avoidance behaviors.
- **Appearing more capable in some situations than others:** A student with characteristics of PDA may exhibit abilities in some contexts but not others, depending on whether they feel in control.

Students who are autistic and display characteristics of PDA likely have a range of reasons that may influence their difficulty with meeting demands, each of which is connected to a common characteristic of an autism diagnosis:

- **The differences in the ways autistic individuals use and interpret social language** can make it difficult for them to interpret the intent of a request; some have a heightened anxiety/fear response that can trigger a survival response for even minor requests.

- **Unexpected changes can cause significant anxiety for autistic individuals.** Often, the unexpected changes might be to a routine or plan they had in their minds, so it is difficult to predict when a request or change might initiate an anxiety response. They might resist tasks that disrupt their routines or expectations.
- **An aspect of the comfort many autistic individuals experience with routine** involves areas of special interests. The flip side of this is the difficulty they may face when they are asked to engage with a task that isn't an area of personal interest. It can be extremely hard for them to complete these tasks.

When it comes to supporting students with PDA tendencies, the consensus is that traditional autism approaches may not work or could even be counterproductive (O'Nions and Eaton 2020). This is where the importance of integrating independence and autonomy, such as through the strategies we suggested for co-regulation, comes into play. Coupled with strong relational connections with the adults in their lives, accommodations can help many autistic learners with characteristics of PDA be successful in the academic setting. Integrating a component of autonomy and control can provide them a feeling of safety or an opportunity to tie a task to an already established area of success.

The PDA Society suggests a variety of communication and anxiety-reducing techniques to support autistic individuals with this type of demand avoidance. They created the acronym PANDA to provide a range of strategies to help (PDA Society 2021). Many of the strategies are accommodations and supports that teachers can provide in the way they communicate and arrange learning for all students.

- **Pick battles.** Explaining the reasons for requests along with enabling choice and control can help clarify expectations and provide a sense of autonomy.
- **Manage anxiety.** Reducing uncertainty and managing sensory needs to ease stress can help lower anxiety; lowered anxiety helps individuals attempt tasks that could be seen as demands.

- **Negotiate and collaborate.** Utilizing trust and fairness as tools to find shared common ground can empower students to feel more comfortable with expectations and requests.
- **Disguise and manage demands.** Using declarative language to frame requests in nondemanding terms can provide space for students to process the information without triggering a heightened response to the request.
- **Adapt.** Using flexibility, novelty, and creativity to come up with ways to accomplish a task or objective that wasn't originally planned can reduce paralysis or panic about a request or demand.

Other Causes of Demand Avoidance in Neurodivergent Learners

Beyond PDA, there are many other reasons why neurodivergent learners might experience or show traits of demand avoidance:

- **Anxiety:** If a learner experiences high levels of anxiety, they might avoid situations or tasks that trigger these feelings. This could be due to fear of failure, fear of making mistakes, or fear of the unknown.
- **Discomfort with ambiguity:** Not feeling confident about how to do a task or feeling uncertain about the goals of a task can lead to hesitation and avoidance of the request. Frequently, this discomfort with ambiguity is also influenced by difficulty with describing the problem or asking for help.
- **Difficulty with executive function skills:** Learners who have trouble with attention regulation, task initiation, or other executive function skills may find it challenging to start and complete tasks. What appears to be demand avoidance might actually be executive functioning difficulties. These difficulties are frequently noticeable with ADHDers and non-PDA autistic students.
- **Skill deficits/learning disabilities:** If a learner struggles with certain skills due to a learning disability, they may avoid tasks that heavily rely on those skills.

Many of the strategies that are helpful in supporting autistic students with PDA tendencies can be used with other neurodivergent students who show traits of demand avoidance. Understanding why students show demand avoidance absent of PDA can help you determine which strategies would best support and accommodate those learners. These are some more strategies to support demand avoidance:

- **Use declarative language.** This can be specifically helpful because it removes the demand language that can trigger students' fight/flight/freeze/fawn responses.

- **Use co-regulation.** When difficult interactions or situations arise, model for the student how to name their frustrations and feelings by stating your own.

- **Provide choices.** Giving the student control over some choices can reduce anxiety.

- **Create predictable routines.** A predictable routine can help the student know what to expect and feel more in control, reducing anxiety about transitions or new, unexpected demands.

- **Use collaborative goal setting.** Work with the student to set achievable goals that they feel invested in. This helps them feel ownership over their learning path.

- **Use their interests.** If you can link demands to something the student is interested in, they might feel more motivated to engage.

- **Avoid power struggles.** If a student is resisting a demand, consider whether it is essential at that moment. Engaging in a power struggle can escalate anxiety and avoidance. Sometimes, it might be more effective to back off and later approach the situation differently. Power struggles rarely end with positive results, and the long-term negative impact they have on the relationship between a student and their teacher is very difficult to overcome.

- **Empathize and validate feelings.** Acknowledge that the demands may be genuinely difficult for the student, even if they might seem simple to others. Expressing understanding can build trust and make the student more willing to collaborate.

Intersecting Identities

Students who are also members of marginalized groups, especially those who are Black or Latine, risk having their behavior pathologized more frequently than White students. This is further influenced by students' socioeconomic backgrounds, and the discrepancy in disciplinary actions they receive increases as students get older (Gopalan and Nelson 2019).

Neurodivergent students with these intersectional identities are at an even higher risk of having their behavior, such as demand avoidance, be interpreted as a cause for discipline. Additionally, they are less likely to have a neurodivergent label because of barriers they may face in accessing supports and services. Awareness of the possibility of neurodivergence when supporting or determining disciplinary consequences is crucial.

Rejection Sensitivity

Rejection sensitivity is another area where a unique approach to supporting neurodivergent students' behavioral needs is necessary. Rejection sensitivity—also called rejection awareness or rejection perception—is a term that describes the heightened feelings of anxiety or fear of rejection that some neurodivergent learners experience. In essence, rejection sensitivity is like having a heightened radar for potential rejection or criticism, which causes these learners to respond more emotionally than others in the same situations. Rejection sensitivity is often discussed in neurodivergent spaces as rejection sensitivity dysphoria (RSD) and within the context of ADHD, though it is not exclusive to ADHDers (Zhou et al. 2018; Zhang et al. 2021). It is important to note that RSD is not an official diagnosis but rather a term used to describe this heightened response many neurodivergent people experience and how they might behave when experiencing it. Some recent research shows that ADHDers show different levels of brain activity when exposed to positive reinforcement (less activity) versus negative feedback or criticism (heightened activity). This seems to suggest that the brain chemistry of ADHDers may foster these experiences of intense rejection sensitivity (Babinski et al. 2019).

A point of caution here is the potential to pathologize normal reactions. We all react negatively when we feel criticized or rejected, particularly during times of stress. It's important to remember that everyone is different, and not all strong responses to perceived rejection are indicative of a pattern of rejection sensitivity. Neurodivergent learners are likely to have a history of negative feedback from social situations, perceived failures related to executive function skills, or disappointment related to academic performance (especially in comparison to their ability). These past experiences can accumulate and lead to a trauma-like response to perceived rejection, including hypervigilance for possible rejection or emotional reactions that are out of proportion to the situation (Grossman, Hoffman, and Shrira 2022). Factors such as differences in interpreting social cues and heightened anxiety responses can also influence neurodivergent students' responses to rejection (Goodall et al. 2022).

Rejection sensitivity can manifest in a variety of types of situations, with both minor and more significant responses. This list includes a few examples of situations where rejection sensitivity might show up at school and how students may react:

- **Group projects:** A student with rejection sensitivity might be highly anxious when choosing groups for a project, fearing they'll be the last chosen or not included at all. They may preemptively isolate themself or refuse the groupwork outright to avoid the possibility of feeling rejected.
- **Feedback on assignments:** Upon receiving a grade lower than expected, a student with rejection sensitivity might become particularly upset, perceiving it as a personal failure or a rejection from the teacher rather than constructive criticism meant to improve future work.
- **Social interactions:** If friends choose to sit at a different lunch table or play a different game at recess, a student with rejection sensitivity may perceive this as a personal rejection and respond with intense sadness or withdrawal.
- **Class participation:** If a student's answer is corrected or refuted during a class discussion, they may interpret this as a personal rejection or an embarrassment. As a result, they may become reluctant to participate in future discussions to avoid similar instances.

- **Peer relationships:** Misinterpreting neutral or ambiguous comments as negative or rejecting can be common in students with rejection sensitivity. For example, if a friend is simply having a bad day and is less talkative than usual, the student might take this as a personal slight and feel hurt or rejected.
- **New situations or changes:** If there's a change in seating arrangements, a student with rejection sensitivity might feel anxious about sitting next to unfamiliar peers because of worries about potential rejection. They may resist the change or exhibit signs of distress.
- **Asking for help:** Students with rejection sensitivity may avoid asking teachers or peers for help with schoolwork, fearing they will appear unintelligent or be judged or ridiculed. This fear of rejection may lead to academic struggles if they can't overcome the challenges of the work on their own.

Rejection sensitivity may also manifest in ways other than those described above, depending on the student and situation. The key is to recognize these reactions for what they are—responses to perceived rejection—rather than intentional overreactions or misbehavior. Empathy and understanding can go a long way in supporting students who might be dealing with rejection sensitivity. Using explicit communication and providing opportunities for discussing reactions, fears, and feelings can help build confidence in students who experience rejection sensitivity. Co-regulating with them when they begin to experience this stress will help them develop skills for self-regulation in the future.

Double Empathy Problem

Rejection Sensitivity Dysphoria

The situation: A neurodivergent student is waiting for feedback on a group project in class. The teacher is giving constructive feedback to each group, pointing out areas for improvement along with the positives. The student is particularly sensitive to criticism and is apprehensive about how they will react to the teacher's comments.

Perspective of others: The students' classmates and teacher see the neurodivergent student as particularly invested in the project. When the teacher offers constructive criticism to the group, they notice the student becoming visibly upset, and they perhaps mistake it for an overreaction to minor feedback. The teacher and other students see the neurodivergent student's response as a sign of being too sensitive or not being able to handle constructive criticism. They are unaware of the intensity of the emotions the student is experiencing due to their sensitivity to perceived rejection.

Perspective of the neurodivergent student: The student experiences the feedback session with heightened emotional intensity. They perceive the teacher's constructive criticism as a profound personal rejection, triggering intense feelings of failure and inadequacy. Despite understanding intellectually that the feedback is meant to be helpful and is directed at the group as a whole, not them personally, they can't help but feel deeply hurt and embarrassed. This intense emotional response might lead to a strong urge to withdraw from the situation or an inability to focus on the rest of the lesson. The student struggles to regulate these overwhelming feelings, which seem disproportionate to the situation at hand, causing significant distress and impacting their ability to engage in the learning environment.

Possible follow-up: Recognizing that the student is an ADHDer, the teacher realizes that the student may be experiencing rejection sensitivity. They talk to the student about their reaction and work to find ways to offer feedback that work for this student, such as providing any feedback in a one-on-one setting where they can discuss strengths and areas for growth without others present. Allowing the student to process the information and ask questions about it in this way mitigates the intense emotional reaction and builds trust and rapport between student and teacher.

What to Remember

- Teachers' perception of behavior is based on the outward signs of their students' internal emotional experiences. To support neurodivergent students in expressing themselves, teachers need to be proactive, curious, and compassionate allies, not reactive disciplinarians.
- Rethinking punitive behavior management systems, like behavior charts, is critical in a neurodiversity-affirming environment. When students aren't in charge, these systems can cause shame, make students feel called out, and perpetuate inequity and bias that disproportionately affect neurodivergent students.
- Prioritizing co-regulation is key to creating neurodiversity-affirming environments that recognize behavior as communication, value each student's unique experiences, engage students in recognizing and regulating their internal emotions, and give them the skills they need to navigate learning and social interactions.

Chapter 7

Building Emotionally Competent Classrooms

 Points to Ponder

- How do your emotional regulation skills interact with your students' social and emotional skills?
- Does your classroom include a hidden curriculum?
- How can an emotionally competent classroom foster effective student self-advocacy?

Emotional competence is key in neurodiversity-affirming classrooms. When you're creating a space that recognizes and values the needs and strengths everyone brings to the table, it's important that you are understanding, empathetic, and flexible enough to connect with each student in their unique way. Showing your students the importance of managing emotions isn't always easy if you haven't begun critically examining your own emotional regulation skills.

It's worth noting that emotional competence and emotional regulation aren't the same. Emotional competence is about understanding and managing both your own emotions and those of others, including recognizing feelings and handling social interactions wisely. Emotional regulation, on the other hand, is more specifically about controlling your emotional reactions in different situations to help you meet goals, stay balanced, and adapt to changes. Teachers who foster students' emotional competence and ability to self-regulate start by modeling both skills themselves.

This chapter explores the impact of an emotionally competent classroom and strategies for strengthening your and your students' emotional competence. It shares how understanding family emotions and concerns around a student's diagnosis is part of an emotionally competent classroom and guides you through our Four Es Framework that you can share with families and students to lead them through this process.

From Self to Students: The Impact of Teacher Emotional Regulation

We've talked a lot thus far about rethinking and reframing behavior, but we also want to acknowledge this doesn't apply just to students. All people have "behavior" that serves a function for them, including educators. But when you're so focused on understanding what's behind your students' behavior and how to approach it, it can be easy to overlook yourself. When students act, those actions can cause you to react. If you don't take the time to care for yourself and your own emotional well-being, you can end up in an action-reaction cycle that doesn't serve anyone well.

If you're rolling your eyes and thinking, "Yeah, yeah, everybody talks about self-care," you're not wrong. People do talk a lot about making time to care for oneself in the midst of stressors and busy schedules. What is often not acknowledged is that good self-care isn't just a bubble bath or a night out. Often, the most important types of self-care are intentional and deliberate, and they have a long-lasting impact.

One component of self-care is recognizing the need to build your own emotional competence and awareness. It's like the old "put on your own oxygen mask before helping others" adage—if you don't develop and work on your emotional regulation skills, you can't help students build theirs. As one study of the impact of teachers' emotional regulation found, it's a teacher's responsibility to create and manage the emotional climate of their classroom (Taxer and Gross 2018). That's probably not surprising to you. But what might be surprising is that the study considers the emotional climate of the classroom to include both co-regulating (helping your students deal with and manage their emotions) *and* self-regulating (using techniques to manage your own emotions in positive ways). Effectively managing and reflecting on your emotions has a positive impact on students' emotional well-being and learning outcomes. It also helps build stronger student-teacher relationships, especially with students whose behavior is often classified as "disruptive" (Gallagher and Mayer 2006; McGrath and Van Bergen 2019).

Some of this is due to the power of mirror neurons. Mirror neurons are why, when people watch displays of emotion, the regions in their brains involved in the control and regulation of their emotions are activated almost as if they'd experienced the emotion themselves (Bonini et al. 2022). That's a powerful finding, especially if you think about the fact that both neurodivergent and neuro-normative students are watching others to gauge what's "typical" as they form their own reactions.

Basically, when you're modeling emotional regulation strategies—positive or negative—your students' brains practice what they're seeing. That allows them to do it more easily themselves. So how you manage your emotions matters not just for your own well-being but also for the well-being of your classroom. To put it plainly, your ability to model emotional regulation skills has the power to change your students' brains.

Using the CASEL Framework to Examine Your and Students' Skills

Emotional competence isn't just one skill, it's many—each of which plays an important role in your ability to relate to others and build an emotionally competent classroom. These skills are reflected in the five core competencies of the Collaborative for Academic, Social, and Emotional Learning's (CASEL) framework of SEL: self-awareness, self-management, social awareness, good decision-making, and the ability to develop and maintain relationships. Figure 7.1 on the next page shares what's included in each of these core competencies.

Though the CASEL competencies are most often targeted in K–12 curricula and programs for students' social and emotional learning, they're not relevant only to students. When students' social and emotional skills need more work, they're more likely to struggle in the face of a challenge or conflict. The same is true for teachers

FIGURE 7.1 A Look at CASEL's Core Competencies

Competency	Definition	Skills
Self-awareness	the ability to recognize and understand your own emotions, thoughts, strengths, areas for growth, and values, as well as knowing how they influence your behavior in varying contexts	• recognizing and naming your emotions • understanding and being able to articulate your personal values • matching your actions and thoughts to your values • recognizing you have biases and having a willingness to examine them • feeling confident about your strengths • having an awareness of your challenges and a growth mindset about them
Self-management	the ability to effectively manage your emotions, thoughts, and behaviors in varying contexts to achieve both personal and collective goals	• demonstrating impulse control • having and using effective stress-management techniques • being motivated to set and meet personal and professional goals • being able to plan, organize, and communicate in productive ways
Social awareness	the ability to recognize social norms and take the perspective of, empathize with, and be compassionate toward others, even (and especially) when their backgrounds or experiences differ from your own	• seeing and being open to different perspectives, even if you don't agree with them • seeking out various perspectives to better understand situations • respecting diversity in all its forms • approaching and responding to others with empathy • understanding social and ethical norms and how systems influence them, sometimes in unjust ways • recognizing other people's strengths and acknowledging their feelings

Competency	Definition	Skills
Responsible decision-making	the ability to think about how your behavior and actions affect you and other people, with the goal of making sound, ethical, and safe decisions that take into account the benefits and consequences to everyone involved	• using critical thinking to identify, analyze, and solve problems • examining the impact of your actions • taking accountability for the consequences of your actions, be they positive, negative, or neutral • being curious and open-minded and taking available information into mind before making a decision • recognizing your role in supporting well-being in yourself and the communities in which you participate
Relationship skills	the ability to create and maintain strong, mutually supportive relationships with other people, including those who have life experiences and perspectives that differ from your own	• having effective communication skills • listening to others, hearing them, and reacting appropriately to what they say • being able to stick to and explain your own opinions and positions instead of simply adopting others' ideas • being both a help-seeker and a help-giver • attempting to resolve conflict when necessary

(Garcia 2019). The following sections outline how each of the competencies impacts your teaching, situations that you might find challenge your ability to use the skillset, and ways to incorporate the competencies in a neurodiversity-affirming classroom. And pages 180–181 share eight ways you can strengthen your emotional competence.

The Impact of Self-Awareness on Your Teaching

We've all had the experience of being upset by students' words or behavior and taking it personally. In those moments, it's easy to react to students rather than take the time to respond. Reactions often happen quickly, without a pause to reflect, and they put your own feelings about what's happening first. Responding, however, takes more self-awareness. It means you take a beat before doing anything and ask yourself, *What is it about this situation that's making me so upset?* (Figure 7.2 shares more about the distinction between reactions and responses.)

When you don't practice self-awareness, it can easily feel like a student's actions are directed *at* you. But rather than being intended to upset you, it is much more likely that the student's words or behavior are a result of a limited ability to communicate effectively or regulate emotions. This is an important distinction, because when you interpret a student's behavior in a personal way, it is easy for emotions (and the situation) to escalate.

As the adult in the room, you need to remember the importance of self-reflection, understanding your own feelings, and thinking through how to express them appropriately. It can be difficult to maintain that level of self-awareness in the daily hustle and bustle of the classroom. It's a lot of mental exercise to perform before you respond to the student, and the truth is, you're going to have off days, just like your students do. But keeping that in mind and communicating it to them is another part of being self-aware.

Incorporating Self-Awareness into Your Classroom

Neurodivergent students, particularly those who camouflage or mask, aren't always as self-aware as educators expect. You can model self-awareness for them (and all students) by communicating how you are evaluating and thinking about your emotions. Students can't gain or improve skills that have not been explicitly taught. And you also can't

FIGURE 7.2 Reaction vs. Response

Reactions...	Responses...
happen quickly, without a pause to reflect, and often reflect your own feelings about what's happening	happen in the moment, but with pause to think about what you know about the student and *their* reactions
don't allow you to think through the full impact of what you say or do	allow for consideration of the short- and long-term impacts of what you are about to do or say
reinforce a power dynamic in which things happen *to* students, not *with* them	reinforce high expectations for your students and your belief that they can control and change their own responses
lead to punitive consequences	lead to logical consequences and teaching of skills

expect them to pause and think through their responses and actions if you're unwilling to be vulnerable and share what it looks like when you struggle to emotionally regulate. That vulnerability can look like this:

- You're aware that having emotional reactions is healthy and you tell students that it's okay for them to have them too.
- You name your emotions in front of students and deliberately build their emotional vocabularies by giving them tools, such as feelings wheels, to help them name their own.
- You recognize how your emotions impact your actions.
- You use the "think aloud" strategy to model that recognition and reflection (Zhang and Zhang 2019).
- You're honest with students that you're all developing these skills together and that not everybody will develop them at the same pace.

The Impact of Self-Management on Your Teaching

Keeping your emotions under control in a busy classroom isn't always as easy as recognizing them, especially when you're teaching during a time that the US Secretary of Education, Miguel Cardona, has acknowledged as being one in which teachers are facing "intentional toxic disrespect" (2023). Both teachers and students have reasons for struggling with managing emotions—including external and internal pressures that are separate from stressors at school. Social comparison, eco-anxiety, social and racial injustice, stressors at home and in the community, and the lack of cultural representation in curriculum and classrooms can all make it more difficult for teachers and students to regulate emotions, both inside and outside the classroom.

As an adult, you've likely developed strategies for coping with these stressors. But your students are still learning those skills, and these external stressors can be real barriers to their self-management. Neurodivergent students often have some additional barriers, including struggling to understand both the presented curriculum and what's known as the "hidden curriculum." The hidden curriculum is the unspoken expectations around behavior, social norms, and supposed shared understanding of how classrooms and society work (Alsubaie 2015). This hidden curriculum can vary across educational settings, but there are some commonalities. For example, most classrooms and school settings have expectations around communicating with peers and teachers, executive function and critical-thinking skills, intra- and interpersonal norms, and social accountability (see figure 7.3 for more).

Teachers expect students to know this hidden curriculum. But if you don't make hidden curriculum explicit, then that expectation is unreasonable, particularly for students who come from cultural backgrounds that differ from the majority and those who have difficulty reading social cues and nuance (Alsubaie 2015). Assuming students can and will adhere to unspoken expectations is a challenge that can impact not only *their* ability to self-manage but *yours* as well. When students aren't able to regulate because they don't understand the unspoken expectations, it can cause friction and misunderstanding. Their actions may seem willful to you because you're holding them to those expectations, and your reactions may not make sense to them because they don't understand what they've "done wrong."

FIGURE 7.3 Uncovering the Hidden Curriculum

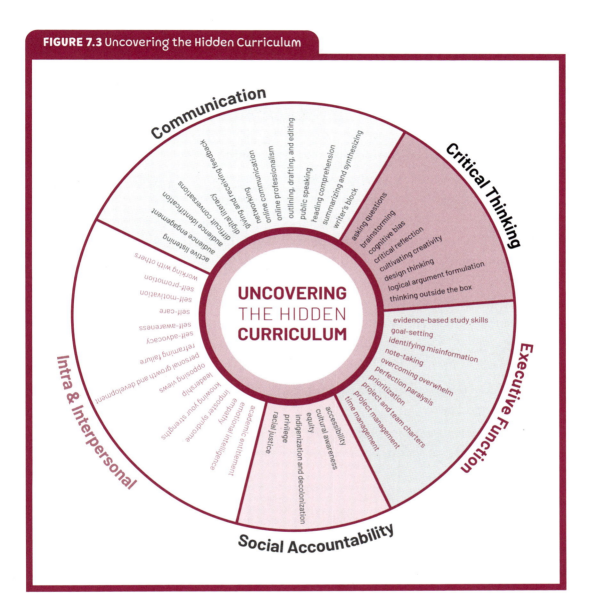

Copyright © 2024 by Uncovering the Hidden Curriculum, licensed under CC BY-NC-SA, at https://hiddencurriculum.ca/about-us

Incorporating Self-Management into Your Classroom

When students are struggling to learn the presented and/or hidden curriculum, it can make you feel like you're not good at your job, which, in turn, can cause stress and frustration for all (Wray, Sharma, and Subban 2022). It may not always feel like it, but these moments of frustration can serve as opportunities for you and your students to build self-management skills. In practice, here are some things you can try:

- **Acknowledge the complicated world we're living in** and keep in mind the factors outside of your classroom and control that impact your and your students' ability to manage strong emotions.
- **Keep in mind that neurodivergent students may have emotional reactions based on past experiences** or a history of repeated failure because their needs haven't been appropriately met.
- **Make your classroom expectations, routines, and operations explicit** so that students know and can work toward following them.
- **Review and discuss interactions** that you or your students wish had been handled differently.
- **Model how to revisit those interactions** and explain the *what* and *why* of what you're doing.
- **Use tools to support executive function skills,** such as planners, graphic organizers, note-taking apps and strategies, color-coding systems, and more.

Double Empathy Problem

Interrupting in Class

The situation: In a high school class discussion, a neurodivergent student who struggles with self-awareness and self-management frequently interrupts the teacher with questions or comments that seem off-topic. These interruptions are causing some disruption in the flow of the class.

Perspective of others: The student's classmates and teacher perceive the behavior as intentionally disruptive or inattentive. Because they are interpreting the behavior through the lens of their own self- and social-awareness skills, they view the interruptions as a lack of respect for the class rules or as an inability to stay focused on the subject being discussed. This assumption that the neurodivergent student is intentionally not following the hidden curriculum leads them to feel frustrated and impatient with the student.

Perspective of the neurodivergent student: The student's questions and comments are their way of processing the information being taught. Though seemingly off-topic, the "interruptions" are this student's attempt to connect new information to what they already know or to clarify points they find confusing.

Possible follow-up: When the teacher takes the time to discuss the behavior with the student and learn about their thought process, the teacher can appreciate the student's unique way of learning and processing information. They are then able to collaborate with the student to find more effective ways to integrate their contributions into the class discussion without disrupting the flow of the class.

The Impact of Social Awareness on Your Teaching

In a neurodiversity-affirming classroom, social awareness is one of the most important skills for teachers and students to develop. For many neurodivergent students, building and maintaining strong relationships is challenging. They may struggle with perspective-taking, reading other people's cues, being tolerant of ways others approach the world, and understanding that differences in values don't mean a friendship can't flourish. To some degree, those struggles mirror more traditional classroom set-ups and expectations in which there are "right" and "wrong" ways to approach the work and think about the material, as well as parameters for how to interact with teachers and each other based on power hierarchies.

That said, many teachers are taking more progressive approaches to building equitable classroom cultures that provide space for varying perspectives, allow many ways of working, respect cultural differences, and affirm a diversity of value systems. These socially aware classrooms promote strong teacher-student relationships built on empathy, equity, and mutual respect.

This is not to say that it's always easy to see or respect a student's perspective, especially if it shows up in the form of interruptive behavior or a disagreement during which the student—neurodivergent or otherwise—becomes dysregulated. Even the most socially aware teacher can become so frustrated that they dismiss a student's thoughts or opinion not because of *what* the student is expressing but because of *how* they're expressing it.

Incorporating Social Awareness into Your Classroom

Getting to know what interests your students, what excites them, and what they want to do, both inside and outside the classroom, is a good way to start building an atmosphere that encourages the development of social awareness skills. This helps you figure out ways to provide real-life relevance in your instruction and also teaches students the value of getting to know people on a personal level. For neurodivergent students, it has the additional benefit of showing them that you're interested in their authentic selves. See page 179 for a list of good questions to help you get to know your students. Below are some ways to incorporate social awareness into your practice:

- **Ask students for input** on the classroom environment and to explain how their suggestions could support their and others' learning.
- **Work with students to create classroom rules** that value and consider the varying personalities, needs, strengths, and cultures represented in your group.
- **Normalize conversation** about people's differing perspectives and concerns.
- **Incorporate the phrase "Tell me more . . ."** into your classroom vocabulary to help you *and* your students learn to dig deeper to better understand each others' perspectives and experiences.

The Impact of Responsible Decision-Making on Your Teaching

As a teacher, every day you likely make more decisions than you can count. Whether small or large, these decisions are impactful. You might decide how to handle challenging behavior, how to present content and material, how to manage your and students' time, and even how to make decisions. Ideally, you've decided that creating a neurodiversity-affirming classroom includes implementing Universal Design for Learning (chapter 4) or incorporating elements of it. If so, you're consistently teaching students how to be responsible decision-makers too.

When students are expected to be expert learners, they're also expected to make decisions about how to show what they know, how to access the material, and what accommodations they may need to accomplish those things. That means *you* need to be able to make decisions about how you're going to provide them with the skills and resources to make those choices, while also making decisions about your instructional design and how you will teach to meet academic outcomes, improve standardized test scores, and/or increase graduation rates.

Teaching responsible decision-making and practicing it yourself takes honesty, humility, and discretion. As you share your process and the factors you consider in the decisions you're making with students, you also need to be humble enough to let them challenge your thought processes and even point out or provide additional information that you hadn't considered. There are, of course, some things you won't be able to share with students to protect everyone's privacy. But it's powerful to say that out loud. This is especially helpful for students who are concrete thinkers and those who have a strong sense of justice.

Incorporating Responsible Decision-Making into Your Classroom

Helping students become decision-makers means being able to acknowledge that the ways they think about things may be different from the way you think about them—and that you may not always understand how they came to a conclusion. The power of the question *What makes you think that?*—when asked with true curiosity—gives students confidence that there's more than one way to think about things, that there's more than one correct decision, and that you really care about how their minds work. Thinking aloud about how your choices impact yourself and others models for students how to think about their own thinking. It makes implicit thought processes explicit and helps neurodivergent students, in particular, understand that other people aren't always thinking the same way they are.

The Impact of Relationship Skills on Your Teaching

Humans are wired to want social connection. Neurodivergent students who struggle to build relationships may think, understandably, that this comes easily to everyone else, but of course that's not the case. Therefore, it can be especially important for them to see you putting in the work to develop meaningful connections with them, their peers, and your colleagues.

Building relationships requires you to be emotionally expressive, able to ask for help, and willing to give support when asked. It requires vulnerability and trust. It means showing students that there's value to building relationships with people you may not understand or choose to be friends with, but with whom you spend time. Most of all, building relationships takes practice.

Incorporating Relationship-Building Skills into Your Classroom

Students often don't see how you interact with people outside the classroom, but they can benefit from observing how you engage with them during class. These are some key strategies:

- **Be openly curious** about the reason behind a student's words or actions before responding to them or passing judgment.
- **Set and communicate boundaries,** emphasizing that they are guidelines for your own well-being rather than strict rules dictating how others should act.
- **Acknowledge that building relationships can be hard**, while stressing that students shouldn't assume it is easy for someone just because it appears that way.
- **Model how to ask clarifying questions** about emotions, behavior, decisions, and even facial expressions so students understand that how they interpret something may not be what the other person is trying to express.
- **Solicit, listen to, and respond to feedback** from your class to make sure you're engaging in ways that are comfortable to all students.

- **Build in time for you and your students to get to know each other** without an academic outcome or goal. (See questions that can help you get to know your students below.)

Fifteen Questions to Get to Know Your Students

1. What do you like to do when you have free time?
2. Do you have favorite books, TV shows, or movies? What are they and what makes them your favorite?
3. Do you like to listen to music? What kind and when?
4. Do you play a sport or an instrument? Would you like to?
5. Who do you look up to? Why?
6. If you could describe yourself in five emojis, which ones would you use?
7. What is something I don't know about you that you wish I knew?
8. Is there anything about you that I know that you wish I didn't know?
9. What is one thing you want to know about me?
10. If you're having trouble in class, do you have ideas for how I can best help you?
11. What do you like best about learning?
12. What do what you like least about learning?
13. Will you tell me three things that make you laugh?
14. Will you tell me three things that stress you out?
15. Can you tell me about a time when you felt like someone really *got* you?

BONUS QUESTION: Which of these questions do you think I shouldn't ask anymore?

Eight Ways to Strengthen Your Emotional Competence

Strengthening your emotional competence helps you manage your own emotions and respond effectively to students' emotional needs, creating a supportive learning environment. It enables you to foster positive relationships, reduce classroom conflicts, and improve student engagement. As an emotionally competent teacher, you'll be better equipped to handle the stresses of the classroom and support your students. Here are some ways to get started:

1. **Practice open-minded self-reflection.** Allow yourself to examine your thoughts, emotions, and reactions through a nonjudgmental lens. When you look at how you think or react without putting a moral judgment of "good" or "bad" on it, you get a better sense of the triggers and patterns that inform your actions. Consider journaling, drawing, or recording your reflections so you're able to look at them again to gain perspective and follow your progress over time.

2. **Increase your emotional literacy.** This goes beyond having a strong emotional vocabulary. Learning to name emotions effectively is just one part of emotional literacy. You also can improve your ability to recognize and understand how your emotions feel to you and look to others, which gives you an opening into having a solid understanding of the causes of your emotions and how they affect your relationships. Emotional literacy also means being able to accurately identify and label emotions in others.

3. **Build your stress-management tool kit.** Developing and learning new strategies and techniques to manage stress can help prevent emotional overwhelm. Adding activities that bring you joy, such as exercise, a night out with friends, or a favorite hobby, to your tool kit can increase your sense of mental well-being.

4. **Prioritize self-care.** Keep in mind that self-care isn't indulgent, extravagant, or selfish. Taking care of yourself is key to ensuring your emotional well-being, building resilience, and increasing your ability to support others. Self-care can be as simple as making sure you eat regularly, get enough sleep, and take time to do things you love.

5. **Establish a community of care.** Your community of care is your support system. Colleagues, friends, and family are part of your community of care, but it also includes resources like health care professionals, professional development networks, mentors, and other people or systems that you can turn to when you need guidance and support.

6. **Create a "don't-do" list.** We all have a to-do list, but few of us have a "don't-do" list—a list of activities and behaviors that are unproductive or not worth the time and energy. Consciously choosing not to engage in these activities can make space for more meaningful endeavors. For instance, your "don't-do" list might include reading the news in the morning, answering emails after a certain time of day, saying yes to things you don't have time for, or spending time with people whose company you don't enjoy.

7. **Challenge negative or unhelpful thoughts.** This is also known as cognitive reframing. It asks you to examine the validity of thoughts that may be causing you emotional distress. Try to find evidence that supports or contradicts the thoughts, and if you can't support them, look for a more realistic way to frame the situation to help regulate your emotional state.

8. **Identify healthy coping strategies.** Different coping strategies work for different people. The key is to make sure that what you're doing to cope isn't causing you additional distress or harm. Healthy coping strategies are positive and constructive ways to deal with stress, challenges, and difficult emotions. They can include things like social connection, mindfulness techniques, exercise, practicing gratitude, or other actions that maintain your well-being.

Understanding Family Emotions and Concerns

Another facet of building emotionally competent, neurodiversity-affirming classrooms is understanding students' families, and particularly the fears and concerns neurodivergent students' families may have around their children's diagnoses and what those diagnoses might mean for their children's experiences in school.

It's not uncommon for parents to worry about labeling a child as neurodivergent. One big fear parents may hold is that the label will mean their child will be treated differently in the classroom based on what teachers know about the specific diagnosis and not on what they know about the specific child. Some parents may also worry that a label provides their child with an excuse as to why things are difficult for them, and instead of being motivated to try new ways of learning, their child will instead just not try, leading to learned helplessness.

Some of this fear has to do with parents' own emotional competence. Some parents may not be able to name how they're feeling or have the self-awareness to realize that how they react to a diagnosis impacts their child's response to the news as well. Many families feel pressured to make decisions about their children's education before they've had a chance to seek out enough information, process the news, and think through the short- and long-term implications of the decisions they're being asked to make. Without strong family-school communication, these fears and worries may—like the hidden curriculum—stay unspoken and lead to misunderstandings that challenge everybody's ability to self-regulate.

The Four Es Framework

Cyrus

Cyrus, an autistic student, wasn't diagnosed until he was nine years old because his cognitive giftedness made it easy for him to meet the academic demands of school. Despite that, his difficulty with communication, emotional and sensory dysregulation, and challenges with cognitive flexibility meant his early school years were very difficult. His dysregulation was viewed as a "behavior problem," which led to additional outbursts of frustration. Because he was often dysregulated, he had a hard time keeping friends and getting along with others. And because many of his teachers reacted to him as if he were being deliberately difficult and as if his frustration were personally aimed at them instead of responding using their own self-regulation skills and emotional competence, Cyrus didn't trust teachers.

He got into trouble because people thought he was being a "wise guy" and disrespectful. He felt misunderstood, lonely, and always in trouble. His mother, too, felt misunderstood, lonely, and as if she were in trouble for not getting Cyrus's perceived behavior "problem" under control. She spent a lot of time talking to teachers and, as her understanding of Cyrus grew, the way she approached those conversations changed.

At first she talked about Cyrus's difficulty with self-regulation as a way to excuse his "behavior." Once he was diagnosed, she began to explain how autism contributed to his trouble with self-regulation. Eventually, she began to talk to Cyrus's teachers about what being autistic looked like for him and educated them about how they could all work together to help Cyrus be successful. Once the teachers had a better sense of why Cyrus was struggling with self-regulation, they began to respond instead of reacting. And because they knew more about how being neurodivergent impacted Cyrus's development of emotional regulation skills, they provided Cyrus a higher level of support in learning them.

Being identified or diagnosed as neurodivergent leads each person through a unique process of accepting the limitations that come along with it and learning to advocate for support. In the case of children and teens, their families also have to process the information and their emotions about it. The vignette about Cyrus shows how his mother progressed through learning and understanding his diagnosis. Not all caregivers will go through the same emotional journey of acceptance that Cyrus's mother did, but it's important for you to understand the impact of a diagnosis on students' families and caregivers. For Cyrus's mother, his diagnosis led her through the first three Es of what we are calling the Four Es Framework:

1. **Excuse** yourself from doing the task.
2. **Explain** why the task is hard.
3. **Educate** someone about the skill you have trouble with and how that gets in the way of doing the task.
4. **Empower** yourself to self-advocate for support.

As educators, it's our responsibility to support students and their caregivers not only in making it past the excuse, explain, and educate stages of accepting a neurodivergent diagnosis but also in moving to the fourth E: empowerment.

When students' teachers or caregivers excuse, explain, and educate, they're doing things *about* students, not *with* them. They sit in meetings discussing signs of dysregulation and support strategies (*How can we learn to recognize signs of frustration? What if we try a social skills group?*), but they often don't ask students what they think or empower them to self-advocate. To empower students, educators and parents need to move from talking about them to talking with them. This can be as simple as asking things like, "How can we help *you* recognize your signs of frustration?" and "Do *you* think a social skills group might help?"

To move toward empowerment, you can start by talking to your whole class (as well as students' families) about the Four Es Framework, using an example from your own life of something you find difficult and how it impacts you. For example, you might tell students about how you have a hard time concentrating. You can then talk them through what it sounds like when you use it to **excuse** why you can't do a task, **explain** to them why struggles with concentration make the task hard, **educate** them on what it means to have difficulty concentrating and why that gets in the way, and finally share what it sounds like when you are **empowered** to self-advocate for support. Then invite students to think about the four Es in relation to something they struggle to do. What does it sound like when they excuse, explain, educate, and are empowered to self-advocate?

Amanda's Four Es Story

Amanda: I have two sons who identify as autistic. Even though one had already been identified, it was still a shock and a readjustment for me when, eight years later, my other son was diagnosed. I remember worrying about his teachers, so much so that I brought it up to the developmental behavioral pediatrician, who laughed at me.

She told me, "He's never going to know what it's like to be any other kid. He is who he is, and he's going to succeed and thrive because he doesn't know you expect him to be anybody else." This was eye-opening for me. It made me look back at my life and realize that all the ways I thought I was quirky, all the ways I thought I was just a kid, were actually neurodivergent traits that I've had my entire life. Being able to frame things this way, to say, "I don't know what it's like to be any other way," to see how my identity has been shaped by being neurodivergent, has been a real relief for me.

Emily: How do you think your shift in perspective has influenced how your son sees his own identity?

Amanda: Now, he's loud and proud. He's very self-aware. He knows he's autistic; he knows he has ADHD. He's able to say, "I'm having trouble concentrating because of my ADHD," or "I'm having trouble paying attention just because I'm not interested in what you're saying."

I think my shift in talking about his neurodivergence with him openly, in encouraging him to speak openly to his teachers about it, has been really important. It gives him agency over how he wants to talk about autism and ADHD, how he views them affecting him, and how they shape his identity.

Emily: A concern that people often have is that they're worried that if kids are given a diagnosis, they'll use it as an excuse. What are your thoughts on that?

Amanda: I think that's sometimes true, because kids are kids. You give any kid anything, and they can use it as an excuse. That doesn't have anything to do with neurodivergence. It's just how kids are. But we do need to teach students, as educators or as parents, to go beyond the excuse phase. They need to understand that their diagnosis is a reason a particular task is hard for them, but it's not an excuse to simply not do it.

Emily: One of the things that I often tell kids about self-advocacy is that they should approach it with a specific question and a possible solution. This moves it away from being an excuse and toward problem-solving.

Amanda: Yes, but only if the person on the receiving end of that advocacy understands the possibilities of what might work and how to respond positively to the advocacy. We so often tell kids to self-advocate without knowing whether the person they're talking to knows what to *do* when kids speak up. If a student says, "This is a problem, this is a challenge I'm having, I don't know what to do," the teacher should be able acknowledge how hard it may have been for the student to speak up for themselves, and perhaps even offer some solutions that have worked for others in the past. This is how you start empowering kids to say, "Those options sound fantastic. Let me try this one for three weeks and see what happens."

Emily: I think that, as parents, we often have many expectations, fears, and anxieties around whether our kids' teachers understand neurodivergence and understand our kids for exactly this reason.

Amanda: Oh, so many of my concerns for my son were about school. I was worried about what his schooling would look like. What if he couldn't figure out how to "do school"? What would it mean if he couldn't follow the routine or pay attention in the expected way?

My worries weren't about his life outside of school. It was mostly about what this diagnosis meant for his educational future and whether the teachers he'd have would have the skills to recognize the value of him being himself. I think that if teachers understand that my son doesn't know what it's like to be anybody but himself, and let him be himself, that understanding could alleviate some of my worries.

What to Remember

- Teachers can enhance students' social and emotional competency by fostering self-awareness, managing emotions, promoting understanding of others' perspectives, making responsible decisions, and nurturing strong relationships, all of which help students and educators alike navigate challenges and conflicts.
- Teachers can better support the development of students' emotional competence by working on and modeling their own efforts to build emotional competence.
- The Four Es Framework can be used by students and their families to accept and address limitations, with a particular emphasis on empowering students by engaging them in conversation about their needs and self-advocacy, rather than merely talking about them.

Chapter 8

Meeting Sensory Needs

 Points to Ponder

- What classroom-wide changes can you implement to reduce potential sensory overwhelm for all students?
- What are some signs of unmet sensory needs that you see in your students?
- How can you integrate fidgets and other sensory-soothing tools into your routine?

Understanding of how sensory needs impact neurodivergent individuals' self-regulation has grown significantly in recent years (Butera et al. 2020). Like other topics in this book, there's a lot of variance. While some individuals find that sensory input helps direct their focus and attention, others are frequently distracted by sensory stimuli. They are unable to tune out sensory input and struggle with regulating their focus and attention. Individuals who are hypersensitive to sensory input are stressed and overwhelmed when faced with sensory input that is too intense for them, and they may try to avoid certain spaces and situations. When educators recognize the unique range of sensory needs of their students, they can adapt classrooms and schools to provide environments and accommodations that allow students with sensory sensitivities to thrive. This chapter tells you how to do just that.

Building Awareness of Sensory Integration Differences

Think of a time when you were in a situation that was extremely uncomfortable—maybe you were in an environment that was really hot, with no reprieve from the sweaty sensation of still air. Or maybe the volume of the surrounding noise was overwhelming and there was no escape. How did you feel? What emotions did you experience? Did you feel helpless, anxious, or stressed?

For many neurodivergent individuals, environments that many others would consider "typical" or "normal" can be overwhelming. Getting through a day in a school building may require incredible stamina and camouflaging for students with sensory sensitivities. This often reduces the "window of tolerance" these students have for additional stressors, and it takes very little for the effort needed to maintain regulation to push beyond their ability to manage the sensory stimuli. Sensory integration differences have a direct impact on emotional regulation, communication, and executive functioning skills (Mallory and Keehn 2021). See figure 8.1 for some ways this might manifest in students.

Although most frequently associated with autism, sensory integration differences are not exclusive to it. Autism is, however, the only diagnosis that includes sensory differences as part of the diagnostic criteria. Criteria B for an autism diagnosis in the *DSM-5* relates to autistic individuals' preference for routines and repetition; one of these is listed as a "hyper- or hyporeactivity to sensory input or unusual interest in sensory aspects of the environment" (APA 2013).

Other types of neurodivergence can impact the ability to process sensory input as well. Although sensory integration differences are not included in the *DSM-5* related to ADHD diagnoses, many ADHDers experience heightened sensory-seeking behaviors and increased sensory sensitivity (Kamath et al. 2020). People with obsessive-compulsive thoughts (OCD) show a heightened awareness and response to sensory stimuli, and research also shows that individuals who are cognitively gifted can experience increased sensitivity to sensory input (Poletti et al. 2022; Rinn 2021). Of course, each person has a unique sensory integration profile. Educators' awareness of sensory needs can benefit all learners, not only those who are neurodivergent.

FIGURE 8.1 Impact of Unmet Sensory Integration Needs

Area of Impact	Possible Manifestations
Emotional Regulation	<ul><li>increased irritability</li><li>outbursts related to frustration/anger</li><li>attempts to escape/elope</li><li>increased need for stimming actions to help calm</li></ul>
Communication	<ul><li>situational mutism</li><li>decreased ability to negotiate/compromise</li><li>increased difficulty with perspective-taking</li></ul>
Executive Functioning	<ul><li>easily distracted; poor focus and concentration</li><li>reduced metacognition and cognitive flexibility skills</li><li>trouble with task initiation, persistence, and completion</li></ul>

Our Eight Sensory Systems

To be able to recognize and accommodate students' sensory needs, it's important to first understand the body's sensory systems. Most of us are familiar with the five sensory systems we learned about in elementary school: visual (sight), auditory (hearing), tactile (touch), olfactory (smell), and gustatory (taste). However, there are three

FIGURE 8.2 Sensory Systems and Examples of Processing Differences

Sensory System	Overresponsive/Hypersensitive Example
Visual	preference for environments with low lighting; overwhelmed by rooms with a lot of visual "noise" (such as décor or clutter)
Auditory	inability to tune out background noises; emotional dysregulation prompted by overwhelming auditory stimuli
Tactile	fearful or startle response to unexpected touches; discomfort due to certain types of clothing or fabrics
Olfactory	anxiety when familiar spaces or things smell "different" (such as they've recently been cleaned with scented cleaning products or when a new fabric softener is used)
Gustatory	strong aversion to certain tastes or textures; amplified perception of bitterness, spiciness, or sweetness
Proprioceptive	discomfort with certain types of touch or pressure; disorientation in crowded spaces
Vestibular	overreaction to movement, such as feeling nauseous or dizzy with slight shifts in position; discomfort with activities like swinging
Interoceptive	heightened awareness of psychosomatic symptoms of emotional dysregulation, such as stomachaches or headaches

Underresponsive/Hyposensitive Example	Discrimination Difficulty Example
appearing clumsy due to missing details in their scope of vision (like missing a step or curb)	difficulty identifying objects that are partly hidden, especially in a cluttered environment
lack of response to verbal cues or instructions; unbothered by disruptive noises such as loud music or sirens	difficulty differentiating between voices to determine a speaker; difficulty regulating volume of voice
high pain threshold or little to no response to pain; limited awareness of temperature changes	difficulty identifying or describing objects based only on touch
insensitivity to certain smells others may find offensive; preference for stronger scents to compensate for reduced olfactory sensitivity	difficulty identifying the source of odors or recognizing certain smells
reduced awareness of different tastes or textures of food	difficulty distinguishing taste or texture of foods
limited sensitivity to pressure or force; poor body awareness leading to frequent bumps or falls	difficulty writing without watching one's hand (impacts copying down information from a display onto paper, etc.)
insensitivity to motion; preference for movement experiences (such as being in an upside down or inverted position, or pacing while thinking)	difficulty perceiving distance or elevation
lack of awareness of internal body signals such as heart rate or breathing that are closely associated with emotional regulation	difficulty interpreting body signals such as needing to use the restroom or feeling hungry

additional sensory systems: vestibular (body movements), proprioceptive (body spatial awareness), and interoceptive (internal body signals). Each of these eight systems can be hyposensitive (underresponsive) or hypersensitive (overresponsive) to the sensory information it receives and interprets. Additionally, sensory integration differences can lead to discrimination difficulties—difficulty distinguishing between similar sensory inputs. The impact of sensory integration influences many other skills students need to be able to be successful in almost every setting (Mallory and Keehn 2021). Figure 8.2 shares examples of how someone might be hyper- and hyposensitive to each sense, as well as discrimination difficulties they might experience.

Understanding that students are responding to input from eight sensory systems instead of five helps put into context why students are hyposensitive or hypersensitive even in situations that you may think are "sensory safe." By accommodating sensory needs, you can better support students' ability to succeed in various settings and proactively address potential challenges in sensory discrimination that impact essential skills.

Types of Sensory Integration Differences

Sensory integration differences can affect any of a person's eight sensory systems. There are three categories that a sensory integration difference can fall into: sensory modulation, sensorimotor, and sensory discrimination (Ptak et al. 2022).

Sensory Modulation Differences

Sensory modulation differences involve difficulty regulating responses to certain stimuli.

- **Overresponsive (hypersensitive) sensory reaction:** When most people find a certain type of sensory experience manageable or tolerable, individuals with an overresponsive sensory reaction are likely to react to a short exposure to the stimuli, or they may require an extended period of time to regulate after the exposure. *Example: A student startles and becomes significantly emotionally dysregulated when a fire alarm goes off.*

- **Underresponsive (hyposensitive) sensory reaction:** Sensory experiences that typically cause a reaction or shift in focus are experienced differently by people who have underresponsive reactions to that type of stimuli. The experience may go unnoticed, it may take longer for the person to notice it, or the person may react with lower intensity than someone else. *Example: A student does not self-report an injury that needs care because they have an underresponsive reaction to some kinds of pain.*

- **Sensory craving:** Many people seek out sensory experiences (think riding roller coasters, doing high-intensity exercise, and eating spicy foods). The persistent need to experience or seek out intense or frequent sensory stimulation followed by emotional dysregulation after too much of the sensory-seeking is characteristic of sensory craving behavior. *Example: A student likes to spin in circles but has a difficult time stopping and is very silly, stressed, or overstimulated following the activity.*

Sensorimotor Differences

Sensorimotor differences influence balance and motor coordination.

- **Postural differences:** These are closely tied with general awareness of the body and are influenced by difficulty with body awareness and core muscle control. An individual who struggles with postural differences has a hard time stabilizing their body to match the demands of the movement they are trying to do. This can impact endurance and strength. *Example: A student struggles with balancing tasks in PE.*

- **Dyspraxia:** Individuals who struggle with thinking about, planning, and implementing certain motor movements may have dyspraxia. This can impact a wide range of daily living activities, from directional awareness to athletics to writing. *Example: A student requires a significant amount of time to complete motor tasks, like tying their shoes, even though they've known how to do so for years.*

Sensory Discrimination Differences

Sensory discrimination differences influence each of the eight sensory systems. They involve difficulty with interpreting subtle differences between sensory experiences. Difficulties discriminating between sounds through the auditory system or between information gathered through the visual system are called Auditory Processing Disorder or Visual Processing Disorder, respectively. Difficulties within the other sensory systems may manifest as trouble identifying or recognizing different sensory stimuli, like telling the difference between two smells (olfactory sense) or being able to describe a texture through touch only (tactile sense).

Intersecting Identities

Many neurodivergent individuals struggle with sensory needs related to the clothing they wear. Various types of fabric can influence someone with hypersensitivity to this type of stimuli. School uniforms—pants versus shorts versus dresses—come into play here too. Some religious traditions emphasize certain expectations for clothing, such as headwraps, scarves, or skirts and dresses for girls. Some of these expectations may alleviate sensory needs; for example, wearing dresses or skirts may be more comfortable for some neurodivergent girls, whereas boys may not have that opportunity. Gender roles from a student's culture may also affect reactions to clothing-based sensory needs. For example, a girl who is most comfortable wearing leggings (and refuses to wear other clothing) may not draw as much attention as a boy who only wants to wear shorts and refuses to wear pants.

Alexithymia

Alexithymia is a sensory integration difference related to difficulty with recognizing, identifying, and expressing one's emotions, and it is closely connected to hyposensitivity to the interoceptive sense (Jakobson and Rigby 2021). Alexithymia is not an official diagnosis; it's a way to describe a pattern of behavior. It is more prevalent in autistic individuals, though not exclusive to them. About 10 percent of people are affected by alexithymia to varying degrees (Goerlich 2018). It is frequently seen in individuals who tend to be hyposensitive to their internal body signals. Since they don't respond as strongly to somatic experiences, they may have a more difficult time using those experiences as a way to recognize or regulate their emotions.

The Toronto Alexithymia Scale (TAS-20) is a self-report questionnaire that is used to help identify characteristics of alexithymia. Although the TAS-20 was created for adults between the ages of twenty-one and sixty-four, it is still a useful tool to discuss to understand the factors that influence how alexithymia manifests. It delineates three areas where signs of alexithymia can be noticed: difficulty identifying feelings, difficulty describing feelings, and externally oriented thinking (Bagby, Parker, and Taylor 1994):

- **Difficulty identifying feelings:** This area describes how well an individual is able to identify and label their feelings. A high score on this scale indicates that the person may have trouble distinguishing between feelings such as anger or fear.
- **Difficulty describing feelings:** This area looks at how easily a person can articulate their emotions verbally. Students who struggle with describing their feelings may use vague terms like *good* and *bad* rather than more nuanced emotion language.
- **Externally oriented thinking:** This area examines a person's preference to focus on external events, facts, and objects instead of their own internal emotional experience. Individuals who lean toward externally oriented thinking tend to value facts and practical matters over the internal experience of emotions.

In addition to causing difficulty in identifying and expressing one's own emotions, alexithymia has some secondary impacts. One big one is that it can affect emotional regulation. Having a hard time identifying emotions can lead a student to be confused and struggle to manage their reactions when strong feelings arise. It can also influence their ability to problem-solve in certain situations. For example, think of the different strategies you would use in a social situation depending on whether you felt confused, excluded, or embarrassed. Alexithymia can lead to misunderstandings when a student is unable to easily articulate their emotions when communicating. This can make it difficult for the student to form strong bonds and relationships. Alexithymia can also make it harder for the student to identify emotions in others, which makes understanding others' perspectives a struggle, since an awareness of a wide range of emotions is required to predict how another person may react or feel. Students with alexithymia may need specific support and strategies to improve their self-insight. Additionally, traditional talk-based therapeutic techniques may not be as effective for individuals with alexithymia, since these most often focus on emotional awareness and expression.

Students who experience alexithymia are likely to be misunderstood by teachers and peers. Learning about alexithymia can help teachers understand why a student may react (or *not* react) in expected ways, which can then help them understand a student's reaction without assuming it is a sign of indifference. Although students may experience difficulties related to alexithymia, educators can work with them without pathologizing this sensory integration difference. They can know that there is nothing "wrong" with the person with alexithymia, while recognizing the barriers it causes and working to find strategies that will help students communicate their needs and wants without trying to change who they are.

A number of strategies are particularly helpful in supporting students with alexithymia, though these strategies can be used with all students:

- **Provide opportunities for students to learn about themselves.** Understanding oneself is foundational in being able to communicate and self-advocate. All students can learn about the range of emotions they experience on a day-to-day basis, and students who appear to have difficulty similar to alexithymia can be provided specific information about the characteristics of it.
- **Use tools and visual aids to help identify emotions.** For example, an online search for "wheel of emotions" yields quick-and-easy printable feelings word banks. An emotions wheel is often segmented into five or six sections, with basic emotions (like happy, sad, scared) closest to the center. As you move outward on the wheel, more nuanced emotions are introduced within each category.
- **Use strengths-based strategies to help students develop a connection between their experiences and emotions.**
  - For students who prefer to think and process verbally, shift the focus from their internal experiences of emotion to their internal dialogue. When students develop an awareness of their internal dialogue, it can help them tie those thoughts to their overall mood. If possible, help them build awareness of the body signals they are experiencing as they talk through their thoughts.
  - For students who tend to think in pictures or have stronger visual-spatial abilities, explore ways to express their feelings in images. For example, perhaps a student struggles with describing the feelings in their body, but they can easily demonstrate a feeling with an image (like a scribble for feeling angry or a spiral for feeling worried).
  - Some students may connect emotionally with music. Finding or composing a song to associate with their emotions may provide them an opportunity to connect with and express their feelings.

Alexithymia

The situation: In a classroom discussion about a sensitive topic, students are asked to share their feelings and personal viewpoints. A neurodivergent student with alexithymia participates, but they struggle to express their emotions. Instead, they stick to factual, blunt statements that lack an emotional component. At one point, when pressed to elaborate on how they feel, they respond with "I don't know."

Perspective of others: The neurodivergent student's classmates and teacher misinterpret the student's behavior and responses. They perceive the blunt, emotionless statements and the "I don't know" response as signs of disrespect or defiance, especially in the context of a sensitive topic. They might think the student is deliberately being uncooperative or dismissive of the importance of the discussion. This misunderstanding leads to frustration among peers and possibly to reprimands from the teacher, who believes the student is showing disdain and disrespect for the topic by intentionally disengaging.

Perspective of the neurodivergent student: The student with alexithymia genuinely struggles to identify and articulate their emotions, finding it hard to express feelings in a way that others expect or understand. When asked about their feelings, their response of "I don't know" is a truthful expression of their internal state, not a sign of disrespect or defiance. They feel pressured and misunderstood, and this pressure only exacerbates their difficulty identifying and communicating emotions. The student may also feel unfairly judged and isolated because of their inability to express emotions in a conventional manner, leading to a sense of alienation in what they perceive to be a hostile or unaccepting environment.

Possible follow-up: The teacher finds an opportunity to talk individually with the student to explore what the student's experience during the class discussion was like. Starting from a neutral place of curiosity, the teacher learns that the student's matter-of-fact statements and reduced affect are not related to a lack of care about the topic but reflect a difference in processing information and emotions. The student and teacher develop tools to help the student self-advocate in the future to avoid misunderstandings.

Emotional Regulation and Somatic Awareness

The field of psychotherapy is witnessing a notable shift in its approach to emotional regulation and therapeutic interventions (Palmieri et al. 2022). Traditionally, cognitive-behavioral therapy (CBT) has been widely practiced. This "top-down" method focuses primarily on addressing cognition and thought processes as a way to regulate emotions. From this CBT foundation, counselors and educators have focused on recognizing and reframing one's thoughts about a situation to build emotional regulation skills. Recently, recognition of the significance of somatic awareness and "bottom-up" methods of emotional regulation has grown, emphasizing the role of the body and sensory processing in understanding and regulating emotions.

Somatic awareness is sometimes referred to as body awareness. It's about being able to notice and name what your body is feeling physically and connect this with your emotions. "Bottom-up" methods of emotional regulation focus on regulating somatic experiences to influence emotions and thoughts. Breathing, grounding, and other exercises that aim to calm the fight/flight/freeze/fawn response first are examples of bottom-up approaches, as are the strategies for creating sensory-friendly classrooms on page 203. This shift from "top-down" to "bottom-up" methods of emotional regulation has far-reaching implications, particularly for how educators and counselors support neurodivergent students. Understanding and incorporating somatic approaches can provide effective strategies for supporting these students in their educational and personal journeys.

Guiding students in growing somatic awareness is key to helping them develop a deeper understanding of the bodily sensations associated with their emotional states. You can support students in becoming mindful of how their bodies feel in different situations, which can be important for managing stress and emotions, and for overall well-being. In addition to helping students become aware of this connection, offer accommodations to help them regulate both their bodies and feelings. Using the somatic experience as an entry point to emotional regulation allows you the opportunity to provide tools and accommodations for sensory needs (see figure 8.3). Most of these tools and accommodations are much more concrete than the typical CBT focus on recognizing and shifting thoughts.

There are some additional benefits to implementing somatic approaches to supporting students. Somatic approaches to emotional regulation are closely aligned with the trauma-informed practices already in place in many schools. Additionally, by helping neurodivergent students develop somatic awareness, educators and counselors can support these students' abilities to identify and communicate their emotional needs effectively. This fosters a sense of agency in neurodivergent students, promoting their self-advocacy in educational settings and beyond.

Supporting Sensory Needs in Schools

The ways a student reacts to sensory integration challenges aren't always easy to see from the outside, or at least the outward-facing signs and behavior may not be what you expect to see when a student is over- or underreacting to sensory information. You may not hear the buzzing of the fluorescent lights that is causing your student to put their hands over their ears and may instead wonder why the student is trying to block you out. You may not know that a student won't pick up the book you gave them because the texture of the cover is truly unbearable to them. All you can see is the reaction, not that their nervous system is sensitive to and perhaps misinterpreting information from the eight senses.

If you would like to complete an audit of your classroom to identify potential sensory triggers for your students, use this QR code to download a PDF of our Neurodiversity Audit of Classroom Environment Checklist.

Creating sensory-friendly classrooms is essential for accommodating diverse sensory and learning needs, and accommodations are frequently easy to implement. Noise-muffling headphones to help reduce the impact of external stimuli are easily available at minimal cost. Providing space for a student to pace in the back of the classroom and ensuring the room is clear of clutter and visual distraction are free.

Additionally, integrating "bottom-up" methods of emotional regulation, such as mindfulness and relaxation techniques, into the daily routine can greatly benefit students with sensory needs. Teaching them about the connection between their minds and bodies helps them identify and manage their feelings. It's important to be adaptable with these strategies; for example, allow students who are uncomfortable closing their eyes during mindfulness exercises to keep their eyes open and focused on a point on the wall or floor.

Developing a shared language around emotional regulation and sensory experiences is also beneficial. Using a scale from 1 to 10 for students to rate their emotional and physical comfort can help you identify students' sensory needs and their causes. Providing movement breaks and fidgets supports students in managing restlessness or a need for movement. This approach recognizes the importance of being aware of the body's signals and responding appropriately.

Finally, offering sensory tools and accommodations can assist with sensory regulation. You might create and stock a calming corner with flexible seating options, a weighted blanket, noise-muffling headphones, soft items, snacks or gum (if permissible), or an unheated lava lamp. Figure 8.3 shares some more accommodations and tools for supporting sensory needs.

FIGURE 8.3 Accommodations and Tools for Sensory Needs

Sensory Need	Suggestions	
Visual	<ul><li>sunglasses</li><li>section of the room with dim lights</li><li>section of the room with bright lights</li></ul>	<ul><li>fairy light jars</li><li>hats with brims or visors</li><li>colored overlays for reading</li><li>highlighted or bold-lined paper</li></ul>
Auditory	<ul><li>noise-muffling headphones or earplugs</li><li>music (using headphones or ear buds)</li></ul>	<ul><li>white noise machine or app</li><li>sound balls (like tickit® Sensory Reflective Sound Balls)</li><li>fidget cubes with sound elements</li></ul>
Tactile	<ul><li>play dough</li><li>silly putty</li><li>bendable colored wax sticks (like Wikki Stix®)</li><li>pipe cleaners</li><li>coiled keychains or tangle toys</li><li>squishy stress balls</li></ul>	<ul><li>Velcro strips (attached to an index card for portability)</li><li>fidget cubes</li><li>unscented lotion to rub on hands or arms</li><li>pop cubes</li><li>pencil grips</li></ul>
Olfactory	*Make sure to consider students' allergies or sensitivities first:*<ul><li>scented lip balms (also known as "smellies" by some teachers)</li><li>essential oil rollers</li></ul>	<ul><li>scented hand sanitizer</li><li>scratch-and-sniff stickers</li><li>scented markers or pencils</li><li>pocket-sized potpourri sachets</li><li>herbal tea bags</li></ul>

FIGURE 8.3 Accommodations and Tools for Sensory Needs

Sensory Need	Suggestions	
Gustatory	• chewelry • chewable pencil toppers • gum	• crunchy snacks • sour, mint, or spicy hard candies • flavored water
Proprioceptive	• pencil grips • slant boards • raised-line paper • sensory bottles • water bottles with built-in straws	*Consult with an occupational therapist to find the correct:* • Therabands to attach to chair or desk legs • weighted lap pads • weighted vests • wiggle cushions
Vestibular	• balance boards • fidget cubes with switches, gears, or rolling balls • beanbag chairs	• therapy balls (instead of desk chairs) • wiggle chairs or wiggle cushions • swivel chairs • standing desks
Interoceptive	• scheduled breaks for the restroom • alarms/reminders to drink water/eat snacks	• visual or auditory cues to check in with the body

Fidgets as Tools, Not Toys

Fidgets are another tool that can help you support students' sensory needs. It's key to think of fidgets as tools and to communicate that to your students. Many items that can be used as fidgets to support sensory regulation are also common toys, like play dough and Koosh balls. In fact, fidget spinners, initially designed to help with focus, became so popular as toys that they have been banned in many schools, unfortunately for the students who truly benefited from them (Taylor 2017).

The fact that fidget spinners proved to be both overstimulating and a distraction for so many students demonstrates not only that educators need to set the ground rules for fidgets from the beginning but also that the type of fidget really does matter. The problem is that teachers often have go-to fidgets that they hand to students without providing any context or directions, and then they get upset when students use them as toys instead of the tools teachers want them to be.

A true neurodiversity-affirming classroom provides every student with the opportunity to use a fidget when they need one, but that means making sure every student knows that a fidget is a tool to help them thrive. So have clear expectations about how to use fidgets in your classroom and take the time to talk over the rules with your students.

Not sure what those rules should be? Here are some to start with:

- **Make meaningful decisions.** Before using a fidget, think about whether you need it to support you or want it because it looks fun.
- **Fidgets are for focus.** You can use a fidget to focus your mind or your body. A fidget that is being used for fun will be taken away.
- **Fidgets can't get in the way of other people's work.** If the use of the fidget detracts from other students' ability to focus or work, you can first move to a different work area. If it continues to distract other people, choose a different fidget or talk to the teacher about what other strategies are available to help you self-regulate.
- **Fidgets go back in the toolbox when you're done.** Just like any other tool, fidgets should be put back where they belong. If you don't put it back where it goes, the tool will be missing when someone else needs to use it. (This rule also helps reinforce the "tools, not toys" concept.)

There's no "one-fidget-fits all" solution for students. When you have students making decorations on their desks with Wikki Stix or playing catch with a squeezy ball, it's time to reevaluate what else will meet those students' regulatory needs. Matching the type of fidget to the type of sensory need makes it easier to establish a culture in which fidgets are tools all students can use when they need them. Here are some basic things to explain:

- **When used correctly, fidgets can help students feel ready to learn.** They can improve focus, sustain attention, and calm the brain and body.
- **When used incorrectly, fidgets can make it harder for students to learn.** They can make it harder to focus, difficult to sustain attention, and even increase body movements in unproductive ways.
- **It's important to pay attention to when a fidget is needed or helpful.** Some students may need to fidget during quiet work time but find that a fidget makes it harder to learn during group work.

Seeing Stimming as Purposeful

It's almost impossible to talk about sensory needs in school without also talking about self-stimulatory behavior, or stimming as it is more commonly known. Stimming is when a person engages in repetitive movements, sounds, or behaviors. Many neurodivergent students, especially ADHDers and autistic students, stim to communicate or self-regulate.

It's not unusual for schools to include goals around reducing stimming in learning plans for students. This is often phrased in terms of "eliminating" or "extinguishing" stimming behavior or finding "more appropriate" or "less visible" replacement behavior. The phrase "quiet hands," a way of reminding students to suppress their need to flap their hands, clap, tap, or use other nonverbal stimming gestures, is an example of trying to eliminate stimming.

Autistic advocates criticize practices such as "quiet hands," making it clear that "loud hands" serve meaningful communication needs (Bascom 2012). In fact, one survey of nearly 350 autistic adults' experiences of being asked to suppress stimming throughout their lifetimes and in school is poignantly titled, "It feels like holding back something you need to say" (Charlton et al. 2021). We've all had the experience of having to hold back or wait to express ourselves, and it can be uncomfortable. So we ask you to consider the question, *Why are educators trying to eliminate or replace a student's stims?*

Clearly, when stimming is self-injurious, it's important to help a student find a replacement behavior so that they don't hurt themself, but many stims don't involve self-harm. Some teachers will say stims need to be extinguished because they don't want students to feel embarrassed or out of place when their stimming is noticeable. Or they may say it's because the stims are distracting to the rest of the class. If we're bravely truthful, though, one of the biggest reasons we seek to stop stimming is because it makes us—the adults in the room—uncomfortable.

Here are six stimming behaviors you might see in your classroom:

1. **Hand flapping:** A student repeatedly opens and closes their hands or pats the air.
2. **Rocking or swaying**: A student moves forward and backward or side to side while sitting or standing. (You might see a student rock only their torso or twist at the waist—it's not always the whole body.)
3. **Spinning:** A student rotates or twirls their body or an item.
4. **Finger flicking/wiggling:** A student rapidly flicks or wiggles their fingers at their sides, in front of their eyes, or in other ways that don't involve the rest of the body.
5. **Tapping:** A students repeatedly taps their feet, fingers, hands, or items, sometimes on a surface, but also on another part of the body, like the thighs or head.
6. **Vocal stimming:** A student makes repetitive sounds or vocalizations such as throat-clearing, sniffing, whistling, huffing breaths, humming, or repeating words or phrases.

Why do students stim? Most people who stim do it to self-regulate in certain situations. Do you shuffle from foot to foot when you're waiting in line somewhere? Or tap your fingers on a table when you're thinking? Maybe you inhale and exhale to calm yourself when you're anxious or to communicate frustration when someone is annoying you.

All these repetitive behaviors serve a purpose when you engage in them. They're just more socially acceptable than some of the stims you might see from neurodivergent students. Here are some of the reasons your students might stim:

- **To provide a sense of comfort and self-soothing.** The repetitive nature of stimming behaviors can provide comfort and predictability, which can help ease anxiety, stress, or nervousness.
- **To help regulate sensory input.** Repetitive movements or actions can provide proprioceptive and vestibular input that helps students feel more grounded, regulate sensory arousal levels, and reduce or prevent sensory overload.
- **To communicate.** Some stimming serves as a way of conveying emotions, needs, or preferences.

Neurodiversity-affirming environments see stimming as purposeful and seek to understand the purpose of the behavior. Creating an environment in which stimming is considered healthy and useful shows you respect and understand the needs behind the behavior. It doesn't matter if it makes you uncomfortable. What matters is whether it's making students *more* comfortable.

"Whole Body Listening" Is Not Neurodiversity-Affirming

Perhaps you have seen the traditional posters showing a diagram of a student who is using "whole body listening." A lot of teachers probably have one hanging in their classroom right now (or did at one time). The image shows a happy student sitting, facing forward, hands folded on their (clean) desk, their feet flat on the ground, eyes staring directly outward from the poster (supposedly making eye contact with the speaker).

This idea and image are well-intentioned; the goal of the poster is to help students be aware of what focused listening looks like. However, the image undermines a neurodiversity-affirming environment because it only focuses on one thing: what the student looks like to others observing them.

When neurodivergent students mask their sensory needs, they may *look* like the child in that poster. However, the appearance of making eye contact, refraining from fidgeting, and sitting completely still in their chair in no way guarantees that a student is focused on what is occurring in the lesson. Their mind might be completely focused on maintaining that posture, working to manage the anxiety associated with getting in trouble for not listening, or thinking about the *Titanic*, their favorite animal, or the math test next hour.

It is important that students know what actually works to help them focus. Does having a fidget fulfill a need for movement? Does drawing help them stay focused on what is being said? Does pacing in the back of the classroom help them regulate their emotions, or does rocking help them process the information being shared? Asking all students to look like the child in the "whole body listening" poster is ableist and denies the sensory needs many neurodivergent students require to effectively learn. Using disciplinary or behavioral techniques to force compliance with what others expect from your students may accomplish the goal of getting students to look like the child in the poster, but they undermine your goal of helping children learn.

It is a mind shift for many educators to move away from the common expected behaviors most of us grew up with when we were in school, and it is a fair critique to note that the sensory needs of some may be in opposition to the sensory needs of others. Flexibility and creative problem-solving can help you create an environment that is supportive of all learners.

What to Remember

- Sensory integration differences aren't solely seen in autism; they're common in other neurodivergent conditions as well, and they can also impact students who aren't neurodivergent. Accommodating sensory needs creates an environment in which all students have better regulation skills.
- There are eight sensory systems through which humans take in information. Three are nonapparent: vestibular (body movements), proprioceptive (body spatial awareness), and interoceptive (internal body signals). When students are experiencing difficulty processing information in those senses, you may see reactions that seem disproportionate to the situation.
- Accommodations and tools like fidgets can be effective in supporting sensory regulation. Teaching students to use and recognize them as tools instead of toys can provide neurodivergent students with new ways to self-regulate and self-soothe.

Chapter 9

Neurodiversity-Affirming Communication

Points to Ponder

- What is the value of recognizing and supporting neurodivergent communication styles in your classroom?
- How can you rethink communication to meaningfully engage with the nonspeaking students in your classroom?
- Do you currently focus on teaching social skills or social acuity to neurodivergent students?

The variety of student minds, experiences, and cognitive processes in our schools makes a compelling case for the adoption of more inclusive and compassionate communication frameworks. Traditional methods of communication, built on a narrow understanding of what is considered neuro-normative, can inadvertently stigmatize and alienate neurodivergent students. By working to build neurodiversity-affirming communication, you can foster a more inclusive environment where every student feels valued and understood, regardless of their neurological wiring.

Adopting neurodiversity-affirming communication is also a strong step toward creating empathetic citizens. When students learn the importance of adjusting their communication to ensure mutual understanding and respect, they carry these lessons into adulthood. The ripple effects of such a shift can be profound, perhaps even leading to communities and societies that prioritize understanding, acceptance, and shared growth over divisive assumptions and misunderstandings.

In this chapter, we'll explore the nuances of neurodiversity-affirming communication and its transformative potential for education, setting the stage for a more inclusive future.

What Is Neurodiversity-Affirming Communication?

At its core, neurodiversity-affirming communication is an approach that respects, acknowledges, and values the diverse ways human brains function. Imagine if educators tried to teach every student using a single, rigid method. Not only would it be impractical, but they'd also miss out on the wide range of perspectives that students bring to the classroom. The same holds true for communication. Neurodiversity-affirming communication is built on a foundation of flexibility and adaptability, understanding that each student processes information, expresses themself, shows what they know, and perceives the world in a way that's unique to their neurological makeup.

Because communication is the connection and exchange of information between people, we must consider all the stakeholders who are communicating and the influence of each group in promoting neurodiversity-affirming communication in our schools and classrooms.

- **Educators and school staff:** Teachers and other adults in the school are the foundation for modeling neurodiversity-affirming communication. In addition to supporting the regulation, communication, and social needs of neurodivergent students, they model this type of communication to the other students in the school.

- **Neurodivergent students:** With communication styles and needs that differ from what educators may expect, a both/and approach to supporting communication is appropriate. In addition to accepting their authentic communication preferences, educators can work with neurodivergent students to help them learn to interpret communication that isn't automatic for them and communicate in ways that get their wants and needs met.

- **Neuro-normative students:** Peer support plays a pivotal role in neurodivergent learners feeling and being accepted and understood at school. Helping all students understand and value the diverse ways people communicate provides a strong foundation for an inclusive learning environment. It's important for students not only to respect and empathize with their neurodivergent peers but also to engage in and adapt to diverse communication styles. This fosters understanding and acceptance and equips neuro-normative students with versatile communication tools and skills that will benefit them beyond the classroom.

Intersecting Identities

The diversity of languages and cultures in our world means people have unique styles of communication based in their home language and cultures. Some cultures, for example, use communication that requires "high context," meaning they rely more heavily on understanding hidden social rules, underlying meaning and tone, and nonverbal communication to interpret what is said and what is meant (Hall 1959, 1976). This can be a barrier for neurodivergent people who don't understand or easily pick up on those aspects of communication. France, China, and Japan are examples of countries that have high-context cultures. Other cultures require "lower context." Some examples include the United States and Germany. These cultures use communication that tends to be more direct with wording and intent, although there is still plenty of room for confusion (Hall 1959, 1976). Students who are neurodivergent and whose primary culture or language at home differs from that of the majority population and educators in your school may find adapting to academic language and communication expectations at school difficult.

Setting the Stage for Neurodiversity-Affirming Communication

Effective communication, at its core, is a two-way street, demanding patience, flexibility, and a sincere intention to understand and connect. By employing the following strategies, you can enhance the way you engage with neurodivergent students, ensuring every interaction is rooted in respect, empathy, and a deep appreciation for the richness that neurodiversity adds to our interactions and collective experiences.

Assume Positive Intent

At times, neurodivergent students may say or do things that come off as abrupt, rude, or out of context. However, more often than not, this isn't a manifestation of ill intent. Rather, it's rooted in a difference in communication or processing style. Assuming positive intent can help you reframe these moments. Instead of viewing them as cause for discipline, you can pause and seek clarification. If a student impulsively calls out in class while you're speaking, assume this interruption is because the student is engaged and interested in the topic. Rather than disciplining the behavior, engage with the student and continue to work with them on methods of communicating that don't disrupt the class and don't damage your rapport.

When neurodivergent students feel their teachers are approaching their words and actions with an intent to understand rather than judge, they're more likely to engage and contribute in class (Grolnick 2018). Recognizing instances when a student might simply be eager to participate but struggles with timing or phrasing can help educators develop strategies to foster clearer communication. This proactive approach not only mitigates potential disruptions but also emphasizes the student's value in the learning process and community.

Establishing a classroom culture that consistently assumes positive intent breeds understanding and acceptance. It emboldens students to take risks, share openly, and collaborate, because they know they're in a space where their experiences, ideas, and ways of being are valued. This sentiment, when genuinely nurtured, sets a precedent for all students to approach their peers with empathy and a desire to understand.

> **Isaiah**
>
> Isaiah often corrects his classmates and teacher during lessons. His behavior, stemming from his detail-oriented nature and literal interpretation of information, could be misinterpreted as challenging authority or rudeness. However, Ms. Garcia recognizes that Isaiah's behavior is a reflection of his strength in noticing and remembering specific details. She assigns him the role of fact-checker for class activities, allowing him to contribute positively and feel appreciated. This also helps Isaiah's peers understand and value his unique perspective and skills, fostering a more inclusive and respectful classroom environment.

Ask for Clarification and Elaboration

One component of assuming positive intent is asking for clarification and elaboration when there's a misunderstanding. This practice champions the idea of listening to understand rather than to respond. When educators make a genuine effort to understand their students' perspectives, they foster trust. Students feel that their viewpoints are valid and worth exploring. This leads them to feel more secure in sharing their thoughts because they don't fear immediate rejection or ridicule.

Listening to understand requires encouraging students to elaborate on their perspectives. This not only promotes critical thinking but also asks them to reflect more deeply on their responses. This reflection also helps students solidify their understanding of the topic at hand. Over time, these insights can guide your teaching strategies, ensuring you deliver content in ways that resonate with each learner.

Lastly, by actively seeking to understand and asking genuine questions, teachers model a behavior of respect and curiosity. This approach, when consistent and sincere, fosters a classroom culture where respect becomes the norm. Students begin to emulate this behavior, leading to a more collaborative and understanding community of learners.

Offer Multiple Communication Modes

Another strategy to promote inclusive communication is to recognize and incorporate multiple modes of communicating. The underlying philosophy of this is rooted in the understanding that neurodivergent students might not always communicate best through traditional verbal means. In some cases, they may find nonverbal methods more effective and expressive.

Educators can offer flexibility and variety in accepted communication methods. When a student is feeling overwhelmed by emotion, verbal communication might be particularly difficult. Offering the opportunity to write their thoughts or draw on a dry-erase board can help them effectively communicate. In addition to changing the ways they receive communication from neurodivergent students, educators can modify how they express their thoughts too. Matching the communication style of a student is one way to meet them where they are in the current moment, which aligns with co-regulation strategies (see chapter 6).

Additionally, the digital age has equipped us with a plethora of tech tools that can bridge communication gaps. Apps and software that convert speech to text, digital art platforms, and even simple presentation tools can be invaluable for neurodivergent kids.

Sol

Sol, a student in Mr. Ortiz's social studies class, experiences anxiety and emotional dysregulation due to heightened sensitivities to environmental stimuli or social interactions. Feeling overwhelmed during discussions, Sol often shuts down, unable to express themself verbally. Rather than pushing Sol to communicate or "use their words" when dysregulated, Mr. Ortiz offers alternative communication methods, recognizing that traditional verbal communication can be challenging for Sol. By allowing Sol to express themself through hand signals and writing notes on a dry erase board, Mr. Ortiz validates Sol's feelings and provides a comfortable medium for communication. This not only supports Sol's emotional regulation but also builds a trusting relationship—so Sol is able to calm from emotional dysregulation more quickly.

Encourage Self-Advocacy

We believe that one of the most impactful techniques educators can adopt is to encourage students' self-advocacy. This is about more than teaching students to speak up; it's about empowering them to articulate their needs, preferences, and boundaries.

You can actively teach students how to self-advocate, offering specific procedures and techniques. This way you aren't just passively waiting for students to come forward. You might set aside time during the day for check-ins or feedback sessions or create communication boxes where students can drop written notes about their learning experiences. Scripts can also be a useful tool for helping students plan what they'd like to say when they self-advocate and can reduce the anxiety around unstructured conversations. Email or chat apps can be additional pathways for students to share their needs and preferences. Neurodivergent students will benefit from learning self-advocacy skills, whatever their age, and feel empowered when their needs are met.

Integrate Declarative Language

Declarative language is another useful tool to support neurodiversity-affirming communication. As you learned in chapter 6, declarative language involves sharing observations or information without giving a direct command or asking a direct question. This shift, subtle as it may seem, can have profound effects.

One of the reasons this approach is so effective with neurodivergent students is because it promotes a sense of autonomy and allows them to make decisions (Jang, Reeve, and Deci 2010). When students hear a statement about the world around them, they're given the chance to assess and decide how they want to respond. They aren't just following orders; they're processing information, making judgments, and taking action—they are empowered. Using declarative language also reduces pressure for students who feel on edge with direct commands. For more information on how to use declarative language in your classroom, see page 152.

Recognize Unconventional Reactions to Hierarchies

Neurodiversity-affirming communication requires you to have an understanding of how neurodivergent learners might perceive and react to power hierarchies—as this can be perceived as particularly challenging by many educators. Traditional classroom and social structures can create a perception of authority that is intimidating to or misunderstood by neurodivergent students. For instance, an autistic student might not immediately grasp social hierarchies, leading them to interact with teachers and peers in a way that seems uninhibited by traditional norms. Or an ADHDer might impulsively challenge illogical or inconsistent classroom rules without intending to disrespect or undermine their teacher's authority.

Schools operate based on layers of power hierarchies, stretching from the top tiers of administration down to students. For many neurodivergent learners, especially autistic or ADHD students, navigating this intricate web can be perplexing due to its often unspoken, inconsistent, and illogical nature. One major stumbling block is the unspoken rules and norms of a school—the hidden curriculum (see chapter 7). While many students might intuitively grasp these expectations, neurodivergent students might find their nuances arbitrary and baffling. Adding to the complexity of these power dynamics is the fact that they can also be riddled with inconsistencies, such as a behavior that's overlooked in one setting but reprimanded in another. For learners who flourish with clarity and consistency, these variances can seem like a maze of contradictions.

It is also worth noting that many neurodivergent individuals lean toward a more literal interpretation of information (Kalandadze et al. 2018). A statement meant to encourage inclusivity, like *This is your classroom as much as mine*, may be taken at face value, leading to potential misunderstandings. Additionally, some neurodivergent learners, especially ADHDers, have a heightened radar for injustice. When they sense that power hierarchies are being wielded unfairly, they may not stay silent. This is driven by a genuine inability to reconcile what they perceive to be illogical actions, not mere defiance.

So rather than perceiving behaviors that challenge or ignore power hierarchies as intentional disruptions or defiance, educators should consider that neurodivergent students may simply understand or respond to power hierarchies differently than neuro-normative students do. One approach that can help is to explicitly clarify the rationale behind classroom rules or structures, ensuring that students understand their purpose. Reframing authority in terms of mentorship and guidance, rather than dominance, can be particularly helpful. When students view their educators as allies and guides, they are more likely to form cooperative relationships, fostering a more harmonious classroom atmosphere (Plantin Ewe 2019; Rucinski, Downer, and Brown 2017). The following vignette and Double Empathy Problem feature share how a neurodivergent individual's unconventional reactions to hierarchies can impact communication with teachers and peers.

Alyssa

Alyssa, in Mrs. Harris's class, is autistic. Alyssa's logical understanding of relationships means that she doesn't abide by the hidden rules associated with social hierarchies and positions of power, sometimes leading to what appears to be confrontational behavior. Alyssa's direct questioning of classroom rules and instructions is her way of seeking clarity. Mrs. Harris understands this and responds by explaining the logic behind the classroom structure, turning potential conflicts into educational dialogues. This approach not only helps Alyssa understand and adapt to the classroom environment but also teaches the rest of the class about the value of clear, logical explanations and the importance of considering diverse perspectives and communication styles.

Double Empathy Problem

Social Standing Among Peers

The situation: In a high school setting, there are unspoken social hierarchies among students, with certain groups considered more popular or influential than others. A neurodivergent student interacts with individuals from various groups without regard to these social standings, treating everyone equally regardless of their perceived status within the school's social hierarchy.

Perspective of others: Classmates might find the neurodivergent student's behavior unusual or confusing. They may perceive the student's disregard for the social hierarchy as either a bold statement or a lack of social awareness. Some students might see this as a refreshing approach, while others could interpret it as a challenge to the established social order. The neurodivergent student's actions might be seen as either admirable or naïve, depending on each peer's view of the social dynamics at play. It could potentially lead to the neurodivergent student being bullied by those who feel threatened by their approach.

Perspective of the neurodivergent student: The neurodivergent student does not place much significance on arbitrary social hierarchies. They may not fully recognize or understand these unspoken social rules, or they might simply not value them. To them, interacting with all peers equally seems logical and fair. They approach social interactions based on personal interest, shared activities, or genuine connection, rather than social standing. This leads them to treat everyone with the same level of respect and consideration, which might be at odds with the typical social dynamics of their environment. The neurodivergent student may be unaware of the impact of their actions on these social structures, or they might be aware but unconcerned about conforming to the arbitrary norms.

Possible follow-up: Depending on how the neurodivergent student is received and the impact on the student, the follow-up for this situation may vary. Education for the neuro-normative students about accepting differences and creating a welcoming environment for all students can help them accept this student, as can schoolwide bullying prevention practices and policies. The neurodivergent student can be supported by having a teacher-mentor who helps interpret any unexpected reactions from other students.

Neurodivergent Communication Styles

Neurodiversity-affirming communication requires recognizing that there isn't a singular correct way for people to express themselves. For educators, this goes beyond adapting your teaching methods—it's about creating a classroom environment where a wide range of communication styles are understood and valued.

Neurodivergent individuals' methods of communication might differ from what you are accustomed to. When you grasp these diverse communication styles, you are better equipped to foster a learning environment that caters to each student's unique strengths and needs. The following sections describe some common neurodivergent communication methods.

Info-Dumping

Some students communicate via sharing vast amounts of information on a specific topic, sometimes without pause or awareness of their listeners' engagement. This behavior is known as info-dumping.

Common among many neurodivergent individuals, especially those on the autism spectrum, info-dumping isn't merely over-talking without purpose. It represents a person's passionate engagement with a subject or a genuine desire to communicate interests and knowledge. They might share in-depth details about a topic because it's an area of expertise or fascination for them, and they believe it's equally as intriguing to you.

Info-dumping isn't exclusive to neurodivergent individuals; it's something many people do at one time or another, especially when they're engrossed in a topic they're passionate about. Have you ever had a friend, for example, who couldn't stop talking about a new movie, a hobby, or a recent vacation? That's a form of info-dumping. It's a way of connecting, of sharing something that excites us or resonates with our experiences. We all have moments when we're so engrossed in something that we want the whole world to know about it. When a student is in the midst of an info-dump, they are often at their most passionate and engaged. In this way, an info-dump offers a unique opportunity to enter the student's world and see things from their perspective.

During info-dumps, many of the typical social language "challenges" students might face are lessened. Their speech may flow more fluently, their vocabulary can be impressively expansive, and their eye contact might differ from usual, all because they're delving into a topic that excites and captivates them. By tuning in and participating in their enthusiasm, you can leverage info-dumping as a tool for relationship-building, paving the way for more productive and harmonious interactions in the classroom.

Autistic Students' Engagement and Communication

The differences in engagement and communication between an autistic student's areas of special interest and topics outside of those areas can be stark. This disparity isn't due to a lack of ability, but rather the intrinsic nature of how their attention and interests are wired.

One common misconception is that the social language differences exhibited by many autistic individuals stem from an inherent deficiency in understanding or producing language. In reality, much of the difficulty arises from the misalignment between their personal interests and the topics of general social discourse (Murray 2018; Schaeffer et al. 2023). When engaging in topics they're passionate about, perhaps through an info-dump, autistic people frequently illuminate their unique linguistic strengths and expertise. This engagement contrasts with broader social communication contexts, where their approach might diverge from the norm. This is not due to a lack of understanding, but rather is a reflection of their distinct neurodivergent perspective on interpersonal interactions. When the conversation shifts to areas outside their immediate interests, their engagement wanes, leading to what may seem like disinterest or difficulty in communication. Recognizing and respecting this aspect of their neurodivergence can lead to more effective teaching strategies and improved interpersonal interactions.

Echolalia

Some students frequently repeat sounds, words, or phrases—a communication method known as echolalia. Common among many autistic individuals, echolalia isn't mimicking without purpose. In fact, it often serves several important roles (Davis 2017). For some students, echoing words can be a way to communicate; they might use a remembered phrase to convey a thought or feeling because it's the best tool they have at that moment. Think of it as a student using a learned formula: it's a starting point. Many autistic kids use echolalia as a bridge in their language journey, progressing from this echoed speech to more unique and spontaneous language over time.

Echolalia isn't exclusive to autistic individuals, though; it's a behavior observed in many neuro-normative people as well. When children are first learning to talk, they often parrot back what's said to them. This is a fundamental part of language acquisition. As children grow into adulthood, they continue echoing phrases or idioms in everyday conversations, especially ones that are catchy or hold cultural significance. This continues throughout a person's lifetime. How many times have you repeated a line from a popular movie or a catchy jingle from a commercial almost unconsciously? Echolalia is a communal way of connecting or sharing an inside joke. Additionally, in stressful or unexpected situations, even adults might repeat a question or statement they've just heard, using that moment of repetition to process and react.

The classroom can be an overwhelming place. So, sometimes echolalia can act like a comfort blanket for a student. Repeating familiar sounds or phrases might help the student manage anxiety or navigate the sensory overload that the bustling classroom brings. Some students echo words as a way of processing information—a little like when you ask someone to repeat something because you didn't catch it the first time. Some students use echoing as an attempt to connect with peers. Even if this is not in the "typical" way you'd expect, they're trying to participate and reach out. Other students might find the act of repeating words or sounds pleasurable, like how some people hum or tap when they're deep in thought, or use repeated phrases to express emotions, like quoting a line from a movie that perfectly captures how you're feeling. It's an innovative way to communicate when words don't come easily.

It may feel unfamiliar to respond to echolalia, but a good starting point is to see these echoes as insights into the student's world. When a student repeats a line from a book, that might be their way of highlighting an interest or sharing something they find comforting. Are they seeking clarity? Echoing your sentiment? Or just finding solace in familiar words during an overwhelming moment? These are only a few examples of why a student might engage in echolalia, but through rapport-building and frequent interactions, you will get to know the patterns of your students' communication styles. Once you understand the purpose of the student's echolalic communication, you can respond appropriately, by clarifying your point, acknowledging their agreement, or offering reassurances for overwhelm. Engaging with echolalia, rather than simply correcting or ignoring it, allows you to build rapport and encourage continued communication.

Nonverbal Communication

Neurodivergent individuals might be nonspeaking for various reasons, even when they possess the cognitive ability to understand and produce language in other forms. One reason is that sensory processing differences can cause spoken language to feel overwhelming or unmanageable. Another reason includes motor planning challenges that make the coordination of speech muscles difficult. Additionally, anxiety or social communication differences can influence a student's comfort or desire to use spoken language (Donaldson, corbin, and McCoy 2021; Sarris 2020).

Importantly, a student being nonspeaking doesn't equate to an inability to communicate. Many such students find alternative and effective means of expression. Gestures, sign language, or the use of AAC (augmentative and alternative communication) devices may resonate more deeply with them. These communication methods are not secondary to speech but authentic and preferred ways of communicating.

When engaging with nonspeaking neurodivergent students, the way you respond is pivotal. It's essential that you recognize and understand the meaning of a student's signs and gestures so you can respond appropriately. You might even incorporate some basic sign language into your classroom routines and interactions. Replying to a student's nonverbal communication using clear, concise spoken language, or through mirroring their nonverbal cues, provides encouragement and builds relationships.

It's also beneficial to weave AAC devices and visual aids seamlessly into classroom settings. By doing so, you normalize the use of these tools and ensure that all students, regardless of their communication style, have equal access to learning resources. Moreover, structuring classroom activities to encompass varied methods of interaction—like hands-on experiments, art projects, or interactive tech solutions—ensures that spoken language isn't the only pathway to participation.

Situational Mutism

Some neurodivergent speakers might experience situational mutism. (*Situational mutism* is a more neurodiversity-affirming term than the more common *selective mutism*, which implies choice and intent when an individual is unable to speak.) Situational mutism is characterized by students who can speak in certain environments but are unable to produce spoken language in others due to anxiety or stress.

When addressing situational mutism, educators should remember that it's not about a student's preference for silence or a consistent communication style they have. Instead, it is a reactive response to specific situations that feel overwhelming. To support these students, it is paramount that you create a reassuring classroom environment. This could mean carving out a quiet space in the room where students can relax or pairing them with trusted buddies who help them navigate classroom interactions. Offering alternative means of communication, like AAC devices or an option for written responses, can also alleviate the immediate pressure of verbal participation.

As students develop confidence in their verbal communication and comfort in their relationships with teachers and peers, they may be able to use verbal language with increased frequency. However, one rule stands out: never force speech. Pressuring a student with situational mutism to talk can exacerbate their anxiety. Instead, prioritize understanding and patience. Small steps forward are significant victories. Ensuring these students feel supported, whether they speak or not, is an integral piece in creating a neurodiversity-affirming environment.

Fostering Peer Support and Understanding

In addition to understanding diverse communication methods and styles yourself, you can educate your students about them. Students understanding and accepting that peers might interpret nonverbal cues in ways that differ from their own interpretation or might find direct eye contact or other social "norms" uncomfortable is important for creating a neurodiversity-affirming environment. The more students know, the easier it is for them to adapt and understand.

Teachers can lead by example. Integrating simple strategies into the daily routine of the classroom—like using visual aids for those who benefit from them, allowing more "think time" for students to process verbal instructions, or incorporating tech tools—can go a long way. This not only supports neurodivergent students directly but also demonstrates for the entire class how to be flexible in communication.

When fostering peer support and understanding, an environment of patience is key. Sometimes, a student might need something repeated or rephrased. Sometimes, they might communicate in a way that's unconventional. When you emphasize patience and understanding, not only do neurodivergent students feel more at ease, but their peers also learn the importance of taking the needed time to understand another person.

Social Acuity Over Social Skills

When discussing the needs of neurodivergent students, particularly within the realms of social development and communication, it's essential to differentiate between teaching social *skills* and fostering social *acuity*. The distinction is crucial and carries significant implications for neurodivergent students' well-being and personal development.

Social skills, as commonly taught in many educational settings, often boil down to a list of prescriptive behaviors designed to fit a specific social mold. In contrast, social acuity refers to the development of a genuine understanding of social contexts and cues. Instead of forcing neurodivergent students into a one-size-fits-all mold, educators work to help them recognize and interpret various social situations in a manner that's true to their unique experiences. This doesn't mean abandoning the idea of teaching helpful social strategies altogether. Instead, it focuses on adaptive, personalized approaches that prioritize the individual's comfort and understanding.

Shifting the focus from mere skills to true acuity respects neurodivergent students' authenticity. It acknowledges that there isn't one "right" way to be social. By fostering environments that celebrate differences and teaching students to navigate the social world in ways that feel right for them, educators can champion both inclusion and well-being.

The idea of teaching neurodivergent students about social nuances, without expecting consistent compliance, can seem counterintuitive to traditional educational methods. However, understanding and application are two very different things. This distinction is vital, and self-advocacy plays a pivotal role in ensuring a comfortable environment for these students. By teaching neurodivergent students about social nuances and cues, you are equipping them with a map of the social landscape. They become aware of why certain behaviors or responses are expected in certain situations. However, and this is crucial, understanding the *why* behind a social norm doesn't mean that adhering to it becomes any more comfortable or intuitive for them. Think of it like learning a complex dance step. Knowing the steps doesn't instantly make a person a dancer. Some may find the rhythm and flow quickly, while others may struggle. And that's okay. The same principle applies here. Neurodivergent students may grasp why eye contact is seen as a sign of attentiveness but still find the act itself overwhelming or distressing.

This is where self-advocacy comes into play. Being able to articulate their feelings and discomforts can be transformative for neurodivergent students. For instance, if a student finds group activities overwhelming, they could be taught to communicate this to their teachers and peers. They might say, "I understand why group discussions are important, but I feel more comfortable contributing in smaller groups or one-on-one." Respecting their self-advocacy allows neurodivergent students to set boundaries, ask for accommodations, and suggest alternatives that work better for them. This not only fosters a sense of agency and autonomy but also helps teachers and peers understand and respect a student's unique needs. It's a proactive approach, shifting the narrative from mere compliance to mutual understanding.

Moreover, allowing neurodivergent students the space to understand social norms without pressing them to constantly emulate these norms does another significant thing: it normalizes difference. It sends the message that while it's beneficial to understand societal expectations, it's equally valid to recognize and honor one's limits, preferences, and needs.

In a practical setting, teachers can integrate lessons about societal expectations within broader discussions about diversity, tolerance, and understanding. Role-playing can be a useful tool where students can practice both understanding and self-advocacy in controlled scenarios.

When educators focus on fostering social acuity over skills, they're not just benefiting neurodivergent students—they're enhancing the entire learning environment. By moving away from rigid social scripts, all students get the opportunity to develop a richer, more nuanced understanding of human interactions.

What to Remember

- Recognizing and respecting neurodivergent communication styles not only makes students feel welcome in the classroom but is also key in deconstructing preconceived notions and biases around "appropriate" or "expected" ways to communicate.
- The ability to produce spoken language shouldn't be confused with the ability to understand or communicate. There are many reasons why neurodivergent students might be nonspeaking, and many nonspeaking students have the cognitive ability to understand and produce language in other forms. It's up to educators to see those other forms of communication as being as rich and valuable as verbal language.
- Focusing on teaching social acuity instead of teaching social skills creates an environment in which neurodivergent students can more easily unmask, learn the neuro-normative landscape, and make informed decisions about how they want to approach social interactions.

Chapter 10

Strengths-Based Instruction

Points to Ponder

- How can you move away from focusing on deficits and toward fostering and leveraging strengths as a way to support neurodivergent learners?
- What classroom strategies are useful to shift instructional practices to be more strengths-based?
- What are some common strengths that you see in your neurodivergent students?

Within traditional educational settings, neurodivergent learners' diverse cognitive profiles have been mistakenly viewed through the lens of deficits, hindering their growth and potential. Each neurodivergent individual possesses unique strengths and cognitive abilities that can contribute to their personal growth and success. By adopting a strengths-based approach, educators can identify and harness individual strengths, unlocking the full potential of neurodivergent learners. Recognizing and leveraging students' strengths promotes academic achievement and also allows students to develop a sense of purpose and fulfillment.

What Is Strengths-Based Instruction?

At its most basic level, strengths-based instruction is an approach to education that focuses on integrating a student's strengths into the way they receive instruction or show what they've learned. Often, *strengths-based instruction* is interpreted to mean "interest-based learning." That is one form of strengths-based instruction, but we share many more possibilities in this chapter. For neurodivergent learners, providing strengths-based instruction is an accommodation that can leverage their strengths to build areas of weakness.

When students experience success and are recognized for their talents, they develop a positive self-identity and become more engaged in their learning journey (Kumar and Mohideen 2021). This, in turn, enhances their motivation to learn, as they feel valued and understood. In a neurodiversity-affirming school where students with diverse cognitive profiles coexist, fostering a positive sense of self is vital to creating an inclusive and accepting community.

The concept a neurodiversity-affirming school is grounded in the idea of providing students with holistic development. By focusing on strengths, educators can cater to the diverse learning needs of students while simultaneously addressing their challenges. For instance, a dyslexic student may struggle with reading but exhibit exceptional visual-spatial skills. Educators can incorporate visual aids or encourage project-based learning, which tap into the student's strengths, while providing support in their areas of difficulty. This approach nurtures well-rounded development, so students flourish academically, socially, and emotionally.

Neurology Justifies Strengths-Based Supports

Lots of students are able to focus and direct their attention to whatever task they are being asked to complete, whether or not they are interested in it. They comply with requests because they know they are expected to do so, and they have the self-regulation skills to initiate tasks and complete them. However, for many neurodivergent learners, kickstarting this motivation can be difficult. They may struggle with self-directed motivation for academic or other required tasks that educators want them to do but that they aren't interested in doing, and they are often intensely motivated by the things they are passionate about. This isn't because they don't care about what educators want them to do; it is directly tied to differences in how their brains function. These include the following:

- **Neural connectivity differences:** Neurodivergent individuals may exhibit differences in neural connectivity, meaning the patterns of communication and integration between their brain regions may be atypical. These connectivity differences can affect the transfer of information, processing efficiency, and motivation (Wylie et al. 2020).

- **Dopamine differences:** Dopamine is a neurotransmitter associated with motivation, reward, and pleasure. Neurodivergent individuals may have atypical dopamine functioning, such as lower dopamine levels or difficulties with dopamine receptor functioning. This can impact their motivation levels and make it more challenging for them to engage in tasks that don't provide immediate or stimulating rewards (Véronneau-Veilleux et al. 2022).

- **Serotonin imbalances:** Serotonin is another neurotransmitter involved in mood regulation, happiness, and motivation. Neurodivergent individuals may experience imbalances in serotonin levels or abnormalities in serotonin receptor functioning, which can affect their motivation and overall mood (Xi and Wu 2021).

- **Noradrenaline (norepinephrine) differences:** Noradrenaline is a neurotransmitter that plays a role in arousal, attention, and focus. Neurodivergent individuals may have difficulties with noradrenaline functioning, leading to challenges in maintaining attention and motivation for tasks that require sustained effort (Xi and Wu 2021).

These differences in brain function mean that there are also biological reasons to pursue strengths-based instruction to help neurodivergent students engage with and master the tasks school asks of them.

Starting with Strengths

The adage *A rising tide lifts all boats* provides a compelling analogy for strengths-based education. Just as the rising tide makes all boats ascend uniformly, leveraging a student's existing strengths—their personal "rising tide"—can help uplift and support their weaker areas. This approach doesn't only support students' individual growth; it also champions the diverse ways each student thinks and learns, celebrating the unique potential in every learner.

In practice, a neurodiversity-affirming school prioritizes strengths-based instruction. Instead of focusing solely on where students might need extra help, educators first identify what each student excels at. For instance, if a student excels in creative writing, that strength becomes the foundation for the rest of their education. Using creative writing as a starting point to improve an area of weakness, such as executive functioning skills, provides the framework for growing the area of difficulty within the context of the strength. When the teacher weaves skills like planning and organization into a creative writing task, the student gets real-life practice in successfully implementing those executive functioning skills, making the entire learning process more meaningful.

Neurodivergent students are often able to understand the theoretical concepts of the skills they are working to build. For example, they can clearly articulate specific skills and strategies for managing social relationships or handling disappointment. However, when asked to apply these skills in their day-to-day actions, they falter. This is typically the outcome when educators teach skills in isolation, without real-world application. By channeling students' inherent strengths, educators can bridge this gap, providing them a more intuitive pathway to mastery. For example, learning about social awareness and acuity in a small-group setting can build knowledge; putting it into practice in robotics club, where the student has a deep knowledge of and passion for the topic, is much more effective.

Many neurodivergent learners have large discrepancies in their abilities. If you were to look at a profile of one student's areas of strengths and difficulties, it would look like a mountain range with large peaks and valleys. Identifying each student's strengths is the first step toward being able to leverage them in the classroom. The strengths of neurodivergent learners are as diverse as they are. However, there are some areas of strength that may be common among them. The following sections explore common strengths in neurodivergent students, what they might look like, and some ideas for how they can be used to support student learning.

Monotropism

Primarily associated with autism, monotropism is often referred to as "special interests," or SpIns. Many neurodivergent individuals are passionately interested in learning about one or more areas, to the exclusion of other areas. This narrow interest and laser-like focus is sometimes called an attention tunnel. A neurodivergent student's special interests can last for months or years. Brains with monotropic focus have a hard time engaging with and finding motivation to complete tasks outside the area of interest (Dwyer et al. 2024). People with monotropic interests typically have an unrivaled passion and depth of knowledge surrounding their topic of interest.

In the classroom, monotropism might be observed as a student being deeply engrossed in a single subject or activity. For instance, they might spend all their free time drawing detailed maps of a historical period instead of varying their activities. When conversing with another person, they may gravitate toward the topic or engage in info-dumping (page 221). These topics can range from the history of wars to a fantasy series to animals, and everything in between.

Because many students whose interests are monotropic have a difficult time regulating their motivation to tasks that are not within the realm of their SpIn, these students greatly benefit from linking their primary interest to other subjects or areas of study. Engaging with the student about their preferred topic is key to building rapport and trust. Additionally, finding peers with similar interests (regardless of age or grade) is an important aspect of helping neurodivergent students find friends. Many of the social difficulties experienced by autistic people are significantly mitigated when engaging with others who have similar interests.

Double Empathy Problem

Monotropism

The situation: In an elementary school setting, a neurodivergent student shows a special interest in astronomy. They are often found reading about planets, drawing space scenes, or talking about space exploration. This interest is so consuming that the student primarily engages in activities related to it, often neglecting or showing little enthusiasm for subjects or activities that are not connected to their special interest in astronomy.

Perspective of others: The neurodivergent student's teacher and peers notice the student's intense focus on astronomy and their relative disinterest in other topics. The teacher might interpret this as a lack of motivation or a one-dimensional approach to learning and feel concerned about the student's disengagement in other areas of the curriculum. Peers might see the student's singular focus as odd or limiting, wondering why they aren't interested in a broader range of activities. There could be a perception that the student is not well-rounded or is unwilling to try new things.

Perspective of the neurodivergent student: For the neurodivergent student, their fascination with astronomy is not a hobby; it's a profound interest that captivates their mind and imagination. This special interest provides a sense of comfort, joy, and deep engagement. While they find immense satisfaction in exploring this topic, they may struggle to find similar enthusiasm for subjects or activities outside this interest. Their apparent lack of motivation in other areas is not a choice but a manifestation of how their attention and enthusiasm are channeled. The student might feel misunderstood or pressured to conform to typical interest patterns while also experiencing frustration or anxiety when unable to engage with their SpIn.

Possible follow-up: Offering opportunities for the student to engage with, communicate about, and learn though their special interest provides the student authentic and strengths-based learning opportunities. Additionally, finding ways for the student to interact with others with similar interests and knowledge can help them form authentic, positive social relationships. The other students can learn about why some people have these laser-like interests and engage with the neurodivergent student in kind and respectful ways.

Hyperfixation

Hyperfixation is often confused with monotropism. However, they involve different patterns. Whereas monotropism is long-term interest in a topic or subject, hyperfixations are shorter-term and tend to shift more frequently. When engaged with their hyperfixations, individuals may become so engrossed that they have a difficult time transitioning to new tasks and their attention is frequently brought back to the topic when not engaged in other activities (Dwyer et al. 2024).

Although the difference between them is subtle, monotropism includes difficulty engaging at all with topics outside of the primary focus, while hyperfixations make the transition between activities the primary difficulty. Like monotropism, hyperfixation provides a foundation for intense and deep focus on a topic of interest that can propel students to success in the classroom.

These students might spend multiple class periods, or even weeks, engrossed in a specific topic or project. If the class is studying ancient Egypt, a student who is hyperfixated on the topic might not only complete the assignments but go above and beyond them, reading multiple books on ancient Egypt and bringing in extra projects or presentations about it. If their hyperfixation is related to something outside of school, they may get distracted and engage with the interest instead of what's going on in the classroom.

You can use the subject of the student's hyperfixation as a gateway to explore related topics. For instance, if a student is hyperfixated on a specific book or genre, introduce them to different literature or writing exercises related to it. When a student is actively and productively engaged with a topic associated with their hyperfixation, provide them time to stay engaged and be aware that expecting them to transition with little advance notice will likely be difficult.

Verbal Ability

Verbal ability is the ability to wield language effectively—both using language orally or in writing and understanding language that one hears or reads. Verbal ability can include having a wide vocabulary, being able to share thoughts clearly, and being able to understand and describe abstract concepts using words.

Because school is a highly verbal environment, many students who show verbal ability perform well academically. However, some neurodivergent individuals who have very high overall verbal ability also struggle with social language pragmatic skills (understanding the nuanced use of language in social situations, such as reading between the lines). Some neurodivergent individuals are hyperlexic (page 49), though hyperlexia can be coupled with difficulties with reading comprehension (especially related to reading fiction and inferencing) as text gets more complex throughout the school years.

A student with high verbal ability might frequently raise their hand to provide detailed answers or elaborate on subjects. They're often the first to engage in class discussions, offer nuanced insights, or even correct minor linguistic errors in reading materials or presentations. Verbal ability might manifest as an intense focus on word choice or the specifics of linguistic constructs. Students might get caught up on the specific phrasing of a question or enjoy exploring synonyms and antonyms beyond the standard curriculum. They may strongly prefer to process information or emotions through writing.

Most schools' curricula are highly verbal in what they present to students and how students share what they've learned. For neurodivergent students with strong verbal ability, providing opportunities for them to reflect on experiences, emotions, or executive functioning through writing or speaking can help them gain insight into their experiences.

Visual-Spatial Ability

Students with strong visual-spatial ability have the capacity to understand and interpret visual information, as well as easily grasp spatial relationships between objects. This can include tasks like reading maps, visualizing objects in three dimensions, or imagining rotations of shapes. Because much of the content in school is presented in ways that are accessible to students with high verbal ability, students whose strengths lie within the visual-spatial realm may not have the same ease with academics (Lakin and Wai 2020).

When given tasks like puzzles, map reading, or geometry problems, these students often excel. Their work is often intricate and nuanced. They might create complex designs in art class, or, when asked to visualize a science concept, they can accurately describe or draw it from multiple perspectives. These students may love to complete puzzles, build LEGO structures, or solve Rubik's Cubes.

Any time you can, work to integrate visual-spatial tools into your lessons. Diagrams, flowcharts, and mind maps provide a comfortable framework for students with strong visual-spatial skills. Offer opportunities for tasks like model building or spatial puzzles.

Teaching students to integrate their visual-spatial skills when completing assignments or taking notes can also help them retain information. The book *Visual Learning and Teaching* by Dr. Susan Daniels is an excellent resource with many tools and tips on how to use visual-spatial strategies in your classroom and teaching practice.

Logic and Reasoning

Some neurodivergent students have the ability to think rationally, make connections between concepts, and deduce or infer conclusions from given information. Many learners identified for gifted education programs thrive when completing work that requires strong logic and reasoning skills, and many autistic learners are known for their ability to notice and elaborate on patterns.

In group problem-solving tasks or math challenges, these students often propose solutions that are systematic and well thought out. They might approach problems in a highly systematic way, desiring to understand the foundational principles before moving forward. A student might pause a math lesson to try to deeply understand one formula's underlying logic rather than rushing to solve multiple problems. These learners might gravitate to strategy games or logic puzzles during free time.

Incorporate diverse classroom activities, such as problem-solving tasks and logic puzzles, to engage students' systematic thinking abilities. Critical-thinking exercises can challenge them to analyze and synthesize information, while also allowing them depth of exploration. Strategy games can be integrated to develop students' strategic thinking, and group discussions allow them to share their unique problem-solving perspectives, benefiting the broader group. Students who struggle with broad or abstract concepts can be supported by breaking down the material into logical steps or sequences. Their strong analytical skills can help them understand the flow and connections between topics.

Anya

Anya loved coding. The step-by-step logic appealed to them. However, writing essays felt chaotic. Their teacher suggested treating essays like algorithms. Each paragraph had a role, a step in the process. With this structured approach, Anya began crafting coherent, well-organized essays, merging their love for sequential thinking with the art of writing.

Detail-Oriented

Detail-oriented individuals possess the unique ability to focus on minute details, capturing the nuances that many overlook. Their exceptional focus enables them to ensure precision, leaving little room for error.

Students who possess this trait may frequently raise their hands to point out tiny errors in a textbook or on your presentation slides. When working on assignments, they may provide more meticulous and comprehensive answers than their peers do. They take their time to ensure that every project or assignment they undertake is immaculate, often going beyond the scope of what's required for accuracy. They may experience discomfort when faced with imperfections in their work.

Detail-oriented students thrive in environments that demand meticulousness. They are ideal candidates for tasks such as proofreading written content, engaging in intricate research projects, or analyzing datasets for inconsistencies. You can set up challenges that test their precision and thoroughness, rewarding them for the depth and clarity they bring. You can also guide them to utilize their attention to detail to support areas of difficulty. For example, to support a difficulty with executive functioning, you may encourage a detail-oriented student to use their strength to assist with planning and scheduling, ensuring they allocate appropriate time for each task.

Minh

Minh had a skill for spotting the tiniest of details in art and text, yet comprehending overarching themes in literature proved challenging. His teacher took a unique approach. Beginning with a detailed analysis of a small passage, Minh would delve deep, discussing each nuance. Over time, the teacher worked with Minh on zooming out, connecting these details to the broader themes of the story. This scaffolded approach made larger concepts more accessible to him.

Big-Picture Thinking

Some neurodivergent students may be big-picture thinkers, with the ability to see patterns, trends, and connections within a broad context. Big-picture thinkers are able to abstract and generalize from specific details, often leading to innovative solutions and creative ideas. These students may also get bogged down with too many details, especially if they don't know the overarching concept that ties the details together.

These students have the ability to see the overarching narrative or system that allows them to make connections between facts or concepts, leading to deep insights. They might enjoy brainstorming sessions where they can propose innovative solutions and projects that require them to design or imagine new systems.

To support big-picture thinkers, you can incorporate activities that encourage systems thinking and exploring connections between concepts. Project-based learning, where students work on long-term projects that tackle real-world problems, can be particularly beneficial. Tools like concept maps or systems diagrams can help these students visualize and explore complex relationships.

Maya

Maya was the class's social butterfly, always eager to discuss and collaborate. However, written assignments were daunting. One day, Maya's teacher asked her to lead a group discussion and summarize everyone's viewpoints, making connections between the various reflections different people had from the same prompt. Writing about the collective thoughts of peers felt natural to Maya. This approach made written expression less intimidating and more relatable for her.

Literal Thinking

Some neurodivergent students have a tendency to understand words, phrases, or situations in their exact, explicit sense. This ability to focus on precise meanings can lead to a deep comprehension of subjects, especially in areas that demand accuracy and detail.

This form of thinking can be particularly suited to and useful in subjects like math, programming, and science, but it can cause some barriers in understanding and using figurative language.

This student might frequently ask clarifying questions when idioms, metaphors, or figurative language are used. Their knack for direct interpretation can lead to confusion when faced with ambiguities or nuances. They might struggle with literature that heavily relies on symbolism but can provide clear and direct summaries of straightforward texts. Conversely, they excel in tasks where clear-cut answers are required. Their approach to problem-solving might be systematic, relying on concrete data and avoiding assumptions based on implied meanings.

Be clear and direct in your instructions. You might ask these students to act as a "check" to ensure instructions or tasks are clearly defined. When introducing or discussing abstract concepts, pair them with concrete examples. This helps the student bridge the gap between the tangible and the conceptual. Offering opportunities for technical writing, research, and data analysis in assignments can also leverage this strength for academic success.

Comfort with Routine

For many neurodivergent learners, routine can enhance focus, minimize anxiety, and provide a sense of stability in the learning environment. Consistency in daily schedules or classroom activities can anchor these students' day, allowing them to anticipate and prepare for what comes next. This can lead to increased confidence and engagement as these learners know what to expect and can better channel their energies toward mastering the content.

Students who find comfort in routine thrive on consistency. They might be the first to remind you of daily rituals, like scheduled reading time or the order of activities. They might become anxious or unsettled if there's an unexpected change in the classroom routine. These students may also frequently ask about the next activity or the plan for the following day as a way to prepare themselves for upcoming transitions.

Recognizing their comfort with routine is important for supporting these learners. It is useful to help them regulate their emotions by providing advance notice about upcoming changes, with a lot of advance details for what to expect. Visual schedules, color-coded calendars, and task boards they can refer to throughout the day reassure them about what is coming next.

Elijah

Elijah could recite lengthy passages after reading them just once. His memorization skills were commendable. He found comfort in reciting them to the teacher and to himself and in using direct quotes in his work. However, comprehension and making inferences were a hurdle. Elijah's teacher found a way to integrate his strength into work that would also help him learn to handle the ambiguity necessary to interpret certain types of texts. The teacher provided Elijah with two different passages with similar themes and asked him to compare them, finding similarities in wording. She then prompted Elijah to contrast them, finding the differences in style and topics. Finally, the teacher guided Elijah to use this information to answer some open-ended questions related to the passages. This pushed Elijah to process and internalize the material, bridging the gap between rote memorization and deep comprehension.

Preference for Novelty

A desire for new experiences and stimuli, often characterized by a tendency to seek out new information, activities, or challenges, can indicate a student's preference for novelty. While some neurodivergent students find solace in routine, others crave new stimuli. They may quickly grow restless with repeated tasks and often seek new challenges, tools, or ways of exploring a subject, displaying a keen interest in novel approaches or resources.

Students who have preference for novelty may finish work quickly in their eagerness for the next challenge. They might get bored with repetitive tasks and seek out additional resources, subjects, or projects to tackle. They're often the students curious about the latest news, tech, or updates in a subject area.

Lean into students' drive for novelty by providing opportunities for them to explore new ideas and new ways of completing tasks. Allow students to choose different methods or approaches to learning about a topic. Introducing project-based learning, where students can pick projects based on their interests, can also be immensely beneficial. Peer collaboration and group brainstorming sessions can serve as a platform for them to exchange new ideas and provide a dynamic environment that satiates their thirst for the novel.

Understanding your students' strengths is important for being able to choose the right strategies and instructional approaches to support them in your classroom. By matching the appropriate strategy or approach to a learner's inherent strengths and needs, you can amplify their success and cultivate an environment of empowerment. Acknowledging and leveraging students' strengths is key to supporting their learning in your classroom, as are integrating adaptive technology and other tech tools and harnessing students' natural curiosities through interest-based learning.

The rest of this chapter provides information on two strengths-based strategies you're likely already using in classroom: mastery-based learning and novelty.

Mastery-Based Learning

Mastery-based learning is an instructional approach that shifts the focus from rote memorization to comprehensive understanding. Rather than progressing through a curriculum at a uniform pace, in mastery-based learning, students advance only when they've fully grasped a concept. In this way, it's very similar to competency-based learning, in which students are required to demonstrate the skills they've learned in the context of the classroom. However, mastery-based learning differs slightly.

In addition to demonstrating the skills they've mastered in the context of the classroom, students must also show they can apply those skills across contexts or in real-life situations. This approach acknowledges that neurodivergent learners often have unique pacing and processing methods. It also acknowledges the value of alternative learning experiences, such as internships, apprenticeships, and trade school. By allowing each student the time, resources, and varied curricular paths they need to master a subject, mastery-based learning helps you move away from a one-size-fits-all approach and toward an environment where each student's learning journey is acknowledged and respected.

Moving away from that one-size-fits-all approach also means moving away from a one-type-of-grading-fits-all approach. That means not using just the final output and time it takes to get there as your grading rubric. Instead, we suggest using a grading system that takes into account whether a student has mastered the skills, met the learning objective, or can use what they've learned in "real life."

Competency-Based Grading

Competency-based grading, with its personalized learning paths and focus on individual skill and knowledge demonstration, naturally aligns with neurodiversity-affirming practices. This approach allows neurodivergent students to progress at their own pace and choose learning activities that cater to their strengths and interests. By offering multiple opportunities to demonstrate mastery and not penalizing students for the time they take to learn, competency-based grading can reduce anxiety and stress, which may be heightened in neurodivergent individuals. This method also emphasizes the practical application of skills, which can be more engaging and meaningful for students with diverse neurological profiles.

Standards-Based Grading

Standards-based grading, while more uniform in its expectations and pacing than competency-based methods, can still be adapted to support neurodivergent learners. Clear, well-defined learning objectives and criteria for success can provide the structure and predictability that many neurodivergent students find helpful. Additionally, emphasizing the most recent evidence of learning, rather than an average of all assessments, can more accurately reflect the current abilities and understanding of a neurodivergent student who takes longer to grasp certain concepts but can achieve high levels of mastery with appropriate support and time.

Novelty

The human brain is wired to respond to novelty. This is actually a survival mechanism: new stimuli indicate a potential change in the environment, prompting the brain to focus and assess. In an educational setting, novelty acts as a spotlight, drawing students' attention and priming their brains for learning. This is especially effective for neurodivergent learners, who might struggle with traditional teaching methods that don't align with their unique cognitive processing. Integrating novelty in the classroom supports the motivation of all students and leverages the many strengths of neurodivergent students (Stoa and Chu 2023).

Neurodivergent students, such as ADHDers, often experience heightened sensitivity to their surroundings. What might seem routine or mundane to a neuro-normative student could be perceived by a neurodivergent learner as new and stimulating. By consistently integrating novelty into classroom instruction, educators can harness this heightened sensitivity, creating an environment where these students are continuously engaged and captivated. Instead of battling distractions or attempting to fit into a one-size-fits-all model, neurodivergent students can thrive in a space where their natural inclination to seek out and respond to novelty is leveraged as a strength.

For autistic learners, novelty can be a double-edged sword. While certain new experiences might initially cause discomfort due to a disruption in the routine, well-planned introductions of novelty can offer opportunities for these students to expand their comfort zones. By presenting novel experiences in a safe, structured manner, you can encourage students who also thrive with consistency to take on new challenges. In addition to providing a "hook" for students to engage with new ideas and concepts, it can also help them build resilience and adaptability over time.

There are *many* ways to integrate novelty in your classroom. The remainder of this chapter shares a few that we've used.

Ways to Integrate Novelty

Many students struggle with completing homework because it feels redundant and like a waste of time. Additionally, the executive functioning required to complete homework can be a barrier for some. Using a flipped classroom approach is a novel way to encourage students to engage with their homework (Strelan, Osborn, and Palmer 2020). A flipped classroom approach asks students to engage with new material outside of class, usually in the form of video lectures or digital content. Class time is for completing practice activities with teacher guidance. Learning new content outside of the classroom makes "homework" novel, unlike redundant practice work. For neurodivergent students, this blend of independent learning with hands-on classroom experiences can be particularly beneficial, providing both structure and room for exploration.

Tech integration is another avenue for infusing novelty. The abundance of available tech tools, apps, and platforms can be used to make learning interactive and immersive. When applied appropriately, technology can turn a conventional lesson into a dynamic experience. For many neurodivergent students, the multisensory nature of tech-integrated lessons can tap into their individual strengths and interests. Additionally, many neurodivergent students gravitate toward technology and are adept at using it, making learning through technology a natural extension of their existing strengths.

Active learning strategies, such as gamification (incorporating game elements into your classroom and curriculum), are another way to integrate novelty. Gamification especially, with its elements of competition, reward, and progression, can ignite motivation and make the learning process enjoyable for many students. *Note: Competition should be used with caution; some neurodivergent students might struggle with emotional regulation when they lose, and competition can foster perfectionism in some students. Adjusting your methods for each student and/or providing accommodations is useful in this—and all—interventions.*

In a neurodiversity-affirming school, these strategies aren't mere add-ons; they are fundamental shifts that recognize and celebrate the varied ways students perceive, engage with, and absorb the world around them. The following sections share some specific examples of integrating novelty into your neurodiversity-affirming classroom.

Badges and Microcredentials

As educators seek innovative and novel strategies for their neurodiversity-affirming classrooms, digital badges or microcredentials can be a fun tool to use with students. Many professional learning programs have digital badges or credentials that professionals can earn and display in their email signature or on their website. A similar structure can be used and tailored for students' individual goals and achievements, celebrating and leveraging their varied skills, modes of creative expression, problem-solving methods, and even interpersonal strengths.

It is important to use caution with this type of gamification. Digital badges run the risk of becoming just another gold star awarded as extrinsic motivation if you don't have student autonomy and buy-in. Students need to be fully engaged in the process of earning digital badges or microcredentials and have a choice about the badges they are earning and how they are earning them. Setting predetermined (either individualized or group-focused) checkpoints and milestones for badges is one way to ensure that students are the driving force behind reaching the goals. Setting individual goals that students can measure independently (with check-ins with you) also removes sole reliance on teacher feedback.

Incorporating badges isn't just about recognizing achievement. It's about validating the diverse ways in which students learn and contribute. For neurodivergent students, badges offer a visual testament to their journey, one that often involves overcoming unique challenges.

To implement badges and microcredentials in your classroom, follow these steps.

1. **Identify skills and milestones.** Begin by mapping out the skills and milestones you'd like to recognize with badges and microcredentials. Go beyond traditional academic achievements and include varied abilities, creativity, problem-solving, and interpersonal skills.
2. **Design your badges.** Create digital badges that reflect the achievements. Platforms like Canva can be used to design, issue, and manage these. Ensure that each badge has a clear visual meaning.
3. **Introduce the system.** Have a class discussion to introduce your badge system. Emphasize its inclusive nature and how it seeks to recognize individual strengths and learning journeys.
4. **Ask for feedback and make adjustments.** Periodically gather feedback from students about your badge system. Understand what's working and what could be improved. Then make adjustments based on this feedback.

Challenges and Boss Levels

You've likely heard your students talk passionately about video games—about "leveling up" and the adrenaline rush they get from "boss battles." These video game elements can be adapted as a novel and strengths-based intervention for your classroom, and one that is especially beneficial for neurodivergent learners.

When playing a video game, a player starts on easier levels, mastering skills needed in the game before moving on to harder challenges and occasionally encountering a significant obstacles or bosses as they progress through the game's levels. Overcoming a boss is tough but rewarding—and is needed to move to the next stage of the game. Structuring your curriculum in a similar manner, with a game theme or story and assignments that gradually increase in difficulty until they culminate in a challenging "boss battle" assignment or test, can leverage this same drive.

Here are some tips to follow when using challenges and boss levels:

- **Use progressive learning.** Begin with foundational concepts and gradually introduce more complex ideas, ensuring students build confidence as they advance.
- **Allow collaboration.** As in multiplayer games, allow collaborative tasks in challenges and boss levels. This strengthens social bonds and provides opportunities for students to build social and emotional skills.
- **Give opportunities to retry.** As in video games, where players can attempt a challenge multiple times, offer opportunities for students to improve upon their previous work and try challenges again.

Examples of Challenges and Boss Levels

Third grade (science): Ms. Lewis's third grade students are fully engaged by the world of plants and their life cycles. To harness this enthusiasm, she structures her lessons as a "Grow Your Garden" game, with a bulletin board set up to look like a classroom garden. When the group completes a lesson (such as "parts of a plant" or "photosynthesis basics"), they get to add a new plant or element to their garden. At the end of the unit, students face a boss battle: a group project to design a "Dream Garden" using what they've earned throughout the unit. Students discuss and decide which elements from their learning journey they'd like to include in their Dream Garden, which fosters teamwork and consolidates their understanding of the lessons.

Sixth grade (executive functioning): Mr. Harrison is aware that many of his students, particularly those who are neurodivergent, struggle with time management, an essential executive functioning skill. He introduces "Time Travelers' Quest." Every student receives a time machine dashboard—a visual organizer with clocks, timers, and schedules. Throughout the week, students set personal goals related to time management, like completing assignments, preparing for tests, or even organizing their materials. As they meet these goals, they time travel to different historical periods, learning fun tidbits about each era. The boss battle is a "Time Travel Fair" at the end of the month, where students present a day in the life of a historical figure or event they've visited, showcasing both their time-management skills and their historical knowledge.

Seventh grade (math): Mr. Carter struggles with students who find algebra dull and unengaging. He introduces "Algebraic Adventures," a role-playing game (see below) where students are wizards who must use algebra to solve challenges. In this game, each algebraic concept is a level: mastering linear equations might help defeat a dragon, while understanding inequalities unlocks a treasure chest. The culminating boss battle at the end of the semester is in the form of a major quest, where students need to combine their algebraic skills to rescue a mythical creature.

Tenth grade (emotional regulation): Mx. Jacobs recognizes that emotional regulation can be a significant challenge, especially for their neurodivergent learners. They create the "Emotion Islands Expedition." The classroom transforms into an archipelago of islands, where each island represents an emotion, such as Joy Isle, Anger Atoll, and Sadness Shore. Throughout the term, students explore these islands with activities that simulate or provoke certain emotions (like watching emotional film clips, listening to mood-specific music, or role-playing scenarios). After each activity, they reflect on their experiences, discuss coping strategies, and learn emotional-regulation techniques tailored to each emotion. The boss battle comes in the form of a "Stormy Seas Navigation" challenge. In it, students encounter a series of unpredictable emotional storms. Using the strategies they've learned, along with their enhanced emotional awareness and regulation skills, they must navigate their ships safely through.

Eleventh grade (history): Ms. Rodriguez teaches World War II history. She recognizes that the vast amount of information about this period can be overwhelming for students, and especially for neurodivergent learners. She designs a "WWII Strategy Game" in which students are grouped into nations. Every week, based on the lessons about major battles or political decisions, each group makes strategic decisions for their nation. They gain points based on historical accuracy and strategic prowess. The boss battle includes a mock multination conference where each group represents their country as they navigate a series of challenges using what they've learned.

Role-Playing Games

The chances that your neurodivergent students are familiar with popular role-playing games (RPGs) like *Dungeons & Dragons* are high. In RPGs, students get the opportunity to step into the shoes of diverse characters, offering them a structured environment to understand and empathize with various perspectives. This becomes particularly crucial in a neurodiversity-affirming classroom where understanding and empathy play pivotal roles.

Educators can use RPGs for a wide range of lessons. From historical reenactments to business simulations to mock trials, RPGs can be integrated into active learning opportunities in all sorts of content areas. Additionally, they are inherently adaptable. Whether a student has attention challenges or exceptional logical reasoning, an RPG can be tailored to match their needs and strengths. For instance, you can design shorter quests for students who find prolonged tasks daunting. And students can create characters emblematic of their unique strengths, empowering them to see themselves in roles that utilize their abilities.

An RPG's immediate feedback is another advantage. As an educator, you can easily glean insights into areas where a student excels or needs more support based on their in-game decisions and subsequent outcomes. Moreover, as students encounter challenges within a game, they learn resilience. Wrapping up with post-game reflections can bridge the game world and the world of your classroom, allowing students to discuss and draw connections between their in-game experiences and real-world scenarios. You can find lots of short, accessible RPGs online to use or adapt for your curriculum.

If you'd like to create your own RPG and you're not familiar with them, you may need to do some preliminary research to understand the structure and goals of a typical game. Once you feel comfortable with general format of an RPG, you're ready to begin designing your game. The following list describes key questions to consider as your design RPGs for your classroom:

- **Goals:** What is the primary learning outcome of your RPG? What subject or topic does the game need to cover?
- **Age:** What age group and skill level is the game for? This will determine the complexity of the game, the complexity of the language used in it, and the themes it can touch upon.
- **Format:** How long should the game last? A single lesson, a week, or an entire semester? Will it be a tabletop game, a digital game, or a mix of both?
- **Materials:** What materials or technologies are available to play the game (dice, computers, projectors, printed cards)?
- **Limitations:** Are there any subjects or issues that should be avoided? Any space limitations?
- **Curricular goals:** How does the game fit into your larger curriculum? Are there specific concepts or events that must be included in it?
- **Assessment:** How will students be assessed based on their participation or outcomes in the RPG? Is the assessment informal (participation and engagement) or formal (quizzes or assignments related to the RPG content)?
- **Character and setting:** Do you or your students have preferences for specific settings (fantasy, space, historical periods, etc.) or types of characters?

AI can be a useful tool in creating RPGs. For an example of an AI-created game, along with further instructions on how to do this on your own, follow this QR code to download a PDF of *Brainovia*, an RPG for developing executive functioning skills (OpenAI 2023).

Gamifying with Dice

Using various sizes of dice (like those used in *Dungeons & Dragons*) can be a fun and engaging way to gamify tasks and objectives in the classroom. While D6 dice (cubes with six sides) are most commonly used for gaming, sets of dice of varying sizes are easily and inexpensively found online. These sets typically include one of each of the following: D4, D6, D8, D10, D12, D20, and an additional D10 where the sides indicate the numbers 00-90. *Note: Dice are named based on their number of sides; a D8 is an eight-sided die.*

Because many neurodivergent learners thrive on novelty, integrating the randomness of chance with dice builds on their strength of being able to engage more easily with new approaches. It also has the benefit of giving students a sense of agency. Although they aren't completely in control, rolling the dice makes the activity feel less like a demand they are being directed to complete.

Here are a few ways to integrate dice into your instruction and assignments:

- **Random question generator:** Assign different questions or prompts to each side of a die. When it's time for a class discussion or review, roll the die to randomly select a question for students to answer.

- **Dice-based quizzes and assignments:** Assign each question a point value reflecting its difficulty, with a set minimum point goal for each assignment. Students roll dice to find out which questions they'll attempt, with higher rolls pointing to tougher questions but offering more points. Successfully answering these tougher questions can exempt them from the rest of the assignment or quiz, blending luck with skill.

- **Storytelling and creative writing:** Have students use dice to generate random elements for their creative writing. For example, one roll could determine the protagonist, another the setting, and a third the plot twist.

- **Vocabulary practice:** Assign a vocabulary word to each side of a die. When practicing vocabulary, students can roll to determine which word they will use in a sentence or how they'll demonstrate understanding of that word. If you need to ensure they've practiced all the words, include a rule that if a student lands on a word they've already used, they need to roll again.

- **Team challenges:** Place the class into teams and create challenges or review games that involve dice. For example, a team could roll dice to determine how many points they earn for a correct answer.
- **Fitness or movement breaks:** Use dice to determine the number of jumping jacks, push-ups, seconds in a seated stretch, or other physical actions students perform during movement breaks.

What to Remember

- Neurological differences in how their brains receive and respond to stimuli can influence students' motivation and engagement. Integrating strengths-based instructional methods allows educators to help neurodivergent learners engage in learning material in ways that work with their brains instead of against them.
- Strengths-based instruction involves assessing and leveraging individual student strengths, integrating novelty into lessons, and ensuring any adaptations to the instruction still match the learning objectives.
- Strengths-based instruction is more than just interest-based learning; tapping into students' specific areas of ability and skills is an excellent way to engage strengths-based supports.

Chapter 11

IEPs, 504 Plans, and Other Personalized Learning Plans

Points to Ponder

- Does every neurodivergent student need an IEP or 504 plan?
- Why should learning plans have SMART goals?
- How can you reframe learning goals to be neurodiversity-affirming?

There are two main ways that students with disabilities, including neurodivergent students who meet identification criteria, formally receive accommodations, modifications, and other support in public schools in the United States. The first is under the Individuals with Disabilities in Education Act (IDEA), the federal law that "makes available a free appropriate public education to eligible children with disabilities throughout the nation and ensures special education and related services to those children" (US DoE 2024). The second formal way that students with disabilities receive accommodations in school is under 504 plans, which are governed under a federal civil rights law, Section 504 of the Rehabilitation Act of 1973. If a student doesn't meet the eligibility criteria for an individualized education program (IEP) and it's clear they still need additional accommodation, that's when a 504 plan would be considered. Section 504 also requires schools to provide a "free appropriate public education." We'll come back to the idea of "free appropriate public education" (or FAPE) in a bit, but keep the word *appropriate* in mind.

About Individualized Education Programs

IEP can refer to a special education program itself or to the legal document that outlines the special education instruction, accommodations, and related services that a student identified as needing special education will receive to make progress in school. About 7.3 million US students receive special education services in the form of IEPs (National Center for Education Statistics 2023). That means 15 percent of all students in the United States are identified as having a disability that requires specialized instruction. And this number doesn't include students who would benefit from services but haven't been identified and disabled students who don't need special education support.

Your neurodivergent students may or may not be among the 7.3 million kids. Being neurodivergent doesn't automatically make a student eligible for an IEP. A medical diagnosis (such as for autism or ADHD) doesn't even automatically make them eligible. IDEA has two main requirements for eligibility for special education services:

1. A student must have what's called a "disabling condition" under one of the categories of disabilities defined by IDEA and your state's regulations. IDEA outlines thirteen categories (see the next page). Some states have an additional category of "developmental delay" that can be used until a student turns nine, and other states provide gifted education under IDEA.

2. The disability must have an "adverse effect" on a student's education. What constitutes an adverse effect varies from state to state, and even among school districts in the same state. What's important to know is that while most people think about this adverse effect being academic, there is both legal precedent and guidance from the US Department of Education that says social and emotional effects also can be considered as adversely affecting a student's education (Mr. I. ex rel. L.I. v. Maine School Administrative District 2007; US DoE 2021).

Categories of Disability Under IDEA

If a student has one or more of the following conditions, they're considered eligible for an IEP based on the condition that most significantly impacts their learning.

1. **Autism spectrum disorder (ASD):** As an educational identification, autism refers to a neurodevelopmental disability in which verbal and nonverbal communication and social interaction difficulties significantly impair a student's learning.

2. **Deaf-blindness:** A unique category used for students who have both visual and hearing impairments that together cause significant communication and educational needs that can't be addressed by interventions or programs for just one of the conditions.

3. **Deafness:** This category is reserved for students who have hearing impairment so severe that they aren't able to process information through hearing, with or without amplification.

4. **Emotional disturbance:** Some states have changed this category to "emotional regulation impairment." It covers students who exhibit one or more of the following characteristics over an extended period and to a degree that adversely impacts their learning:

    a. "An inability to learn that cannot be explained by intellectual, sensory, or health factors.

    b. "An inability to build or maintain satisfactory interpersonal relationships with peers and teachers.

    c. "Inappropriate types of behavior or feelings under normal circumstances.

    d. "A general pervasive mood of unhappiness or depression.

    e. "A tendency to develop physical symptoms or fears associated with personal or school problems." (IDEA 1990)

5. **Hearing impairment:** This category refers to an impairment in hearing not included under Deafness that may be either permanent or fluctuant.

6. **Intellectual disability:** Under IDEA, intellectual disability (ID) is defined as "significantly subaverage general intellectual functioning, existing concurrently with deficits in adaptive behavior and manifested during the developmental

period," which adversely impacts learning. It is possible to have another qualifying condition in co-occurrence with ID.

7. **Multiple disabilities:** Students who are eligible under this category have co-occurring conditions, which together cause such significant adverse impact that a student's needs can't be served by specialized instruction for just one of the conditions.

8. **Orthopedic impairment:** This category covers students whose learning is adversely impacted by "a congenital anomaly, impairments caused by disease (e.g., poliomyelitis, bone tuberculosis)," and other causes (IDEA 1990).

9. **Other health impairment:** Students eligible under this category have conditions that impact "strength, vitality, or alertness, including a heightened alertness to environmental stimuli," as well as chronic health conditions (IDEA 1990). Many neurodivergent students who have IEPs are eligible in this category, especially those with ADHD, Tourette syndrome, or similar conditions.

10. **Specific learning disability (SLD):** This category covers students who have impairments in the basic psychological processes involved in using or understanding spoken or written language. This can look like difficulty with mathematics, listening, thinking, reading, writing, spelling, or information processing. This category includes dyslexia and other learning disabilities but excludes difficulty with learning that can attributed to intellectual disability, visual or hearing impairments, or "environmental, cultural, or economic disadvantage" (IDEA 1990).

11. **Speech or language impairment:** This covers communication and articulation disorders, such as stuttering or voice impairment, as well as other language impairments.

12. **Traumatic brain injury:** Students covered under this category have open or closed head injuries that are the result of some sort of accident and that cause functional difficulty with thinking, language and speech, memory and attention, motor abilities, emotional regulation, and other executive functioning skills.

13. **Visual impairment, including blindness:** This category includes visual impairments that adversely affect learning (even with correction).

About 504 Plans

Commonly referred to as "Section 504," Section 504 of the Rehabilitation Act of 1973 is a law that bans discrimination based on disability. Like IDEA, it provides rights and protections to students with disabilities and requires schools to provide a "free appropriate public education." However, there are some important differences between the two laws.

For one, Section 504 bars discrimination against people with disabilities in "all programs and activities" that get federal funding, which means it's not limited to preK–12 students, nor is it limited to schools. For example, Section 504 is also applicable to public universities and colleges, national parks, and even some types of housing.

Unlike with IDEA, the word *appropriate* in FAPE doesn't provide for specialized instruction under Section 504. Instead, in federally funded preK–12 schools, the intent is to remove barriers to learning for disabled students in the general education classroom so they get the same benefit from the curriculum that their peers do. Often, that means including in a written 504 plan any accommodations a student needs to effectively access the general education curriculum.

Another difference is that while IDEA provides what's needed to meet a student's "unique needs" (1990)—that's the individualized part of an IEP—Section 504 says that institutions don't have to provide accommodations that would either "fundamentally alter" an activity or create an "undue burden" to the institution (1973). And while IDEA specifically provides for modifications for students if they're deemed necessary by the student's IEP team, a 504 plan typically only covers accommodations.

Accommodations vs. Modifications

Many people talk about accommodations and modifications interchangeably, but they're not the same thing. This is important to know because modifications can get in the way of keeping expectations high for all students. Accommodations are changes that give students what they need to access and learn the same curriculum as everyone else. They don't change *what* the student is learning but *how* they're learning it. A modification, however, changes the material a student is taught or the expectations or goals of a lesson in a way that makes what the student is learning different from what everyone else is learning. In other words, it changes *what* they learn.

Definition of Disability Under Section 504

Interestingly, one way in which Section 504 is more expansive than IDEA is in how it defines disability. The definition is when a person:

(i) "has a physical or mental impairment which substantially limits one or more major life activities,

(ii) "has a record of such an impairment, or

(iii) "is regarded as having such an impairment" (1973).

When it comes to neurodivergent students, the above definition is particularly important for two reasons. The first is that it means that a student doesn't need a medical diagnosis to have a 504 plan. In fact, many neurodivergent students who no longer need specialized instruction but still need accommodations transition from IEPs to 504 plans. The second reason is that if someone assumes a student can't or shouldn't do something simply because of their diagnosis, and treats them that way, that student would qualify for protection under Section 504.

Consider, for example, an ADHDer who, when younger, showed significant impulsivity in ways that caused safety concerns. If that ADHDer has gained skills over the years and there are no longer any safety concerns, it would be discriminatory for a teacher to read their file and then preemptively bar them from unsupervised recess or attending field trips.

Do Neurodivergent Students Need IEPs and 504 Plans?

In an ideal world, there would be no need for IEPs and 504 plans for neurodivergent students since all classrooms would be set up to be neurodiversity-affirming and would use Universal Design for Learning. In our realistic world, neurodivergent students may need IEPs or 504 plans to get the instruction they need to flourish in their educational environment.

Since *neurodivergence* is an umbrella term that covers a broad range of neuro-variations, some students might need only slight changes to the classroom environment or minor adjustments to schedules or routines—things that you can implement for all your students. Other students, such as those who are dyslexic or intellectually disabled, need specialized instruction, accommodations, and sometimes even modifications to get the same educational benefit as their neuro-normative peers.

Even within a specific category of neurodivergence, the range of student needs can be broad. For instance, one dyslexic student might manage well in a general education classroom with minor accommodations, while another might need a more intensive structured literacy intervention. In the latter situation, an IEP would be more appropriate for this student than a 504 plan.

What to Look For in an IEP or 504 Plan

How many times have you sat at your desk when prepping for a new school year, looking over IEPs or 504 plans and not knowing exactly what to look for, what is your responsibility to implement, and how to even do it?

If you're not a special education teacher, you may not have much experience with crafting IEPs and 504 plans. That can make it hard to know what to look for when you're reading one. If this sounds like you, the following sections can help.

Making Sense of a 504 Plan

Though there isn't a standardized form that all schools use, 504 plans are still relatively simple to read. In fact, Section 504 doesn't require schools to create a written plan, though most still do. A typical 504 plan has the student's personal information, including the diagnosis or condition that makes them eligible for the plan, and may have the documentation of disability attached to it.

More importantly, it outlines the accommodations the student needs, in what subject areas they need them, and what that might look like in your classroom. For example, you may see that a student needs three things:

- a small-group setting during testing
- number lines or multiplication sheets during math
- frequent checks for understanding during full-class teaching

The 504 plan also has the name of the student's case manager, who can help you figure out either how to make the accommodations yourself or who in the school you can go to for support if you're not sure how to put those accommodations into place.

Making Sense of an IEP

IEPs are more complicated documents than 504 plans, in part because IDEA requires certain information to be included in every IEP. If that information isn't there, the school will be out of compliance. However, this standardization makes it a little bit easier to know what to look for.

Similar to a 504 plan, an IEP has a lot of personal information about a student, including their eligibility category. But that's not the place to linger—knowing a student's diagnosis or identification doesn't mean you know what they need for support. We can't stress enough that knowing the name of a neurodivergent condition or disability doesn't teach you anything about a specific student. A label only gives you a sense of the potential traits you might see.

While it is important to read the whole IEP, there are some key areas where you should dive deeper to understand more about how to support the student in your classroom.

PLOP, PLP, PLAAFP, PLEP

The IEP may include one of these unusual headers, which stand for present level of performance (PLOP or PLP), present level of academic achievement and functional performance (PLAAFP), or present level of educational performance (PLEP). Ideally, you're looking at a student's PLAAFP, because it includes not only their academic strengths and challenges but also their social and emotional and adaptive functioning strengths and challenges. PLAAFP is often framed as how a student's skills compare to the expected grade-level performance. It tends to try to answer these questions:

- What do the student's skills and knowledge currently look like compared to grade-level expectations?
- What is the expected or actual impact of the student's disability on their ability to make progress in the general education curriculum without additional support?

Keep in mind, though, that a PLAAFP is a snapshot in time. This section reflects the student's skills only as they were at the time the IEP was written. Once you've read the PLAAFP, make sure to also go back and read any teacher reports or comments on report cards that can give you a sense of the student's day-to-day performance. If you don't see that information, take the time to talk to previous teachers to find out more.

Notes

Typically, the notes and comments section is at the very end of an IEP. Yet this section is the first place to look if you want to learn more about your student. We recommend you flip to this section to read teacher reports, which provide information about grades and work habits and generally have additional insights into how a student shows up in class. As you read between the lines in this section, it can give you a sense of what the student's experience was with that teacher or subject, which can impact how the student expects to interact with you.

The notes section is also the place where any thoughts, comments, or concerns from the student's family are captured. Depending on who took notes at the IEP meeting, this section may be very detailed or simple bullet points. Either way, it gives you a good place to start getting to know more about your student outside of school. Knowing what worries a student's caregivers, what strengths they see in their child, and what works to support their child at home helps you begin building a relationship with the student and their family. The notes can also give you information about what interests and motivates the student, as well information about what hasn't worked well in teachers' past attempts at building connections.

Goals

Goals are one of the most critical elements of an IEP. IEP goals are based on a student's PLAAFP and outline what the team who created the IEP thinks is reasonable for the student to accomplish in an academic year. Ideally, IEP goals should be standards based, meaning the expectations align with grade-level academic standards for your school and state. They should also be SMART: **s**pecific; **m**easurable; **a**ttainable; **r**ealistic, **r**elevant, and **r**esults-oriented; and **t**ime-bound.

IEP goals outline the skills the student needs to focus on in applicable subject areas and what the end result should look like. As one of the student's teachers, you'll be responsible for tracking progress on these goals and reporting back to the IEP team.

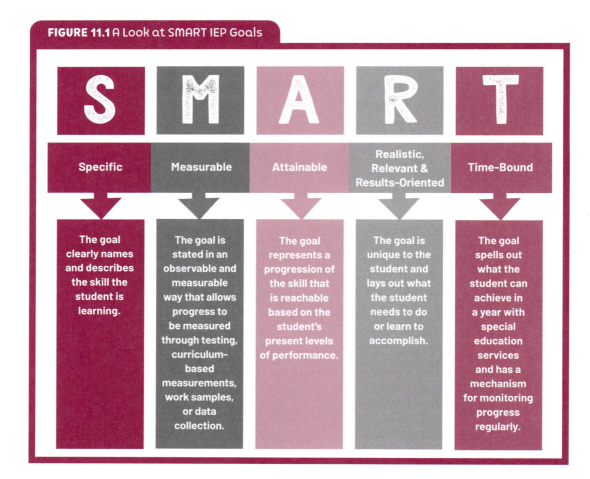

FIGURE 11.1 A Look at SMART IEP Goals

S	M	A	R	T
Specific	Measurable	Attainable	Realistic, Relevant & Results-Oriented	Time-Bound
The goal clearly names and describes the skill the student is learning.	The goal is stated in an observable and measurable way that allows progress to be measured through testing, curriculum-based measurements, work samples, or data collection.	The goal represents a progression of the skill that is reachable based on the student's present levels of performance.	The goal is unique to the student and lays out what the student needs to do or learn to accomplish.	The goal spells out what the student can achieve in a year with special education services and has a mechanism for monitoring progress regularly.

Supplementary Aids, Services, Modifications, and Supports

This section of the IEP is often overlooked, but it's important information for general education teachers, since you'll be responsible for putting any accommodations, modifications, and assistive technology into place in the classroom. All those things are listed in this section, but there's also an opportunity here for the IEP team to provide you training and education about assistive technologies and the student's disability, if needed. If you feel like you need additional professional development around neurodivergence to support the student, this is the place where that can be specifically named. And because an IEP is a legal document, any professional development named in it is required by law to be provided to you.

Special Education and Related Services

This section is what most sets an IEP apart from a 504 plan because it outlines the specially designed instruction (special education) and related services a student needs to make progress toward their goals. Related services include speech, physical, or occupational therapy, counseling, and other services.

In this section of the IEP, you'll learn how often each service will take place, who (by role) will provide the service or instruction, and what your part in it is. In a neurodiversity-affirming environment, these services may happen in your classroom instead of outside of it. That means you'll need to plan your lessons carefully and work with the other educators to make sure schedules match up.

Rethinking Least Restrictive Environment

This concern of students being held apart from peers informs one of the key tenets of IDEA—a concept known as least restrictive environment, or LRE. Most of the time, the first thing people stress about LRE is that despite the use of the word *environment*, it's not talking about the place where a student learns, but the entire educational program. This includes services the student receives and how they are provided. That's because IDEA intended it that way. IDEA says:

> To the maximum extent appropriate, children with disabilities, including children in public or private institutions or other care facilities, are educated with children who are not disabled and special classes, separate schooling, or other removal of

children with disabilities from the regular educational environment occurs only when the nature or severity of the disability is such that education in regular classes with the use of supplementary aids and services cannot be achieved satisfactorily (1990).

So, what does that actually mean? This is where we come back to the word *appropriate*.

IDEA is saying that students with IEPs should be educated alongside nondisabled students as much as possible. Historically, disabled students were educated in separate classrooms from students who didn't receive special education services. IDEA tries to correct for that through the principle of LRE, and when it was added to the law in 2004, many schools began to "mainstream" students to meet the requirements of the law. Put more simply, schools tried to make sure as many students as possible spent as much time as possible in general education classrooms. In this regard, LRE has become more about the place than the program.

But the question of whether the general education classroom is the *appropriate* setting for a student sometimes gets lost in this interpretation of LRE. It's not always in the best interest of students to be in the general education classroom, and not just because they have such severe disabilities that they need specialized programs all day. Some educators and parents feel that this interpretation of LRE doesn't always serve the best interests of neurodivergent students.

Joseph

Joseph, a twice-exceptional, autistic fourteen-year-old, loved to read, read quickly, and felt passionate about having deep discussions about books and their themes. He communicated in a way that worked for him, sharing his opinions and thoughts with confidence while avoiding eye contact and often raising his voice to punctuate his points. His English teacher, Ms. Greene, did not have a lot of experience teaching twice-exceptional autistic students. She had difficulty understanding that Joseph was neither picking up on her gentle hints that it was time to move on from a topic nor reading her nonverbal cues to lower his voice.

While most of the class read at the assigned pace, Joseph was so engrossed in the material that he often read ahead. He was confused about why Ms. Greene asked him to stop reading ahead and not to talk about parts of the book other students hadn't yet read. The two ended up in a cycle in which Ms. Greene took Joseph's tone of voice personally and treated it as a behavior problem. In turn, Joseph's frustration grew, and his emotional regulation skills dropped as he tried to explain his thinking and communication to Ms. Greene.

Eventually, an IEP meeting was held to discuss how to help improve the situation. As the team talked, it became clear that the accommodations the team had already put into place weren't working for either Ms. Greene or Joseph, even after they'd been revisited and revised. The setup and pace of the classroom also wasn't working well for Joseph. While academically it made sense for him to be in the class, there was an adverse impact on his learning because Ms. Greene was asking him to leave class daily when he became emotionally dysregulated. This was also impacting how his peers viewed him.

One team member asked a key question: *Is this classroom really the LRE for Joseph?* The team was split in opinion. Most of them argued that for a student who could keep up with and understand the material at grade level—or even beyond—the general education setting was nonnegotiable as his LRE. Other team members argued that Joseph wasn't meeting grade-level social and emotional expectations in the current environment.

A compromise was made, and the LRE was redetermined: Joseph would spend four days a week doing reading and other work in the library as an independent study and would join the larger group one day a week for discussion. Once this was implemented, Joseph was able to learn at his own pace and self-regulate more easily, and he and Ms. Greene were able to find a way to respect each other's communication styles.

Joseph's story shows that what is "appropriate" isn't always what's obvious, standard, or easy. It demonstrates a need to reexamine your ideas of LRE and advocate for a more flexible understanding and application of the principle to support neurodivergent students in growing not just academically but socially and emotionally as well. It's an example of the fact that while inclusion in the general education classroom is beneficial for many students, it might not always be the best fit for every student. In fact, Joseph's story illustrates that placement without careful thought can defeat the original intent of LRE—making sure students can be included with their peers as much as possible. Being included doesn't just mean being near others. It means being in a place in which you're understood and feel a sense of belonging. In Joseph's case, being in the general education environment caused him to be less included with his peers.

Again, the key word here is *appropriate*. There isn't just one environment that's appropriate for all students. Each student's unique needs and circumstances should determine their placement. Simply placing a student in a general education classroom doesn't guarantee specialized instruction that meets their unique needs. Without proper support, training for general education teachers, or appropriate resources, the student might not benefit from such placement and may even, like Joseph, be harmed by it.

Rethinking IEP Goals to Be Neurodiversity-Affirming

LRE isn't the only element of IEPs that could benefit from being looked at through a neurodiversity-affirming lens. Too often IEP goals are deficit-based and focus on expecting students to conform to neuro-norms for how they should learn or behave. Regardless of a student's disability, an IEP should be personalized to the student's unique strengths and challenges. When it comes to neurodivergent students, that means collaborating with the student, their family, and the entire team to ensure that the IEP goals truly support and affirm the student's neurodivergence. It means focusing on the student's strengths and interests while addressing their areas of need in a way that recognizes how they think, learn, and engage with the world.

Neurodiversity-affirming goals support growth by being respectful of neurodivergence and not expecting adherence to neuro-norms. If you go back to the SMART goals framework, it's neither attainable nor realistic to expect students to mask or to act and learn in ways that go against their neurological makeup. Creating neurodiversity-affirming goals begins by changing the language used in evaluation reports (figure 11.2) to describe skills and deficits.

FIGURE 11.2 Typical vs. Neurodiversity-Affirming IEP Language

Typical Report Language	Neurodiversity-Affirming Report
Ana shows language delay characterized by weaknesses with sentence structure, word structure, expressive vocabulary, following directions, recalling sentences, and basic concepts.	Ana shows language delay characterized by weaknesses with . . . **Strengths identified by testing include** _____.
Ana lacks age-appropriate social communication skills. Ana didn't maintain a topic of conversation, exchange greetings with the clinician, or ask questions when she didn't hear or understand information.	Ana **didn't use or understand typical** social communication skills, as indicated by not maintaining a topic of conversation **as expected** or exchanging **expected** greetings with the clinician. Ana **didn't know** to ask questions when she didn't hear or understand information.
Ana was easily distracted and had difficulty following directions. Ana was observed leaving her seat when she no longer wanted to participate in an activity.	Ana was easily distracted **by** _____ and had difficulty following directions. Ana was observed leaving her seat when she was **no longer able to** participate in an activity.

Goals themselves can be made attainable and realistic by being strengths-based, emphasizing what the student can do and how their way of engaging with the world or areas of interest can help them achieve growth. Figure 11.3 compares a few examples of typical and neurodiversity-affirming IEP goals. Following are some of the skills you might consider when thinking through how to support a student in reaching their goals and in feeling a sense of belonging.

Skill: Self-Advocacy

What it means: Encouraging students to understand and communicate their needs.

What it can look like in a goal: By the end of the academic year, Ana will accurately describe her learning preferences, use specific accommodations, or employ supportive strategies as needed.

Skill: Social Interaction

What it means: Aiming for mutual understanding and genuine connections instead of forcing neuro-normative behavior.

What it can look like in a goal: Ana will engage with peers in ways and at times that are comfortable to her.

Skill: Sensory Needs

What it means: Recognizing and validating sensory regulation needs.

What it can look like in a goal: Ana will use sensory breaks or tools during classroom activities to support her self-regulation.

Skill: Flexible Thinking

What it means: Working on adaptability while respecting a student's unique thinking style.

What it can look like in a goal: Ana will be given the time to explain or demonstrate her strategies or approaches to solving math problems when an approach didn't work so that the teacher can share different strategies.

Skill: Executive Functioning

What it means: Helping students plan, prioritize, organize, and execute tasks in a manner that aligns with their unique cognitive process.

What it can look like in a goal: By the end of the academic year, Ana will utilize her interest in visual aids to organize and plan her assignments, breaking them down into manageable tasks and employing self-identified strategies to complete them on time.

FIGURE 11.3 Typical vs. Neurodiversity-Affirming IEP Goals

Typical Goals	Neurodiversity-Affirming Goals
Ana will maintain a topic of conversation through turn-taking with a minimum of X conversational exchanges. Ana will ask age-appropriate questions about a situation as reported/observed by parents and observed by clinician.	Ana will increase understanding of neuro-normative styles of communication as measured by the ability to identify and/or describe situations in which they could be employed.
Ana shows active listening skills as reported by parents and observed by clinicians and teachers. Ana will respond to teasing/disappointment appropriately as observed by teachers and clinicians.	Ana will clarify unclear communication with a person that she feels safe with, as measured by her ability to verbally or nonverbally indicate her misunderstanding and desire to understand.
Ana will reduce/extinguish/replace vocal stimming and/or participate in an activity by staying seated and still for X minutes.	Ana will be able identify events, situations, or activities in the environment that cause her to feel stressed and use identified calming/coping strategies to feel safe and calm.

Personalized Student Learning Plans

Student learning plans (SLPs) are used to provide personalized education and support to students, but traditionally have targeted different populations of students than IEPs or 504 plans (US DoE 2017). SLPs tend to be more often used in private or innovative charter schools than they are in public schools. Similar to an IEP, an SLP is a personalized document or framework that outlines a student's goals, interests, strengths, and areas for growth in their education.

Different from IEPs, SLPs are not reserved for only students who need special education. Instead, they're designed for every student to help them take a more active role in their learning, set meaningful goals for themselves, and track their own progress over time. SLPs are often used to encourage self-directed learning and to foster in students a sense of ownership and responsibility for their education. Key components of an SLP may include the following:

- **SMART goals:** SLP goals tend to be goals that a student has identified as objectives they want to achieve. These goals don't focus on only academics—they include personal, social, and career-related areas too.
- **Strengths and interests:** SLPs identify a student's strengths, talents, and areas of interest to guide the development of goals and activities that align with their passions and abilities.
- **Areas for growth:** SLPs summarize the areas where a student wants to improve or grow. Again, this doesn't just focus on academic areas.
- **Action steps:** SLPs often break down the steps a student needs to take to achieve their goals. These steps may be specific tasks, projects, courses, classes, or extracurricular activities.
- **Strategies and resources:** SLPs tend to also include suggested strategies, accommodations, tools, and resources that can assist a student in achieving their goals. These resources can include outside-the-box ideas, including mentorship opportunities, online courses, or internships.
- **Progress tracking:** SLPs provide mechanisms for tracking progress and assessing whether a student is making gains toward achieving their goals. This may involve regular reflections, assessments, and updates.
- **Reflection and evaluation:** SLPs often include ways for a student to reflect on their experiences, challenges, and achievements in ways that lead to adjusting or updating goals.
- **Long-term vision:** SLPs often look beyond the near future, addressing and outlining long-term educational and career hopes and ambitions.

SLPs help students become more engaged and proactive learners, fostering skills such as time management, self-assessment, and goal setting.

Unpacking Neurodivergence

Blending IEPs and Personalized Student Learning Plans—A Vision for Inclusive Education

Emily: In schools, we talk a lot about IEPs in a special education context. And then we also talk about personalized student learning plans. Do you see strengths-based tools or ideas being effectively integrated into IEPs, or do you think there's too much focus on deficits?

Amanda: Right now, I believe there's too much focus on deficits. In an ideal world, IEPs would be strengths-based—looking at what a student can do, their interests, and what they excel at—as ways to motivate them and engage them in their own learning, especially in areas where they struggle. But there's a lot of work to be done to get there.

One of the things that gets in the way is compliance. IEPs are legal documents, so there are many regulations around how they must be written, how we should measure progress, and how we can establish a baseline. But I believe there's room to add in what the student is doing really well and how we can address those strengths *and* grade-level expectations, while still meeting the regulations. We're not there yet, but I think we're getting closer, with more and more people interested in making it happen.

Emily: What do you see as the future for SLPs?

Amanda: I'm not sure yet. But I think there's an opportunity to blend IEPs and SLPs, because I believe that IEPs should also be aspirational and motivate student progress. However, I do have concerns about focusing solely on SLPs and overlooking IEPs, because some students do need specialized instruction. I would love to see every student have a personalized learning plan that, if appropriate, also includes the specialized instruction they need.

Some schools are doing experimental things around having SLPs for all students, but we haven't seen enough of it yet, especially in the long term, to know how it integrates with the special education world. I hope we can get to a place where we have an army of teachers with the time and ability to put together personalized plans for all their students. I believe this is a good way that schools are starting to look at a neurodiversity-affirming environment. Each student is unique, with their own strengths and challenges. It's important to discuss these with students so they can understand themselves better and we can understand them better as well.

Creating Neurodiversity-Affirming Learning Plans

IEPs, 504 plans, and SLPs all share the goal of personalizing education for students, but they serve different purposes and are used for different groups of students. On the surface SLPs seem best suited to support neurodiversity-affirming schools. They *are* more inclusive and applicable to all students; they focus on holistic growth, support strengths, and encourage self-directed learning. They also take a lot of time and effort to implement, and they don't carry the same legal protections as an IEP or 504 plan does.

The big question, then, is *How can you take the best elements of each to create plans that celebrate and support neurodivergent students?*

Whatever kind of learning plan you're working with, you can start by approaching it from a perspective that recognizes neurodiversity as a natural variation of human cognition rather than a deficit to be fixed. When you embrace the idea that different neuro-types all have value in contributing to the school and classroom culture, it's much easier to create plans that identify and build on strengths, talents, and interests and that allow the student to excel in the areas where they shine.

In that spirit, many schools are beginning to implement "strengths-based IEPs." These plans look at the whole student, including their academic skills, cognitive patterns, social and emotional skills, background, and interests. It requires a mindset shift when looking at IEPs to ensure that all these components are considered, that strengths are uplifted, and that more weight is given to strengths, interests, and preferences than to deficits (Rawe, n.d.).

By putting the student at the center of the conversation, a strengths-based IEP encourages self-advocacy. It relies on collaboration and conversation between schools, families, and students about what is important to know about the student, how they show up in the world, and what they think of their learning experience. In other words, strengths-based IEPs are primed to be neurodiversity-affirming. Here's how:

- **Strengths-based IEPs start by looking at abilities** before addressing and naming deficits.
- **Strengths-based IEPs look at what students want to be able to do** as well as what the IEP team wants students to be able to do. They also examine how those two things align with the student's strengths and use that information to set shared goals.
- **Strengths-based IEPs puts an emphasis on strengths**, allowing both students and educators to recognize the value of the unique qualities the student brings to the classroom.
- **Strengths-based IEPs ask teams to learn more** about their students, from their students. Students are encouraged to share their interests, preferences for learning and communication, and other information that can help teachers support them in being authentically themselves.
- **Strengths-based IEPs celebrate and encourage self-awareness and self-advocacy** and put into place strategies for building both.

Zenia

Zenia was eight years old when she was evaluated by the school. Her parents had expressed concern that she still couldn't match sounds to letters and struggled to recognize sight words. Her teachers shared this concern and had additional concerns about Zenia's ability to decode and encode when reading and writing. A school evaluation revealed she had characteristics of dyslexia. When the team sat down to discuss the evaluation and next steps, her teacher began the meeting by saying, "Zenia is such a sweet, caring child. She never gives me any trouble." Zenia's mother smiled, put her hand in the air, and said, "Thank you, but we are not here because my child never gives you trouble. We are here to talk about why my child is having trouble. What does she do well that is going to help her be better?"

Too often, IEP teams start the conversation about a student's strengths in a way similar to the example with Zenia. They discuss strengths in the context of what they like about a student, not in actionable ways that can be connected to an IEP. Zenia was indeed a sweet and caring child. She also was tenacious, eager to learn, and loved to make up stories to go with the pictures in books. By reframing the discussion to ask what she did well, Zenia's mother helped the team focus on Zenia's abilities as a way to support her learning moving forward.

Of course, the range of neurodivergent conditions is vast, and every student will have their own unique strengths, but there are ways to reframe some of the traits we might typically think of as deficits to see them through a strengths-based lens. Figure 11.4 on the next page shares some common neurodivergent traits, how they're often described from a deficit-based perspective in learning plans, and how to reframe those descriptions using a strengths-based perspective.

It's key to remember that while neurodivergent students have many strengths, they don't always have superpowers that overshadow their challenges. Too often there's a perception that disabled students must have some exceptional talent that compensates for their struggles. This expectation can get in the way of students getting the extra support they need. This so-called "super-crip" trope makes it hard to keep in mind that it's okay to be average (Alaniz 2014; Grue 2021). The goal of focusing on strengths is to offer a more balanced perspective, promote understanding and acceptance, and create a learning plan that is distinctly suited to the student.

Engaging Students in Creating Learning Plans

Creating a strengths-based, whole-child learning plan necessitates collaboration, and the student must play an active and leading role in any meetings about the plan. A student-led meeting allows your student to speak about themself, while also having your support and that of their family. It shows mutual respect and gives the student agency to make decisions about their own learning. Here are some ways to bring students into the planning process:

FIGURE 11.4 Deficit-Based vs. Strengths-Based Perspective for Common Neurodivergent Traits

Deficit-Based Lens		Strengths-Based Lens	
Trait	**Language**	**Trait**	**Language**
Fixated	can become overly fixated or obsessed, neglecting other important tasks or areas	**Deeply focused**	is able to concentrate intently on a subject of interest for extended periods
Misses the bigger picture	gets bogged down in the small details	**Detail-oriented**	notices and recalls specific details that others might overlook
Struggles to understand others' views	doesn't consider other points of view	**Has a unique perspective**	often sees things from a different angle than peers do, leading to innovative solutions
Gets stuck on specific interest	gets immersed in a single interest to the point of excluding other activities or topics	**Has passions and interests**	can develop deep passions and interests, leading to expertise in specific areas
Doesn't understand social nuance	struggles with understanding or processing emotional nuances or nonverbal social cues	**Very logical thinker**	may approach problems and situations with a structured and logical mindset
Perseverates	fixates and ruminates on past events or conversations	**Has a long and strong memory**	ability to recall specific details or information over time
Easily sensorially overloaded	easily overwhelmed or distressed by sensory stimuli	**Sensitive to changes in the environment**	can notice and observe subtle changes in the environment that others cannot
At-risk for being bullied	gets attached to others and doesn't recognize when they're taking advantage	**Loyal**	often deeply loyal to friends, family, and causes
Rude	offends people by being too blunt	**Honest**	is straightforward and believes in speaking truthfully
Struggles don't break routines	doesn't do well without structure or when faced with change	**Systematic thinker**	recognizes and prefers patterns, sequences, and systems in the world

FIGURE 11.4 Deficit-Based vs. Strengths-Based Perspective for Common Neurodivergent Traits

	Deficit-Based Lens		Strengths-Based Lens	
	Trait	**Language**	**Trait**	**Language**
	"Outside the box" thinker	has trouble thinking or working within established norms	Creative thinker	often has a unique and creative way of thinking
	Inflexible	can be stubborn	Persistent	faces challenges head-on and is often persistent in endeavors
	Limited interests	interests are too specialized	Studies things intensely	dives deeply into areas of interest and develops expertise
	Rigid and unapproachable	comes across as unyielding or standoffish	Sets clear boundaries	clearly articulates personal boundaries
	Doesn't understand euphemistic language or tone of voice	difficulty understanding sarcasm, metaphors, or abstract concepts	Linear and literal thinker	excels in situations that require clear, direct understanding
	Perfectionist	takes too long to complete tasks due to overemphasis on perfection	Thorough	completes tasks with attention and thoroughness
	Socially naive	lacks tact	Authentic	often genuine in interactions and lacks artifice
	Doesn't follow through, has trouble with transitions	neglects other tasks, responsibilities, or social interactions when involved in an activity of high interest	Hyperfocused	ability to focus intensely on tasks, often leading to high productivity in areas of interest
	Struggles to communicate emotions as expected	doesn't show emotion or demonstrate empathy in socially expected ways	Empathetic	possesses a deep empathy for others, and expresses it in their unique way

- **Teach students to read their learning plans and dial back the jargon.** Just like teachers, students should be able to understand the elements of their learning plans and the terms used in them. If you don't know what LRE is, for example, don't assume a student does. Take the time to run through the acronyms and explain things like goals, services, and accommodations.

- **Ask for students' input.** Remember that notes section of the plan? It rarely says "Student is concerned about . . ." or "Student states that . . ." If your student won't be at the meeting, ask them for their thoughts in advance. They can tell you what's going well and what's not working and identify strengths and interests they have that you may not know about.

- **Practice self-advocacy and other meeting-related skills.** Unless someone attends meetings on a regular basis, they don't know what to expect. And students don't go to that many meetings. Help them practice how to introduce themselves, interject, ask a clarifying question, share information, and even how to exit a meeting.

Here are some resources for more on student-led meetings:

- "Implementing Student-Led Conferences in Your School" by Patti Kinney (mlei.pbworks.com/f/SLCPP.pdf)

- "Student Led Conferences Responsibilities and Protocol" (scholastic.com/content/dam/teachers/blogs/john-depasquale/migrated-files/student_led_conference_protocol.pdf)

- "Leaders of Their Own Learning, Chapter 5: Student-Led Conferences" (eleducation.org/resources/leaders-of-their-own-learning-chapter-5-student-led-conferences)

- "The Power of Student-Led Conferences in Primary Grades" (edweek.org/education/opinion-the-power-of-student-led-conferences-in-primary-grades/2016/06)

What to Remember

- Neurodivergent students may need IEPs or 504 plans that lay out special services, ranging from minor accommodations to specialized instruction, depending on the broad and varying needs associated with their specific neurodivergence.
- Rethinking IEPs requires a neurodiversity-affirming approach that emphasizes collaboration, focuses on students' unique strengths and challenges, and ensures attainable and realistic goals that respect students' ways of thinking, learning, and engaging with the world, rather than expecting them to conform to traditional norms.
- Planning holistic IEPs requires collaboration with students, achieved by teaching them to understand their learning plans, seeking their input, helping them practice self-advocacy, and recognizing their strengths without expecting exceptional talents. This inclusion fosters understanding and the creation of tailored learning plans.

Chapter 12

Mental Health Needs

Points to Ponder

- How is the mental health of neurodivergent students impacted by the practices in place in schools?
- What unmet needs and unfulfilled accommodations might negatively impact the mental well-being of neurodivergent students?
- Which classroom strategies that are used to support the mental health of neuro-normative students are effective for neurodivergent students? Which are not?

In chapter 2, we discussed the differences between neurodivergent diagnoses and psychological ones. However, it is important to remember that neurodivergence and mental health needs can and do frequently overlap. You need to consider the mental health needs of your neurodivergent students in order to best support them. Additionally, school counselors are an integral part of creating neurodiversity-affirming schools, and they are often the first responders to many mental health crises.

Understanding the overlap between neurodivergence and mental health needs is vital for creating an environment that supports neurodivergent students.

Many of the mental health needs of neurodivergent students can be mitigated by the strategies already discussed in this book. Providing neurodiversity-affirming schools relieves many of the stressors and situations that can trigger mental health concerns. For example, a student who has a teacher who understands them and peers who accept them is less likely to experience depression caused by loneliness and exclusion (Chapman et al. 2022). A student whose feeling of unease evolves into a clinical anxiety diagnosis might have avoided this diagnosis if they weren't constantly afraid of getting in trouble for their executive functioning difficulties (Pliszka 2019).

In addition to understanding the impact of the school environment on neurodivergent learners' mental health, it's important to recognize that the types of support commonly provided for mental health needs in schools may not be in the best interests of these students. Viewing mental health needs through the lens of neurodivergence helps guide how to choose interventions, whether in the classroom or the school counseling office.

The Connection Between Neurodivergence and Mental Health

The mental health statistics for neurodivergent people are sobering. These are just a few:

- Among autistic adults, 27 percent meet diagnostic criteria for a current anxiety disorder; 42 percent have met criteria for a diagnosis at some point in their lifetime (Menezes et al. 2022).
- A meta-analysis (prior to COVID) showed the lifetime rate of depression among autistic individuals without an intellectual disability was 14.4 percent, compared with only 4.4 percent of the global population (Hudson, Hall, and Harkness 2019).
- Thirteen percent of ADHDers in young adulthood attempt suicide. This is more than four times the rate of suicide attempts among non-ADHD young adults (Nock et al. 2008).

- A meta-analysis of ADHDers in their childhood and teen years found that all the studies reviewed showed an association between ADHD and suicidal ideation and attempts (Garas and Balazs 2020).
- AuDHD adolescents showed rates of depression of nearly 40 percent (Accardo, Pontes, and Pontes 2022).
- One study found that 54 percent of people with learning disabilities met the diagnostic criteria for depression and anxiety (Cooper et al. 2007).
- Students who have been identified as having learning disabilities are 4.5 times more likely to have a diagnosed mental health condition than their peers who do not have learning disabilities (Emerson and Hatton 2007).

The school environment can actively create experiences that are stressful and isolating for neurodivergent students, and the experiences themselves can play a significant role in triggering mental health conditions or exacerbating preexisting mental health vulnerabilities. Many factors—such as neurodivergence, genetic predisposition, personality traits, and coping mechanisms—and their interplay can influence whether a student's mental health needs meet the threshold for a clinical diagnosis. For example, prolonged exposure to stressors such as academic pressures, social challenges, bullying, or major life changes can lead to or exacerbate depression, anxiety, or trauma-related disorders. These stressors may act as a catalyst, bringing mental health conditions to the surface or magnifying them to the point of significant concern. Figure 12.1 provides a few examples.

Sorting Out Emotions from Diagnoses

When we talk about feelings of anxiety or sadness, we're often referring to normal emotional reactions that everyone experiences. These feelings can arise from stress, worry, disappointment, or various other common circumstances. However, having a diagnosis of a mental health disorder like generalized anxiety or depression is not the same as experiencing those emotions. It is helpful to your students if you understand this distinction.

For example, feeling anxious from time to time, like before an important test, presentation, or performance, is a natural part of being human that can help someone

FIGURE 12.1 Overlapping Neurodivergence and Mental Health Needs

Neurodivergent Trait	Example	Mental Health Outcome
Differences in developing social relationships	An autistic student feels disconnected from their peers and, although they desire closer friendships, they are often excluded.	The long-term impact of desiring closer relationships but being unable to attain them can lead to this student's lowered self-esteem, loneliness, and clinical depression.
Trouble sustaining attention when there are outside stimuli	An ADHDer finds it nearly impossible to concentrate during a test. Their difficulty focusing leads to impulsive or incomplete responses on the test.	Repeated poor grades on tests and stress responses during test-taking can lead to performance/test anxiety (a form of social anxiety).
Difficulty meeting academic expectations	When asked to read aloud in class, a dyslexic student stumbles over words and reads very slowly.	Feelings of inadequacy and shame lead to a sense of learned helplessness, unwillingness to take risks, and anxiety surrounding school.
Sensory processing differences	An AuDHDer becomes overwhelmed by the noise and bright lights of the cafeteria. When they begin experiencing panic and anxiety, they are told they must remain in the cafeteria with their class.	The sensory overwhelm of the school environment leads to anxiety in the student, which manifests as school avoidance.

focus on the task at hand (Maric, Bexkens, and Bögels 2018). Generalized anxiety, however, is a persistent and pervasive condition that often interferes with a person's daily life. It's not just about feeling anxious occasionally; it's about consistent and excessive worry that can become crippling. The worry is often hard to control and may seem out of proportion to the actual risk involved.

Similarly, feeling sad or lonely now and then, especially in response to specific events or changes, is typical. Depression is not typical—it is a more severe and chronic condition. Clinical depression is not feeling blue for a couple of days; it's a constant sense of despair and hopelessness that can last for weeks, months, or even longer. People suffering from depression might lose interest in activities they once enjoyed, struggle with sleep, feel fatigued, and even have thoughts of self-injury or suicide (APA 2013).

So how do clinicians differentiate between these different levels? The process typically is aimed at understanding the intensity, duration, and impact of the feelings on a person's life. For a clinical diagnosis, symptoms must typically persist for an extended period, like six months for generalized anxiety and at least two weeks for depression. They must also cause significant distress or impair the person's ability to function in essential aspects of life.

Clinicians also look for other underlying causes or factors. For example, feelings of anxiety or sadness may be attributed to a specific event or situation. In contrast, generalized anxiety disorder and depression may lack clear external triggers, though persistent exposure to stressful environments or unhealthy social relationships can be the initiating event for developing symptoms for those diagnoses (National Institute of Mental Health, n.d.).

Many ADHDers describe the phenomenon of being so stressed out about their lagging executive functioning skills that they overcompensate with hypervigilance and perfectionism. This effort eventually lasts long enough and is impactful enough to qualify for a diagnosis of generalized anxiety (Strohmeier et al. 2016). Some autistic people end up on high alert for changes that will impact their sensory processing or feel so frequently misunderstood when communicating that they withdraw from relationships. The resulting feelings of inadequacy and loneliness can reach the threshold for a depression diagnosis (Kojovic et al. 2019). While neither neurodivergence nor uncomfortable emotions are the sole cause of mental health struggles, they can indeed be influenced by external factors and ultimately add up to a mental health diagnosis.

Misdiagnosis of Neurodivergence and Psychological Conditions

Although schools aren't responsible for diagnosing mental health conditions, there may be times when being able to recognize the difference between a psychological diagnosis and characteristics of neurodivergence is important for educators. The team that determines which assessments to complete for a possible IEP is influenced by what they *assume* is impacting the student. Recognizing how some of the overlaps between neurodivergent and mental health diagnoses might manifest can be helpful in this process.

Masking behavior is a common reason for misdiagnosis among neurodivergent individuals. An autistic student who has learned to mask their struggles with social cues and reciprocal communication might appear excessively shy or anxious in social situations. If educators or clinicians don't recognize the masking behavior, they might explain the areas of concern as social anxiety instead of looking for and recognizing the underlying autism. Similarly, an ADHDer may mask their difficulties with executive functioning by becoming overly meticulous and rigid in their routines. This behavior can be misinterpreted as symptoms of generalized anxiety rather than a coping strategy for ADHD. Research shows that the more an autistic person camouflages, the higher they score on assessments of generalized anxiety, social anxiety, and depression (Hull et al. 2021).

Stigma and misinterpretation play significant roles in misdiagnosis as well. The stigma surrounding autism might lead families (or even clinicians) to prefer a diagnosis of a mental health condition like depression or anxiety over a diagnosis of autism. Because of this, an individual struggling with social connections due to autism might be inaccurately diagnosed with depression, as it is more socially accepted (Lewis 2017; Haney 2016). Additionally, cultural stigma and gender biases may lead to some ADHDers being overlooked or misdiagnosed with anxiety or mood disorders. Their inattentiveness and daydreaming may not align with the stereotypical hyperactive ADHD behavior often associated with male ADHDers, leading to a failure to recognize these students' underlying condition (Corkum et al. 2015).

Lack of awareness and education can further complicate diagnosis. A child with sensory processing differences may become overwhelmed and anxious in certain environments, like a loud classroom or cafeteria. Without understanding this student's underlying sensory sensitivities, adults might assume they have an anxiety disorder and miss recognizing the neurodivergent trait. Some autistic individuals may engage in repetitive behaviors or have specific routines that, to an uninformed observer, might resemble symptoms of obsessive-compulsive thinking. Without recognizing the broader context of autism, a clinician might misdiagnose such people with OCD.

It is important to accurately understand what is impacting a student, since misdiagnosing neurodivergent traits as mental health conditions can lead to misguided interventions. An autistic student diagnosed with social anxiety might be treated with supports aimed at typical social development rather than receiving support tailored to their neurodivergent needs. An ADHDer misdiagnosed with generalized anxiety might receive anxiety-focused therapy, which would fail to address their underlying issues with attention regulation and executive functioning.

The path to correct diagnosis is fraught with complexities that can easily lead to misinterpretation of neurodivergent traits as psychological disorders. Understanding the nuances of masking, recognizing the influence of societal stigma, and investing in proper education and awareness are critical to accurately differentiating between neurodivergence and mental health conditions.

Considerations for Counseling Interventions

In the field of education, particularly for those in the roles of school counselor, school psychologist, or school social worker, the challenge of differentiating between neurodivergent traits and mental health conditions is further complicated by the task of providing support that is both appropriate and affirming of neurodiversity. The traditional counseling methods applied to treat generalized anxiety or depression might not necessarily fit the unique needs of a neurodivergent child with a co-occuring mental health diagnosis, whether they are autistic, are an ADHDer, or have other neurodivergent traits.

A neurodiversity-affirming approach requires an understanding of the student's specific neurodivergent traits, preferences, sensory sensitivities, communication styles, and coping mechanisms. Interventions should be individualized and contextualized, reflecting not only the mental health symptoms but also the underlying neurodivergent characteristics. For example, an autistic student who struggles with social anxiety might benefit from supports that consider both their anxiety and the specific challenges they experience related to autism, such as sensory sensitivities or difficulties in understanding social cues.

Interventions that seek to "normalize" neurodivergent students, making them conform to societal expectations without regard to their comfort or individuality, are unlikely to be effective and are not neurodiversity-affirming. A clear example is the application of behaviorally based strategies, such as behavior modification plans that rely on rewards and punishments (see pages 140–147 for more). Such approaches can lead to masking, which can then lead to increased stress, anxiety, and even more significant mental health concerns. For those working in educational support roles, it becomes imperative to identify and then either avoid or adapt these interventions.

Similarly, traditional social skills groups often focus on teaching neuro-normative social behaviors, such as maintaining eye contact or engaging in small talk. However, these are often inauthentic and uncomfortable for neurodivergent students, who may communicate and socialize in different ways. Reframing these groups to focus on social acuity (see page 226) is a more meaningful and affirming approach. Teaching neurodivergent students to understand social cues and adapt without compromising their genuine selves leads them to have more satisfying social connections—especially when combined with teaching all students to value neurodivergent communication patterns.

Finally, interventions that ignore the strengths and interests of neurodivergent students, focusing only on their areas of deficit or challenge, can lead these students to experience a negative self-image and lack of motivation. Emphasizing and building upon what a neurodivergent student does well (see chapter 10), however, fosters a sense of competence and engagement.

Finding effective counseling interventions for neurodivergent students requires careful consideration of those interventions that may be counterproductive. It calls for a shift from conventional techniques to more personalized, empathetic, and neurodiversity-affirming methods. The focus must always be on understanding and supporting the student in ways that respect their unique neurodivergent traits, rather than attempting to mold them to fit preexisting societal norms. By recognizing the complexity of neurodivergence and being willing to adapt and innovate, educators can create a truly inclusive and empowering learning environment.

Neurodiversity-Affirming Clinical Practices

Luca, age 13, autistic
NON-NEURODIVERSITY-AFFIRMING APPROACH: Luca began working with the mental health counselor at their school due to challenges identified by teachers related to Luca's social interactions and sensory sensitivities. The counselor focused on trying to make Luca behave more "typically," using rigid behavioral interventions. The counselor also disregarded Luca's unique interests and sensory needs, pushing Luca to suppress stimming and engage in social interactions that felt uncomfortable. This led to increased anxiety for Luca and a lack of progress in both counseling sessions and the classroom.

NEURODIVERSITY-AFFIRMING APPROACH: Luca worked with a counselor who understood and respected their neurodivergence. The counselor recognized Luca's unique strengths and interests and used them to build rapport and develop appropriate goals. Together, they worked to create strategies to help Luca navigate social situations in a way that felt authentic to them and addressed their sensory sensitivities with compassion. Luca showed progress in self-confidence and their ability to interact with peers.

Anika, age 15, ADHD
NON-NEURODIVERSITY-AFFIRMING APPROACH: Anika's struggles with focus and organization led to underachievement in school. The school psychologist approached Anika's ADHD as a defect that needed to be fixed, focusing on trying to implement strict scheduling and rigid structure without an understanding of her strengths and abilities. Anika's creativity and energy were stifled, leading to frustration, poor self-esteem, and an unwillingness to attempt new strategies.

NEURODIVERSITY-AFFIRMING APPROACH: Anika's school psychologist embraced her ADHD as part of her unique neurology. Together, they collaborated on developing tools that complemented Anika's energy and creativity while still addressing her organizational needs. Interventions were tailored to leverage Anika's preference for novelty, and the framework was posed in a way that didn't make Anika feel she had failed if a strategy didn't work. Anika's self-esteem improved, and she began to thrive academically and socially.

Chiyo, age 8, autistic with social anxiety
NON-NEURODIVERSITY-AFFIRMING APPROACH: Chiyo's social anxiety was seen as something that needed to be cured by her school counselor, who often pushed her into social situations without proper support or understanding. This one-size-fits-all approach did not account for Chiyo's individual needs and experiences, causing her anxiety to worsen and leading to her disengagement in seeking out the school counselor's support.

NEURODIVERSITY-AFFIRMING APPROACH: Chiyo's school counselor embraced a neurodiversity-affirming model, recognizing that social anxiety was a part of Chiyo's neurodivergent experience. Together, they worked to understand Chiyo's specific triggers, and they created a tailored intervention plan. Gradual exposure and strategies aligned with a comfortable pace for Chiyo resulted in significant improvements in her anxiety and overall well-being.

Dmitri, age 9, Tourette syndrome
NON-NEURODIVERSITY-AFFIRMING APPROACH: Dmitri's tics were viewed as disruptive and something to be controlled by his school's social worker. The social worker attempted a strict behavior modification approach to suppress Dmitri's tics without considering their neurological basis. This

led Dmitri to feel increased stress and anxiety, and his tics became more pronounced.

NEURODIVERSITY-AFFIRMING APPROACH: Dmitri's school's social worker took the time to understand Tourette syndrome and recognized that Dmitri's tics were involuntary. They worked together on strategies to manage situations where the tics might be more challenging, and rather than attempting to suppress them, focused on supporting Dmitri's overall emotional well-being. His time with the social worker became a safe space for Dmitri, leading to increased self-acceptance and improved relationships with peers.

Suicidal Ideation and Nonsuicidal Self-Injury Behavior

In the realm of mental health care, navigating the complex intersection of neurodivergent traits with suicidality and nonsuicidal self-injury (NSSI) is essential but fraught with misunderstandings. Because neurodivergent individuals experience life in a way that doesn't align with neuro-normative expectations, their expressions, behaviors, and emotions might differ considerably and lead to confusion or misinterpretation, especially in the contexts of suicidal ideation and self-injury.

Counselors, social workers, and psychologists in schools are the first line of defense when a student is in crisis. However, depending on these adults' particular role in the school, they may have few to no direct opportunities to support students dealing with suicidal ideation and NSSI. Nonetheless, having an awareness of the differences and influencing factors of neurodivergence on suicidal ideation and NSSI is important in providing information to parents and other educators about how to best support students.

The following sections include some of the major influencing factors surrounding suicidality and self-injury in neurodivergent learners, but in no way is it a comprehensive list. Working to understand neurodivergent students and teaching them how to accurately express their feelings and emotions is key to helping individual students, each with traits specific to them.

Social Communication Differences

Social communication differences are a complex and multifaceted influence to consider when working with neurodivergent students. Such differences often manifest in social pragmatic language difficulties, which can create challenges for the student in understanding social cues and expressing emotions. The presence of alexithymia, a condition commonly found in autistic people that makes it difficult to identify and articulate emotions (see page 196), can further complicate this communication landscape.

An autistic individual might make statements that seem to signal suicidal ideation when, in fact, they are expressing frustration, sensory overload, or social confusion. For example, a statement like "I wish I wasn't here," which could be interpreted as passive suicidal ideation, may actually reflect a struggle with the present environment, a sensory experience that is overwhelming, or a social interaction that is challenging, rather than a wish to die. In another instance, a vague or broad statement of distress may be interpreted as general unhappiness when it is really a specific reaction to a specific social situation.

Without proper understanding and appreciation of these unique communication traits, professionals may misinterpret students' expressions, leading to interventions that do not address the underlying issue. Therefore, it is essential to recognize the impact of social pragmatic language difficulties and possible alexithymia in the assessment process. Professionals must develop a finely tuned sensitivity to the way these individuals communicate their emotional states—which may require specialized training in neurodivergent communication patterns—ensuring that assessments and interventions are tailored to their specific needs and experiences. These might involve the use of adaptive communication tools and collaboration with those who know the individual well.

Ignoring or oversimplifying these communication nuances risks missing vital information, potentially leading to inappropriate or even harmful interventions. In the context of mental health support, this recognition is not merely beneficial but essential, providing a foundation for respectful, affirming, and successful therapeutic relationships.

Impulsivity

Impulsiveness, particularly in ADHDers, is a complex factor that necessitates a nuanced understanding when addressing suicidality and self-injury. ADHDers might have thoughts or even attempts at self-injury or suicide that are characterized by impulsivity and may appear less premeditated compared to attempts by neuro-normative individuals. This impulsivity can arise suddenly in response to an immediate stressor or emotion, rather than being part of a longer-term pattern of ideation.

Such a difference calls for a tailored approach that recognizes and directly addresses the impulsivity itself. Educators need to modify interventions to be neurodiversity-affirming and specific to the student, building skills around impulse control, emotional regulation, coping strategies, and other areas to mitigate risk, as opposed to directly focusing on the suicidal ideation or self-injury.

A safety plan that considers a specific student's unique triggers and impulsivity patterns, and offers clear steps for responding to impulsive thoughts or behaviors, can be a critical part of their mental health support plan. The plan might involve identifying and modifying environments or situations that can trigger impulsivity, helping the student recognize early signs of impulsive thoughts or feelings, and developing a personalized strategy for them to seek help or engage in safer coping mechanisms.

Sensory Differences

Sensory needs have a significant impact on NSSI within neurodivergent populations, particularly in children and teens (Moseley et al. 2020). For example, a child or teenager struggling with sensory processing may engage in self-injury as a means of coping with overwhelming sensory experiences or as part of a sensory stim or repetitive behavior. This engagement in NSSI might be without suicidal intent. Understanding the distinction is vital for professionals working with neurodivergent individuals.

In some cases, NSSI may be related to a sensory stim that serves to regulate emotions or provide specific sensory feedback that the individual finds comforting or calming. Though it might appear to others as self-injury, the stim may be a (maladaptive) coping skill rooted in sensory needs rather than a mental health crisis or indication of suicidal ideation. Labeling it as self-injury can lead to misinterpretation and inappropriate intervention.

NSSI in neurodivergent populations (or neuro-normative populations, for that matter) is not necessarily a sign of future suicidal ideation or suicidal behavior, and most often occurs in the absence of suicidal ideation (Klonsky, Victor, and Saffer 2014). While self-injury can be concerning, interpreting it *solely* as a predictor of future suicidality can overlook the context of the situation and triggers.

Supporting neurodivergent individuals who exhibit NSSI requires a nuanced and empathetic approach that recognizes the complex interplay of sensory needs, repetitive behaviors, and coping strategies. It requires moving beyond surface-level interpretations and delving into understanding an individual's unique experience. By doing so, mental health providers can create interventions that are not only more respectful and affirming but also more effective in promoting well-being and safety.

Nonsuicidal Self-Injury

The situation: A school counselor is informed about a neurodivergent student who has been exhibiting NSSI behaviors, like scratching and biting themself, especially during times of high stress or emotional overwhelm. The student is otherwise quiet and tends to isolate themself during recess or free periods.

Perspective of others: Teachers and classmates might view the neurodivergent student's behaviors with concern, confusion, or even alarm, interpreting the behaviors as attention-seeking or a sign of more severe mental health issues. Classmates might avoid the student due to a lack of understanding or fear, while teachers might feel unequipped to handle the situation and worry about the student's safety and well-being. Without looking at the behaviors within the context of the student's neurodivergence, the teacher or school counselor may miss the appropriate intervention.

Perspective of the neurodivergent student: The student is using these behaviors as a way to deal with stress and to distract from sensory overwhelm. They don't understand why others react so strongly to the behavior because they aren't breaking the skin when scratching or biting their arms. The sensory input helps distract from other overwhelming emotions, and while they are frustrated when they begin engaging in the behaviors, these actions ultimately help regulate their focus.

Possible follow-up: The school counselor and occupational therapist work with the student to find alternate ways to manage dysregulation and meet sensory needs and to develop understanding for why others might misinterpret their NSSI actions.

Assessing Risks and Creating Neurodiversity-Affirming Safety Plans

Assessing risks and creating safety plans for neurodivergent individuals grappling with suicidality or NSSI requires a deep and nuanced understanding of neurodivergent traits. Using a neurodiversity-affirming lens ensures that the unique needs, communication styles, and experiences of neurodivergent individuals are at the core of these processes. Be sure to keep these factors in mind if you are in the position to create a safety plan with a student:

- **Communication preferences:** Proper risk assessment requires acknowledging that a neurodivergent student's expressions might differ from neuro-normative patterns. It's important to interpret statements and behaviors within the context of the student's neurodivergence. This may involve direct inquiries that are clearly worded and specific to the student's communication preferences.
- **Sensory and environmental triggers:** Identifying factors that might lead to distress or overwhelm can be pivotal in understanding the risk of NSSI or suicidality for a neurodivergent student. This involves not only asking the student

about their triggers but also observing and understanding how the student's neurodivergence interacts with their surroundings.

- **Support networks:** Engaging with a student's family members, caregivers, or close friends who understand their unique neurodivergent traits can provide invaluable insights into the student's thoughts and behaviors. It's not about seeking information behind the student's back, but rather creating a cooperative and transparent assessment process.

- **Appropriate assessment tools:** Traditional tools and measures for assessing suicidality might not align with a neurodivergent student's experience. Developing or adapting tools that consider the unique ways neurodivergent people communicate and perceive their experiences can lead to a more accurate and empathetic understanding.

Also consider the following within the context of your district's safety planning and reporting policies when you are creating safety plans for your neurodivergent students:

- **Use an individualized approach:** Tailor safety plans for neurodivergent characteristics, including communication styles, processing preferences, and individual strengths.

- **Include sensory strategies:** Incorporate sensory strategies to align with specific needs for calming and support.

- **Give clear and accessible guidelines:** Use visual aids and/or explicit language to match students' unique cognitive and communicative styles.

- **Involve trusted support networks:** Help neurodivergent students identify the trusted people in their lives who can provide support.

- **Promote autonomy and respect:** Emphasize strengths, respect autonomy, and empower neurodivergent students within the planning process.

What to Remember

- The overlap between neurodivergence and mental health needs leads to some sobering statistics, particularly for ADHDers and autistic individuals. Environments that aren't neurodiversity-affirming can be stressful, isolating, and even harmful to the mental health of neurodivergent people.

- Teaching students the difference between emotions everyone experiences and clinical diagnoses can help neurodivergent students understand that some of the uncomfortable feelings they have are similar to the feelings their peers have.

- Neurodiversity-affirming interventions for mental health needs require an understanding of a student's specific neurodivergent traits so that treatment can be individualized and contextualized through the lens of their underlying neurodivergent characteristics.

CONCLUSION

Building the Future Together

The journey toward creating neurodiversity-affirming schools is both a challenge and an opportunity. Neurodivergent students deserve environments that recognize their unique strengths and needs, just as neuro-normative students do. By embracing neurodiversity-affirming practices, we can create schools where all students are seen, valued, and supported to thrive. As an educator, you play a role in making this vision a reality. This work requires not only patience and persistence but also a commitment to reimagining traditional educational paradigms.

As you embark on this work, remember that change happens incrementally. Small, intentional actions lead to larger transformations. You don't need to overhaul your classroom or school in one day; each step you take toward creating a more inclusive, supportive space is a step toward a more equitable future for all learners.

Collaboration, compassion, and a willingness to embrace discomfort will be your guiding principles. By working together and supporting one another, educators can make a significant difference in the lives of neurodivergent students. Let this book serve as both a roadmap and a source of encouragement as you continue on this path toward meaningful, lasting change.

We understand that the work of creating neurodiversity-affirming schools may seem daunting. You might be wondering how to effectively implement changes, or how to convince your colleagues and administrators of their value. We've been there too, and we know it's not easy.

Throughout this book, we shared conversations we have had with each other as we explored what it means to be neurodiversity-affirming. We want to close the book by recognizing questions you may have for us or may face from others as you advocate for neurodiversity-affirming practices. We hope our answers help justify this shift and empower you to begin or continue this work.

How will you find the time to implement these changes?

The challenge of incorporating new practices into an already packed schedule is real. It's natural to worry about how to incorporate neurodiversity-affirming practices on top of your current teaching, planning, and administrative tasks. We suggest starting small. Choose one or two practices to implement initially, rather than overhauling everything at once, and look for ways to integrate them into existing routines and lesson plans. Remember that many neurodiversity-affirming approaches can save time in the long run by reducing behavioral issues and improving student engagement.

How can you manage such a wide range of needs in one classroom?

Balancing individual needs in a large class can feel overwhelming, especially when focusing on individualized approaches. Remember that what works for neurodivergent students often benefits everyone in the classroom. Try implementing universal design principles. Use flexible grouping strategies to provide targeted support. Empower students to advocate for their needs and support each other. It's about creating an environment where all students can thrive, rather than trying to manage each need in isolation.

Will this approach take away from meeting academic standards?

Contrary to common concerns, neurodiversity-affirming practices support academic goals, since engaged, supported students are more likely to succeed academically. Many of these practices enhance learning for all students. Focus on teaching core concepts in multiple ways to reach diverse learners. By creating an inclusive environment where all students feel valued and have their needs met, you're likely to see improvements in overall academic performance.

What do you do if other teachers or administrators don't support this?
Building a supportive community is crucial when facing potential isolation or pushback. Start by sharing success stories and data that demonstrate the benefits of these practices. Invite colleagues to observe your classroom or collaborate on lessons. Advocate for schoolwide initiatives that support neurodiversity-affirming practices. Remember that change often starts small—your positive results may inspire others to follow suit. Be patient and persistent in your advocacy and look for allies who share your vision.

How will you know if you're doing it right?
Uncertainty about effectively implementing changes is natural. Regularly check in with students about what's working and what isn't. Keep a reflective journal to track your progress and insights. Remember that becoming neurodiversity-affirming is a journey, not a destination. Be kind to yourself as you learn and grow. Celebrate small successes and view challenges as opportunities for refinement. Trust in the process and in your ability to make a positive difference for your students.

What do you do if students resist these changes?
Change can be challenging for everyone, including students, who might not immediately appreciate new teaching practices. Address potential resistance by explaining the reasoning behind changes and by involving students in decision-making processes when possible. Patience and consistency are key as everyone adjusts. Helping students understand how these changes benefit the entire class often leads to greater acceptance. When students feel heard and included in the process, they're more likely to embrace new ways of learning and interacting.

Won't this be too difficult to manage alone?
Concerns about feeling overwhelmed by individual adjustments without systemic support are valid. Remember that you don't have to do everything at once or by yourself. Focus on gradual, consistent progress rather than overnight transformation. Collaborate with colleagues to share the workload and ideas. Advocate for systemic changes that support your efforts. Look for opportunities to build a network of like-minded educators (see page 14) within your school or district. Together, you can create a more sustainable approach to implementing neurodiversity-affirming practices.

What happens if the changes don't work?

Hesitation about trying new approaches is understandable, especially when considering potential unintended consequences. It's important to remember that every classroom is different, and it may take time to find what works best for yours. View setbacks as learning opportunities rather than failures. Be flexible and willing to adjust your approach based on feedback and results. Keep communication open with your students, their families, and your colleagues. If something isn't working, analyze why and brainstorm alternatives. The goal is progress, not perfection, and your willingness to adapt and improve will ultimately benefit your students.

How do you explain these changes to parents or guardians who might be skeptical?

We understand that some families might have concerns or questions about neurodiversity-affirming practices, especially if they're unfamiliar with the concept. Addressing these parental concerns requires proactive communication. Consider hosting an information session or sending out a detailed newsletter explaining the benefits for all students. Use concrete examples of how these practices can improve learning outcomes and student well-being. Be open to questions and feedback and offer resources for parents to learn more about neurodiversity. Remember that parents are often your strongest allies when they understand how your approach can help their children thrive.

It's time to embrace neurodiversity, not just as a concept but as a practice that empowers and uplifts every member of the school community. The future of education is inclusive of all neurotypes. And with your dedication, it can become a reality.

Acknowledgments

We would like to thank the many people who helped shape and bring this book to fruition. Thank you to our editors, Tom Rademacher, who believed so strongly in the concept and need for this book from the very beginning, and Cassandra Labriola-Sitzman, who helped shape the final draft, asked great questions, and endured many questions from us; to publicist Amanda Shofner and the entire marketing team for their support with marketing and promotion; and to publisher Kyra Ostendorf for giving us a platform to share this paradigm shift with educators and schools.

A big thank you to Dr. Ellen Braaten for writing the foreword and for your belief in the power of this book and its concepts.

We also are grateful for our colleagues in schools, practices, organizations, and across sectors for their support, their curiosity, and their understanding as we took on writing this book alongside our day jobs.

We would be remiss in not also acknowledging the myriad podcasters and authors from and with whom we've been privileged enough to learn and share space, and who have allowed us to use their platforms to amplify our message. We are proud to call so many people we admire friends as well as allies.

To all the neurodivergent families, clients, and students we have learned from, thank you for letting us into your lives and for challenging us to do better every day.

And lastly, we're grateful to *Schitt's Creek* for the endless memes that perfectly described the range of emotions authors experience while writing a book; the usually reliable wi-fi in the various airports, conference centers, and hotels where we wrote and revised in fits and starts; and Twitter, may it rest in peace, for building a community that brought us together to create and debate the ideas that went into this book.

Amanda: And a special thank-you to Emily, without whom I absolutely could not have done this. Thanks for pushing me to think outside my comfort zone as we wrote this book together, for not letting me take myself too seriously, for challenging my ideas, for knowing that my preferred mode of neurodivergent communication when under stress is the sending of memes, and for being the best of friends.

Emily: And a huge thank-you to Amanda, my unexpected soul sister in this writing adventure. Who would have thought that weekend drafting sessions and shared deadline panic could forge such a bond? Your relentless questioning pushed me to dig deeper, your confidence in setting boundaries inspired me to do the same, and your thoughtful perspective helped me edit not only this book but also many emails before my impulsive urge to hit "send." Here's to the power of neurodivergent collaboration and the unexpected joys of shared creative struggle!

References

Abeles, Dekel, and Shlomit Yuval-Greenberg. 2017. "Just Look Away: Gaze Aversions as an Overt Attentional Disengagement Mechanism." *Cognition* 168: 99–109. doi.org/10.1016/j.cognition.2017.06.021.

Accardo, Amy L., Nancy M. H. Pontes, and Manuel C. F. Pontes. 2022. "Heightened Anxiety and Depression Among Autistic Adolescents with ADHD: Findings from the National Survey of Children's Health 2016–2019." Journal of Autism and Developmental Disorders 54: 563–576. doi.org/10.1007/s10803-022-05803-9.

Alaniz, José. 2014. "Supercrip: Disability, Visuality, and the Silver Age Superhero." In *Death, Disability, and the Superhero: The Silver Age and Beyond*. Oxford, MS: University Press of Mississippi. doi.org/10.14325/mississippi/9781628461176.003.0002.

Alsubaie, Merfat A. 2015. "Hidden Curriculum as One of the Current Issue of Curriculum." *Journal of Education and Practice* 6 (33): 125–128. files.eric.ed.gov/fulltext/EJ1083566.pdf.

American Psychiatric Association (APA). 2013. *Diagnostic and Statistical Manual of Mental Disorders: DSM-5*. Arlington, TX: American Psychiatric Association Publishing.

American Psychological Association (APA), Coalition for Psychology in Schools and Education. 2015. "Top 20 Principles from Psychology for preK–12 Teaching and Learning." Accessed June 18, 2024. apa.org/ed/schools/cpse/top-twenty-principles.pdf.

Armstrong, Thomas. 2012. *Neurodiversity in the Classroom: Strength-based Strategies to Help Students with Special Needs Succeed in School and Life*. Alexandria, VA: ASCD.

Armstrong, Thomas. 2017. *Neurodiversity: The Future of Special Education?* Alexandria, VA: ASCD.

Aronson, Joshua, Diana Burgess, Sean M. Phelan, and Lindsay Juarez. 2013. "Unhealthy Interactions: The Role of Stereotype Threat in Health Disparities." *American Journal of Public Health* 103 (1): 50–6. doi.org/10.2105/AJPH.2012.300828.

Babinski, Dara E., Autumn Kujawa, Ellen M. Kessel, Kodi B. Arfer, and Daniel N. Klein. 2019. "Sensitivity to Peer Feedback in Young Adolescents with Symptoms of ADHD:

Examination of Neurophysiological and Self-Report Measures." *Journal of Abnormal Child Psychology* 47 (3): 471–484. doi.org/10.1007/s10802-018-0470-2.

Bagby, Michael, James D. A. Parker, Graeme J. Taylor. 1994. "The Twenty-Item Toronto Alexithymia Scale--I. Item Selection and Cross-Validation of teh Factor Structure." *Journal of Psychosomatic Research* 38 (1): 23-32. doi.org/10.1016/0022-3999(94)90005-1.

Baldessarini, Ross. J., et al. 2012. "Age at Onset Versus Family History and Clinical Outcomes in 1,665 International Bipolar-I Disorder Patients." *World Psychiatry* 11 (1): 40–46. doi.org/10.1016/j.wpsyc.2012.01.006.

Bascom, Julia, ed. 2012. *Loud Hands: Autistic People, Speaking*. Washington, DC: Autistic Press.

Baweja, Raman, Susan D. Mayes, Usman Hameed, and James G. Waxmonsky. 2016. "Disruptive Mood Dysregulation Disorder: Current Insights." *Neuropsychiatric Disease and Treatment* 12: 2115–2124. doi.org/10.2147/NDT.S100312.

Bernardin, Courtney J., Timothy Lewis, Debora Bell, Stephen Kanne. 2021. "Associations Between Social Camouflaging and Internalizing Symptoms in Autistic and Non-Autistic Adolescents." *Autism* 25 (6): 1580–1591. doi.org/10.1177/1362361321997284.

Billeiter, Kenzie B., and John Mark Froiland. 2022. "Diversity of Intelligence Is the Norm within the Autism Spectrum: Full Scale Intelligence Scores Among Children with ASD." *Child Psychiatry & Human Development* 54 (4): 1094–1101. doi.org/10.1007/s10578-021-01300-9.

Bolding, Candice W., Luke J. Rapa, and Katherine Mulholland. 2022. "Theoretical Perspectives Guiding the Study of Disproportionality in Education." In *Disproportionality and Social Justice in Education. Springer Series on Child and Family Studies*, edited by Nicholas Gage, Luke J. Rapa, Denise K. Whitford, and Antonis Katsiyannis. Springer Series on Child and Family Studies. Switzerland: Springer Nature. doi.org/10.1007/978-3-031-13775-4_3.

Bonini, Luca, Cristina Rotunno, Edoardo Arcuri, and Vittorio Gallese. 2022. "Mirror Neurons 30 Years Later: Implications and Applications." *Trends in Cognitive Sciences* 26 (9): 767–781. doi.org/10.1016/j.tics.2022.06.003.

Botha, Monique, Robert Chapman, Morénike Giwa Onaiwu, Steven K. Kapp, Abs Stannard Ashley, and Nick Walker. 2024. "The Neurodiversity Concept Was Developed Collectively: An Overdue Correction on the Origins of Neurodiversity Theory." *Autism* 28 (6): 1591–1594. doi.org/10.1177/13623613241237871.

Butera, Christiana, Priscilla Ring, John Sideris, Aditya Jayashankar, Emily Kilroy, Laura Harrison, Sharon Cermak, and Lisa Aziz-Zadeh. 2020. "Impact of Sensory Processing on School Performance Outcomes in High Functioning Individuals with Autism Spectrum Disorder." *Mind, Brain, and Education* 14 (3): 243–254. doi.org/10.1111/mbe.12242.

Cage, Eilidh, and Zoe Troxell-Whitman. 2019. "Understanding the Reasons, Contexts and Costs of Camouflaging for Autistic Adults." *Journal of Autism and Developmental Disorders* 49 (5): 1899–1911. doi.org/10.1007/s10803-018-03878-x.

Cardona, Miguel. 2023. "Secretary Cardona Delivers Remarks to the National Education Association" (speech). U.S. Department of Education, transcript. ed.gov/news/speeches/secretary-cardona-delivers-remarks-national-education-association.

Carey, Alison C., Pamela Block, and Richard K. Scotch. 2019. "Sometimes Allies: Parent-Led Disability Organizations and Social Movements." *Disability Studies Quarterly* 39 (1). doi.org/10.18061/dsq.v39i1.6281.

Centers for Disease Control and Prevention. 2023. Suicide Data and Statistics. Accessed August 19, 2023. cdc.gov/suicide/facts/data.html.

Chafouleas, Sandra M., Isaiah Pickens, and Stacy Gherardi. 2021. "Adverse Childhood Experiences (ACEs): Translation into Action in K12 Education Settings." *School Mental Health* 13 (2): 213–224. doi.org/10.1007/s12310-021-09427-9.

Chapman, Louise, Kieran Rose, Laura Hull, and William Mandy. 2022. "'I want to fit in… but I don't want to change myself fundamentally': A Qualitative Exploration of the Relationship Between Masking and Mental Health for Autistic Teenagers." *Research in Autism Spectrum Disorders* 99: 102069. doi.org/10.1016/j.rasd.2022.102069.

Charlton, Rebecca A., Timothy Entecott, Evelina Belova, and Gabrielle Nwaordu. 2021. 'It feels like holding back something you need to say': Autistic and Non-Autistic Adults Accounts of Sensory Experiences and Stimming." *Research in Autism Spectrum Disorders* 89: 101864. doi.org/10.1016/j.rasd.2021.101864.

Cloitre, Marylene, Bradley C. Stolbach, Judith L. Herman, Bessel van der Kolk, Robert Pynoos, Jing Wang, and Eva Petkova. 2009. "A Developmental Approach to Complex PTSD: Childhood and Adult Cumulative Trauma as Predictors of Symptom Complexity." *Journal of Traumatic Stress* 22: 399–408. doi.org/10.1002/jts.20444.

Cook, Sara C., Kimberly A. McDuffie-Landrum, Linda Oshita, and Bryan G. Cook. 2017. "Co-teaching for Students with Disabilities: A Critical and Updated Analysis of the Empirical Literature." In *The Handbook of Special Education* (2nd ed.), edited by James M. Kauffman, Daniel P. Hallahan, and Paige Cullen Pullen, 233–248. New York: Routledge.

Cooper, Sally-Ann, Elita Smiley, Jillian Morrison, Andrew Williamson, and Linda Allan. 2007. "Mental Ill-Health in Adults with Intellectual Disabilities: Prevalence and Associated Factors." *The British Journal of Psychiatry* 190: 27–35. doi.org/ 10.1192/bjp.bp.106.022483.

Corkum, Penny, Meredith Bessey, Melissa McGonnell, and Anders Dorbeck. 2015. "Barriers to Evidence-Based Treatment for Children with Attention-Deficit/Hyperactivity Disorder." *ADHD Attention Deficit and Hyperactivity Disorders* 7 (1): 49–74. doi.org/10.1007/s12402-014-0154-2.

Coryell, William, Jess Fiedorowicz, Andrew C. Leon, Jean Endicott, and Martin B. Keller. 2013. "Age of Onset and the Prospectively Observed Course of Illness in Bipolar Disorder." *Journal of Affective Disorders* 146 (1): 34–38. doi.org/10.1016/j.jad.2012.08.031.

Cumin, Julie, Sandra Pelaez, and Laurent Mottron. 2021. "Positive and Differential Diagnosis of Autism in Verbal Women of Typical Intelligence: A Delphi Study." *Autism* 26 (5): 1153–1164. doi.org/10.1177/13623613211042719.

Davis, Kylie Grace. 2017. "Echoes of Language Development: 7 Facts About Echolalia for SLPs." *The ASHA LeaderLive*, May 9, 2017. leader.pubs.asha.org/do/10.1044/echoes-of-language-development-7-facts-about-echolalia-for-slps/full/.

den Houting, Jacquiline. 2019. "Neurodiversity: An Insider's Perspective." *Autism* 23 (2): 657–662. doi.org/10.1177/1362361318820762.

Dewinter, J., H. De Graaf, and S. Begeer. 2017. "Sexual Orientation, Gender Identity, and Romantic Relationships in Adolescents and Adults with Autism Spectrum Disorder." *Journal of Autism and Developmental Disorders* 47 (9): 2927–2934. doi.org/10.1007/s10803-017-3199-9.

Digital Promise. n.d. Learner Variability Navigator. Accessed June 18, 2024. Washington, DC: Digital Promise. lvp.digitalpromiseglobal.org.

Donaldson, Amy L., endever* corbin, and Jamie McCoy. 2021. "Everyone Deserves AAC": Preliminary Study of the Experiences of Speaking Autistic Adults Who Use Augmentative and Alternative Communication." *Perspectives of the ASHA Special Interest Groups* 6 (2): 315–326. doi.org/10.1044/2021_persp-20-00220.

Dwyer, Patrick, Zachary J. Williams, Wenn B. Lawson, and Susan M. Rivera. 2024. "A Trans-Diagnostic Investigation of Attention, Hyper-Focus, and Monotropism in Autism, Attention Dysregulation Hyperactivity Development, and the General Population." *Neurodiversity* 2 (1): 1–27. doi.org/10.1177/27546330241237883.

Education Gazette editors. 2023. "Takiwātanga—In Your Own Time and Space." *Education Gazette* 102 (1): 1HAZ8K. gazette.education.govt.nz/articles/takiwatanga-in-your-own-time-and-space.

Emerson, Eric, and Chris Hatton. 2007. "Mental Health of Children and Adolescents with Intellectual Disabilities in Britain." *The British Journal of Psychiatry* 191 (6): 493–499. doi.org/10.1192/bjp.bp.107.038729.

Evans, Joshua A., Elizabeth J. Krumrei-Mancuso, and Steven V. Rouse. 2023. "What You Are Hiding Could Be Hurting You: Autistic Masking in Relation to Mental Health, Interpersonal Trauma, Authenticity, and Self-Esteem." *Autism in Adulthood* 6 (2). doi.org/10.1089/aut.2022.0115.

Fawzy, Camelia Magdalena. 2015. *Authentic Inclusion or Risk of Discrimination: Organizational Context and Employees' Attitudes Towards Colleagues with Neurodivergence, Developmental and/or Mental Health Related Disabilities.* Doctoral dissertation, University of Maryland University College.

Fotheringham, Francesca, Katie Cebula, Sue Fletcher-Watson, Sarah Foley, and Catherine J. Crompton. 2023. "Co-Designing a Neurodivergent Student-Led Peer Support Programme for Neurodivergent Young People in Mainstream High Schools." *Neurodiversity* 1. doi.org/10.1177/27546330231205770.

Gallagher, Kathleen, and Kelley Mayer. 2006. "Teacher-Child Relationships at the Forefront of Effective Practice." *Young Children* 61 (6): 44–49.

Garas, Peter, and Judit Balazs. 2020. "Long-Term Suicide Risk of Children and Adolescents with Attention Deficit and Hyperactivity Disorder—A Systematic Review." *Frontiers in Psychiatry* 11. doi.org/10.3389/fpsyt.2020.557909.

Garcia, Shivohn N. 2019. "How Social-Emotional Learning Helps You as a Teacher." Understood. Accessed June 18, 2024. understood.org/en/articles/how-sel-helps-you-as-a-teacher.

Gartrell, Dan. 2020. "Instead of Discipline, Use Guidance." *Teaching Young Children* 13 (3).

Goerlich, Katharina S. 2018. "The Multifaceted Nature of Alexithymia—A Neuroscientific Perspective." *Frontiers in Psychology* 9: 1614. doi.org/10.3389/fpsyg.2018.01614.

Goetz, Teddy G., and Noah Adams. 2022. "The Transgender and Gender Diverse and Attention Deficit Hyperactivity Disorder Nexus: A Systematic Review." *Journal of Gay & Lesbian Mental Health* 28 (1): 2–19. doi.org/10.1080/19359705.2022.2109119.

Goodall, Emma, Charlotte Brownlow, Erich C. Fein, and Sarah Candeloro. 2022. "Creating Inclusive Classrooms for Highly Dysregulated Students: What Can We Learn from Existing Literature?" *Education Sciences* 12 (8): 504. doi.org/10.3390/educsci12080504.

Gopalan, Maithreyi, and Ashlyn Aiko Nelson. 2019. "Understanding the Racial Discipline Gap in Schools." *AERA Open* 5 (2): 1–26. doi.org/10.1177/2332858419844613.

Green, Jonathan, Michael Absoud, Victoria Grahame, Osman Malik, Emily Simonoff, Ann Le Couteur, and Gillian Baird. 2018. "Pathological Demand Avoidance: Symptoms but Not a Syndrome." *Lancet Child & Adolescent Health* 2 (6): 455–464. doi.org/10.1016/S2352-4642(18)30044-0.

Grolnick, Wendy. 2018. "Motivating the Unmotivated Student." *Psych Learning Curve*, American Psychological Association, July 16, 2018. psychlearningcurve.org/motivating-the-unmotivated-student/.

Grossman, Ephraim S., Yaakov S. G. Hoffman, and Amit Shrira. 2022. "Learning Based PTSD Symptoms in Persons with Specific Learning Disabilities." *Scientific Reports* 12 (1): 12872. doi.org/10.1038/s41598-022-16752-9.

Grue, Jan. 2021. "Ablenationalists Assemble: On Disability in the Marvel Cinematic Universe." *Journal of Literary & Cultural Disability Studies* 15 (1): 1–17. doi.org/10.3828/jlcds.2021.1.

Hadwin, Allyson Fiona, Sanna Järvelä, and Mariel Miller. 2011. "Self-Regulated, Co-Regulated, and Socially Shared Regulation of Learning." In *Handbook of Self-Regulation of Learning and Performance*, edited by Barry J. Zimmerman and Dale H. Schunk, 65–84. New York: Routledge.

Hall, Edward T. 1959. *The Silent Language*. New York: Doubleday.

Hall, Edward T. 1976. *Beyond Culture*. New York: Anchor.

Haney, Jolynn L. 2016. "Autism, Females, and the DSM-5: Gender Bias in Autism Diagnosis." *Social Work in Mental Health* 14 (4): 396–407. doi.org/10.1080/15332985.2015.1031858.

Hehir, Thomas, Silvana Pascucci, and Christopher Pascucci. 2016. *A Summary of the Evidence on Inclusive Education*. São Paulo: Instituto Alana; Cambridge, MA: ABT Associates.

Hines-Datiri, Dorothy, and Dorinda J. Carter Andrews. 2017. "The Effects of Zero Tolerance Policies on Black Girls: Using Critical Race Feminism and Figured Worlds to Examine School Discipline." *Urban Education* 55 (10): 1419–1440. doi.org/10.1177/0042085917690204.

Hudson, Chloe C., Layla Hall, Kate L. Harkness. 2019. "Prevalence of Depressive Disorders in Individuals with Autism Spectrum Disorder: A Meta-Analysis." *Journal of Abnormal Child Psychology* 47 (1): 165–175. doi.org/10.1007/s10802-018-0402-129497980.

Hull, Laura, Lily Levy, Meng-Chuan Lai, K. V. Petrides, Simon Baron-Cohen, Carrie Allison, Paula Smith, and Will Mandy. 2021. "Is Social Camouflaging Associated with Anxiety and Depression in Autistic Adults?" *Molecular Autism* 12 (1). doi.org/10.1186/s13229-021-00421-1.

Individuals with Disabilities Education Act of 2004 (IDEA), 20 U.S.C. § 1400 (2004).34 C.F.R. § 300.502 (c)(1).

Individuals with Disabilities Education Act of 2004 (IDEA), 20 U.S.C. § 1400 (§ 300.8(c)(4)).

Individuals with Disabilities Education Act of 2004 (IDEA), 20 U.S.C. § 1400 (§ 300.8(c)(6)).

Individuals with Disabilities Education Act of 2004 (IDEA), 20 U.S.C. § 1412 (a)(5).

Jakobson, Lorna S., and Sarah N. Rigby. 2021. "Alexithymia and Sensory Processing Sensitivity: Areas of Overlap and Links to Sensory Processing Styles." *Frontiers in Psychology* 12: 583786. doi.org/10.3389/fpsyg.2021.583786.

Jang, Hyungshim, Johnmarshall Reeve, and Edward L. Deci. 2010. "Engaging Students in Learning Activities: It Is Not Autonomy Support or Structure but Autonomy Support and Structure." *Journal of Educational Psychology* 102 (3): 588–600. doi.org/10.1037/a0019682.

Jellinek, Michael. 2010. "Don't Let ADHD Crush Children's Self-Esteem." *Clinical Psychiatry News* 38: 12. doi.org/10.1016/S0270-6644(10)70231-9.

Kalandadze, Tamar, Courtenay Norbury, Terje Nærland, and Kari-Anne B. Næss. 2018. "Figurative Language Comprehension in Individuals with Autism Spectrum Disorder: A Meta-Analytic Review." *Autism* 22 (2): 99–117. doi.org/10.1177/1362361316668652.

Kamath, M. S., C. R. Dahm, J. R. Tucker, C. L. Huang-Pollock, N. M. Etter, and K. A. Neely. 2020. "Sensory Profiles in Adults with and without ADHD." *Research in Developmental Disabilities* 104: 103696. doi.org/10.1016/j.ridd.2020.103696.

Kapp, Steven K., ed. 2020. *Autistic Community and the Neurodiversity Movement: Stories from the Frontline*. Singapore: Springer Nature. library.oapen.org/handle/20.500.12657/23177.

Kapp, Steven K. 2023. "Profound Concerns About 'Profound Autism': Dangers of Severity Scales and Functioning Labels for Support Needs." *Education Sciences* 13 (2): 106. doi.org/10.3390/educsci13020106.

Kapp, Steven K., Robyn Steward, Laura Crane, Daisy Elliott, Chris Elphick, Elizabeth Pellicano, Ginny Russell. 2019. "'People should be allowed to do what they like': Autistic Adults' Views and Experiences of Stimming." *Autism* 23 (7): 1782–1792. doi.org/10.1177/1362361319829628.

Kernbach, Julius M., et al. 2018. "Shared Endo-Phenotypes of Default Mode Dysfunction in Attention Deficit/Hyperactivity Disorder and Autism Spectrum Disorder." *Translational Psychiatry* 8 (1). doi.org/10.1038/s41398-018-0179-6.

Kildahl, Arvid N., Sissel B. Helverschou, Anne L. Rysstad, Elizabeth Wigaard, Jane M. A. Hellerud, Linn B. Ludvigsen, and Patricia Howlin. 2021. "Pathological Demand Avoidance in Children and Adolescents: A Systematic Review." *Autism* 25 (8): 2162–2176. doi.org/10.1177/13623613211034382.

Kim, Rhiannon M., and Alex Shevrin Venet. 2023. "Unsnarling PBIS and Trauma-Informed Education." *Urban Education* 0 (0). doi.org/10.1177/00420859231175670.

Klonsky, E. David., Sarah E. Victor, and Boaz Y. Saffer. 2014. "Nonsuicidal Self-Injury: What We Know, and What We Need to Know." *Canadian Journal of Psychiatry. Revue Canadienne de Psychiatrie* 59 (11): 565–568. doi.org/10.1177/070674371405901101.

Kojovic, Nada, Lylia Ben Hadid, Martina Franchini, and Marie Schaer. 2019. "Sensory Processing Issues and Their Association with Social Difficulties in Children with Autism Spectrum Disorders." *Journal of Clinical Medicine* 8 (10): 1508. doi.org/10.3390/jcm8101508.

Kumar, Aneesh P., and Fahima Mohideen. 2021. "Strengths-Based Positive Schooling Interventions: A Scoping Review." *Contemporary School Psychology* 25 (1): 86–98. doi.org/10.1007/s40688-019-00244-9.

Lakin, Joni M., and Jonathan Wai, J. 2020. "Spatially Gifted, Academically Inconvenienced: Spatially Talented Students Experience Less Academic Engagement and More Behavioural Issues than Other Talented Students." *British Journal of Educational Psychology* 90 (1): 35–53. doi.org/10.1111/bjep.12343.

Leadbitter, Kathy, Karen Leneh Buckle, Ceri Ellis, and Martijn Dekker. 2021. "Autistic Self-Advocacy and the Neurodiversity Movement: Implications for Autism Early Intervention Research and Practice." *Frontiers in Psychology* 12: 635690. doi.org/10.3389/fpsyg.2021.635690.

Lewis, Laura Foran. 2017. "A Mixed Methods Study of Barriers to Formal Diagnosis of Autism Spectrum Disorder in Adults." Journal of Autism and Developmental Disorders 47: 2410–2424. doi.org/10.1007/s10803-017-3168-3.

Lynch, C. L. 2019. "Invisible Abuse: ABA and the Things Only Autistic People Can See." *NeuroClastic*, March 28, 2019. neuroclastic.com/invisible-abuse-aba-and-the-things-only-autistic-people-can-see/.

Mallory, Courtney, and Brandon Keehn. 2021. "Implications of Sensory Processing and Attentional Differences Associated with Autism in Academic Settings: An Integrative Review." *Frontiers in Psychiatry* 12: 695825. doi.org/10.3389/fpsyt.2021.695825.

Manalili, Marie Adrienne R. 2021. "Ableist Ideologies Stifle Neurodiversity and Hinder Inclusive Education." *Ought: The Journal of Autistic Culture* 3 (1): 6. doi.org/10.9707/2833-1508.1072.

Mänty, Kristiina, Susanna Kinnunen, Outi Rinta-Homi, and Marika Koivuniemi. 2022. "Enhancing Early Childhood Educators' Skills in Co-regulating Children's Emotions: A Collaborative Learning Program." *Frontiers in Education* 7: 865161. doi.org/10.3389/feduc.2022.865161.

Maric, Marija, Anika Bexkens, and Susan M. Bögels. 2018. "Is Clinical Anxiety a Risk or a Protective Factor for Executive Functioning in Youth with ADHD? A Meta-Regression Analysis." *Clinical Child and Family Psychology Review* 21 (3): 340–353. doi.org/10.1007/s10567-018-0255-8.

McCloskey, Michael, and Brenda Rapp. 2017. "Developmental Dysgraphia: An Overview and Framework for Research." *Cognitive Neuropsychology* 34 (3-4): 65–82. doi.org/10.1080/02643294.2017.1369016.

McGrath, Kevin F., and Penny Van Bergen. 2019. "Attributions and Emotional Competence: Why Some Teachers Experience Close Relationships with Disruptive Students (and Others Don't)." *Teachers and Teaching: Theory and Practice* 25 (3): 334–357. doi.org/10.1080/13540602.2019.1569511.

McManus, Beth M., Zachary Richardson, Margaret Schenkman, Natalie Murphy, Elaine H. Morrato. 2019. "Timing and Intensity of Early Intervention Service Use and Outcomes Among a Safety-Net Population of Children." *JAMA Network Open* 2 (1): e187529. doi.org/10.1001/jamanetworkopen.2018.7529.

Menezes, Michelle, Christina Harkins, Melissa F. Robinson, Jessica Pappagianopoulos, Robert Cross, Roma A. Vasa, and Micah O. Mazurek. 2022. "Treatment of Anxiety in Autistic Adults: A Systematic Review." *Research in Autism Spectrum Disorders* 99: 102068. doi.org/10.1016/j.rasd.2022.102068.

Milton, Damian E. M. 2012. "On the Ontological Status of Autism: The 'Double Empathy Problem.'" *Disability & Society* 27 (6): 883–887. doi.org/10.1080/09687599.2012.710008.

Milton, Damian, and Sara Ryan, eds. 2022. *The Routledge International Handbook of Critical Autism Studies* (1st ed.). New York: Routledge. doi.org/10.4324/9781003056577.

Moore, Allison. 2020. "Pathological Demand Avoidance: What and Who Are Being Pathologised and in Whose Interests?" *Global Studies of Childhood* 10 (1): 39–52. doi.org/10.1177/2043610619890070.

Moseley, Rachel L., Nicola J. Gregory, P. Smith, C. Allison, and Simon Baron-Cohen. 2020. "Links Between Self-Injury and Suicidality in Autism." *Molecular Autism* 11 (1): 14. doi.org/10.1186/s13229-020-0319-8.

Morin, Amanda. n.d. "The Difference Between Discipline and Punishment." Understood. Accessed June 18, 2024. understood.org/en/articles/the-difference-between-discipline-and-punishment.

Mr. I. ex rel. L.I. v. Maine School Administrative District No. 55, 480 F.3d 1 (1st Cir. 2007).

Murray, Dinah. 2018. "Monotropism—An Interest Based Account of Autism." In *Encyclopedia of Autism Spectrum Disorders*, edited by Fred R. Volkmar. New York: Springer. doi.org/10.1007/978-1-4614-6435-8_102269-1.

National Center for Education Statistics (NCES). 2023. "Students With Disabilities." *Condition of Education*. U.S. Department of Education, Institute of Education Sciences. Accessed May 18, 2024. nces.ed.gov/programs/coe/indicator/cgg.

National Center for Education Statistics (NCES). 2022. Digest of Education Statistics Table 204.30. US Department of Education, Institute of Education Sciences. Accessed May 18, 2024. nces.ed.gov/programs/digest/d23/tables/dt23_204.30.asp.

National Institute of Mental Health (NIMH). n.d. *Generalized Anxiety Disorder: When Worry Gets out of Control*. U.S. Department of Health and Human Services. Accessed May 18, 2024. nimh.nih.gov/health/publications/generalized-anxiety-disorder-gad.

NC State University, Center for Universal Design, College of Design. 1997. "The Principles of Universal Design." Accessed May 18, 2024. design.ncsu.edu/wp-content/uploads/2022/11/principles-of-universal-design.pdf.

Nock, Matthew K., et al. 2008. "Cross-National Prevalence and Risk Factors for Suicidal Ideation, Plans, and Attempts." *The British Journal of Psychiatry* 192 (2): 98–105. doi.org/10.1192/bjp.bp.107.040113.

OpenAI. 2023. ChatGPT (August 3, 2023 version) [Large language model]. chat.openai.com/chat.

O'Nions, Elizabeth, and Judith Eaton. 2020. "Extreme/'Pathological' Demand Avoidance: An Overview." *Paediatrics and Child Health* 30 (12): 411–415. doi.org/10.1016/j.paed.2020.09.002.

O'Nions, Elizabeth, Essi Viding, Caroline Floyd, Emma Quinlan, Connie Pidgeon, Judith Gould, and Francesca Happé. 2018. "Dimensions of Difficulty in Children Reported to Have an Autism Spectrum Diagnosis and Features of Extreme/'Pathological' Demand Avoidance." *Child and Adolescent Mental Health* 23 (3): 220–227. doi.org/10.1111/camh.12242.

Ostrolenk, Alexia, Baudouin Forgeot d'Arc, Patricia Jelenic, Fabienne Samson, and Laurent Mottron. 2017. "Hyperlexia: Systematic Review, Neurocognitive Modelling, and Outcome." *Neuroscience & Biobehavioral Reviews* 79: 134–149. doi.org/10.1016/j.neubiorev.2017.04.029.

Palmieri, Arianna, Katya C. Fernandez, Ylenia Cariolato, Johann R. Kleinbub, Sergio Salvatore, and James J. Gross. 2022. "Emotion Regulation in Psychodynamic and Cognitive-Behavioural Therapy: An Integrative Perspective." *Clinical Neuropsychiatry* 19 (2):103–113. doi.org/10.36131/cnfioritieditore20220204.

Pape, Barbara. 2018. *Learner Variability Is the Rule, Not the Exception.* Washington, DC: Digital Promise Global. digitalpromise.org/wp-content/uploads/2018/06/Learner-Variability-Is-The-Rule.pdf.

PDA Society. 2021. *Helpful Approaches Infographic: PANDA Approaches*. PDA Society Resources. Published 2019, updated 2021. Accessed May 18, 2024. pdasociety.org.uk/resources/helpful-approaches-infographic/.

Phelps, Fiona G., Gwyneth Doherty-Sneddon, and Hannah Warnock. 2006. "Helping Children Think: Gaze Aversion and Teaching." *British Journal of Developmental Psychology* 24 (3): 577–588. doi.org/10.1348/026151005X49872.

Plantin Ewe, Linda. 2019. "ADHD Symptoms and the Teacher–Student Relationship: A Systematic Literature Review." *Emotional and Behavioural Difficulties* 24 (2): 136–155. doi.org/10.1080/13632752.2019.1597562.

Pliszka, Steven R. 2019. "ADHD and Anxiety: Clinical Implications." *Journal of Attention Disorders* 23 (3): 203–205. doi.org/10.1177/1087054718817365.

Poletti, Michele, Eva Gebhardt, Lorenzo Pelizza, Antonio Preti, and Andrea Raballo. 2022. "Neurodevelopmental Antecedents and Sensory Phenomena in Obsessive Compulsive Disorder: A Systematic Review Supporting a Phenomenological-Developmental Model." *Psychopathology* 56 (4): 295–305. doi.org/10.1159/000526708.

Posey, Allison. n.d. "Using UDL to Break Down Barriers to Learning." Understood. Accessed July 5, 2023. understood.org/en/articles/how-to-break-down-barriers-to-learning-with-udl.

Price, Gavin R., and Daniel Ansari. 2013. "Dyscalculia: Characteristics, Causes, and Treatments." *Numeracy* 6 (1): 2.

Ptak, Agnieszka, Diana Miękczyńska, Agnieszka Dębiec-Bąk, and Małgorzata Stefańska. 2022. "The Occurrence of the Sensory Processing Disorder in Children Depending on the Type and Time of Delivery: A Pilot Study." *International Journal of Environmental Research and Public Health* 19 (11): 6893. doi.org/10.3390/ijerph19116893.

Radulski, Elizabeth M. 2022. "Conceptualising Autistic Masking, Camouflaging, and Neurotypical Privilege: Towards a Minority Group Model of Neurodiversity." *Human Development* 66 (2): 113–127. doi.org/10.1159/000524122.

Rawe, Julie. n.d. "Strengths-Based IEPs: What to Know." Understood. Accessed July 5, 2023. understood.org/en/articles/strengths-based-ieps-what-you-need-to-know.

Rehabilitation Act of 1973, 29 U.S.C. § 794 (1973).

Rinn, Anne N. 2021. *Social, Emotional, and Psychosocial Development of Gifted and Talented Individuals*. New York: Routledge.

Rinn, Anne N., Rachel U. Mun, and Jaret Hodges. 2022. *2020–2021 State of the States in Gifted Education*. National Association for Gifted Children and the Council of State Directors of Programs for the Gifted.

Rucinski, Christina, Jason T. Downer, and Joshua Brown. 2017. "Teacher-Child Relationships, Classroom Climate, and Children's Social-Emotional and Academic Development." *Journal of Educational Psychology* 109 (8): 1–12. doi.org/10.1037/edu0000240.

Sarris, Marina. 2020. "An Autism Mystery: Why Is Speech Elusive for Some on the Spectrum?" SPARK for Autism, July 10, 2020. sparkforautism.org/discover_article/speech-elusive/.

Schaeffer, Jeannette, et al. 2023. "Language in Autism: Domains, Profiles, and Co-occurring Conditions." *Journal of Neural Transmission* 130 (3):433–457. doi.org/10.1007/s00702-023-02592-y.

Shaw, Sebastian C. K., Mary Doherty, Sue McCowan, and Jessica A. Eccles. 2022. "Towards a Neurodiversity-Affirmative Approach for an Over-Represented and Under-Recognised Population: Autistic Adults in Outpatient Psychiatry." *Journal of Autism and Developmental Disorders* 52 (9): 4200–4201. doi.org/10.1007/s10803-022-05670-4.

Shaywitz, Sally, and Jonathan Shaywitz. 2020. *Overcoming Dyslexia* (2nd ed.). New York: Knopf.

Siegel, Matthew, Kahsi A. Smith, Carla Mazefsky, Robin L. Gabriels, Craig Erickson, Desmond Kaplan, Eric M. Morrow, Logan Wink, and Susan L. Santangelo. 2015. "The Autism Inpatient Collection: Methods and Preliminary Sample Description." *Molecular Autism* 6: 61. doi.org/10.1186/s13229-015-0054-8.

Silberman, Steve. 2015. *NeuroTribes: The Legacy of Autism and the Future of Neurodiversity*. New York: Avery.

Soler-Gutiérrez, Ana-María, Juan-Carlos Pérez-González, and Julia Mayas. 2023. "Evidence of Emotion Dysregulation as a Core Symptom of Adult ADHD: A Systematic Review." *PLOS ONE* 18 (1): e0280131. doi.org/10.1371/journal.pone.0280131.

Spaeth, Elliott, and Amy Pearson. 2023. "A Reflective Analysis on Neurodiversity and Student Well-being: Conceptualising Practical Strategies for Inclusive Practice." *Journal of Perspectives in Applied Academic Practice* 11 (2): 109–120. doi.org/10.56433/jpaap.v11i2.517.

Sriram, Rishi. 2020. "The Neuroscience Behind Productive Struggle." Edutopia, April 13, 2020. edutopia.org/article/neuroscience-behind-productive-struggle/.

Stanley, Jonathan. 2023. "Designing for Neurodiversity: Leveraging Research to Create Spaces for All Learners." Spaces4Learning, May 9, 2023. spaces4learning.com/articles/2023/05/09/designing-for-neurodiversity-leveraging-research.aspx.

Steele, Claude M., and Joshua M. Aronson. 1995. "Stereotype Threat and the Intellectual Test Performance of African Americans." *Journal of Personality and Social Psychology* 69 (5): 797–811. doi.org/10.1037/0022-3514.69.5.797.

Stoa, Rosalyn, and T. L. (Alan) Chu. 2023. "An Argument for Implementing and Testing Novelty in the Classroom." *Scholarship of Teaching and Learning in Psychology* 9 (1): 88–95. doi.org/10.1037/stl0000223.

Strelan, Peter, Amanda Osborn, and Edward Palmer. 2020. "The Flipped Classroom: A Meta-Analysis of Effects on Student Performance across Disciplines and Education Levels." *Educational Research Review* 30: 100314. doi.org/10.1016/j.edurev.2020.100314.

Strohmeier, Craig W., Brad Rosenfield, Robert A. DiTomasso, and J. Russell Ramsay. 2016. "Assessment of the Relationship Between Self-Reported Cognitive Distortions and Adult ADHD, Anxiety, Depression, and Hopelessness." *Psychiatry Research* 238: 153–158. doi.org/10.1016/j.psychres.2016.02.034.

Tare, Medha, Sarah Cacicio, and Alison R. Shell. 2021. *The Science of Adult Learning: Understanding the Whole Learner.* Digital Promise. digitalpromise.org/wp-content/uploads/2020/12/Adult-Learner-White-Paper-1.pdf.

Taxer, Jamie L., and James J. Gross. 2018. "Emotion Regulation in Teachers: The 'Why' and 'How.'" *Teaching and Teacher Education* 74: 180–189. doi.org/10.1016/j.tate.2018.05.008.

Taylor, Kate. 2017. "A Growing Number of High Schools Are Banning the Hottest Toy in the US." *Business Insider*, May 9, 2017. businessinsider.com/fidget-spinners-banned-from-top-high-schools-2017-5.

Uncovering the Hidden Curriculum. n.d. "About Us." Accessed June 18, 2024. hiddencurriculum.ca/about-us/.

US Department of Education (US DoE). 2017. "Issue Brief: Personalized Learning Plans." US Department of Education, Office of Planning, Evaluation, and Policy Development, Policy and Program Studies Service. www2.ed.gov/rschstat/eval/high-school/personalized-learning-plans.pdf.

United States Department of Education (US DoE). 2021. "Return to School Roadmap: Development and Implementation of Individualized Education Programs in the Least Restrictive Environment under the Individuals with Disabilities Education Act." United States Department of Education Office of Special Education and Rehabilitative Service, OSEP Qa 21-06 September 30, 2021. sites.ed.gov/idea/files/rts-iep-09-30-2021.pdf.

US Department of Education (US DoE). 2024. "A History of the Individuals with Disabilities Education Act." Last modified February 16, 2024. sites.ed.gov/idea/IDEA-History.

US Department of Education (US DoE), Office of Special Education and Rehabilitative Services. 2015. "OSEP Deal Colleague Letter on IDEA/IEP Terms." October 23. 2015. sites.ed.gov/idea/idea-files/osep-dear-colleague-letter-on-ideaiep-terms.

van der Kolk, Bessel. 2015. *The Body Keeps the Score: Mind, Brain, and Body in the Transformation of Trauma*. New York: Penguin.

Véronneau-Veilleux, Florence, Philippe Robaey, Mauro Ursino, and Fahima Nekka. 2022. "A Mechanistic Model of ADHD as Resulting from Dopamine Phasic/tonic Imbalance during Reinforcement Learning." *Frontiers in Computational Neuroscience* 16. doi.org/10.3389/fncom.2022.849323.

Wachtel, Lee Elizabeth, Jill Escher, Alycia Halladay, Amy Lutz, Gloria M. Satriale, Arthur Westover, and Carmen Lopez-Arvizu. 2024. "Profound Autism: An Imperative Diagnosis. *Pediatric Clinics* 71 (2): 301–313. doi.org/10.1016/j.pcl.2023.12.005.

Waizbard-Bartov, Einat, Deborah Fein, Catherine Lord, and David G. Amaral. 2023. "Autism Severity and Its Relationship to Disability." *Autism Research* 16 (4): 685-696. doi.org/10.1002/aur.2898.

Walsh, Reubs J., Lydia Krabbendam, Jeroen Dewinter, and Sander Begeer. 2018. "Brief Report: Gender Identity Differences in Autistic Adults: Associations with Perceptual and

Socio-cognitive Profiles." *Journal of Autism and Developmental Disorders* 48: 4040–4078. doi.org/10.1007/s10803-018-3702-y.

Warrier, Varun, David M. Greenberg, Elizabeth Weir, Clara Buckingham, Paula Smith, Meng-Chuan Lai, Carrie Allison, and Simon Baron-Cohen. 2020. "Elevated Rates of Autism, Other Neurodevelopmental and Psychiatric Diagnoses, and Autistic Traits in Transgender and Gender-Diverse Individuals." *Nature Communications* 11 (1):3959. doi.org/10.1038/s41467-020-17794-1.

Wehmeyer, Michael L. 2013. "Disability, Disorder, and Identity." *Intellectual and Developmental Disabilities* 51 (2): 122–126. doi.org/10.1352/1934-9556-51.2.122.

Weir, Elizabeth, Carrie Allison, and Simon Baron-Cohen. 2021. "The Sexual Health, Orientation, and Activity of Autistic Adolescents and Adults." *Autism Research* 14 (11): 18 2342–2354. doi.org/10.1002/aur.2604.

Wilson, Peter H., Scott Ruddock, Bouwien Smits-Engelsman, Helene Polatajko, and Rainer Blank. 2012. "Understanding Performance Deficits in Developmental Coordination Disorder: A Meta-Analysis of Recent Research." *Developmental Medicine & Child Neurology* 55 (3): 217–228. doi.org/10.1111/j.1469-8749.2012.04436.x.

World Health Organization (WHO). n.d. International Classification of Diseases, Eleventh Revision (ICD-11), 2019/2021. https://icd.who.int/en.

Wray, Emma, Umesh Sharma, and Pearl Subban. 2022. "Factors Influencing Teacher Self-Efficacy for Inclusive Education: A Systematic Literature Review." *Teaching and Teacher Education* 117: 103800. doi.org/10.1016/j.tate.2022.103800.

Wylie, Korey P., Jason R. Tregellas, Joshua J. Bear, and Kristina T. Legget. 2020. "Autism Spectrum Disorder Symptoms Are Associated with Connectivity Between Large-Scale Neural Networks and Brain Regions Involved in Social Processing." *Journal of Autism and Developmental Disorders* 50 (8): 2765–2778. doi.org/10.1007/s10803-020-04383-w.

Xi, Tingting, and Jinlin Wu, J. 2021. "A Review on the Mechanism Between Different Factors and the Occurrence of Autism and ADHD." *Psychology Research and Behavior Management* 14: 393–403. doi.org/10.2147/PRBM.S304450.

Yudin, Michael K. 2015. Dear colleague letter. October 23, 2015. Washington, DC: U.S. Department of Education, Office of Special Education and Rehabilitative Services. sites.ed.gov/idea/files/idea/policy/speced/guid/idea/memosdcltrs/guidance-on-dyslexia-10-2015.pdf.

Zhang, Wen, Na Hu, Xuechen Ding, and Junyi Li. 2021. "The Relationship Between Rejection Sensitivity and Borderline Personality Features: A Meta-Analysis." *Advances in Psychological Science* 29 (7): 1179–1194. doi.org/10.3724/SP.J.1042.2021.01179.

Zhang, Lawrence Jun, and Donglan Zhang. 2019. "Think-Aloud Protocols." In *The Routledge Handbook of Research Methods in Applied Linguistics*, edited by Jim McKinley and Heath Rose, 302–311. doi.org/10.4324/9780367824471-26.

Zhou, Jianhua, Xiaoyu Li, Lili Tian, and E. Scott Huebner. 2018. "Longitudinal Association Between Low Self-Esteem and Depression in Early Adolescents: The Role of Rejection Sensitivity and Loneliness." *Psychology of Popular Media Culture* 93 (1): 54–71. doi.org/10.1111/papt.12207.

Index

f denotes figure

A

AAC (augmentative and alternative communication) devices, use of, 224
ABC Model (antecedent-behavior-consequence), 139–140
ableism
 impact of on neurodivergent kids, 74–75
 internalized ableism, 72–73
 and intersecting identities, 76
 understanding and confronting, 72–73
ableist language, 73*f*
accommodations
 for all, 111
 vs. modifications, 257–258
 normalizing of, 31–32
 and tools for sensory needs, 203*f*–204*f*
action and expression, providing multiple means of, 103–104
actor, as type of camouflaging, 126
#ActuallyAutistic community, 7
adaptive behavior, intellectual disabilities and, 64
adverse childhood experiences (ACE) study, 82
alexithymia, 196–200
allistic, 7, 61
alternative teaching, 92–93
Alyssa (student example), 219
Amari (student example), 62–63
American Psychological Association, addition of diagnosis of Asperger's to *DSM-IV*, 17

Americans with Disabilities Act (ADA), 71
Amina (student example), 46
Anika (student example), 287–288
antecedent-behavior-consequence (ABC Model), 139–140
Anya (student example), 237
apathetic academic, as type of camouflaging, 125
artificial intelligence (AI), as tool for creating RPGs, 250
ASD (autism spectrum disorder), 17, 50, 255
Asperger, Hans, 50
Asperger's syndrome, 17, 50–51
assignments, suggesting ways to complete, 110
attention deficit/hyperactivity disorder (ADHD)
 and attention regulation, 52–53
 characteristics of, 52–54
 and emotional regulation, 54
 and executive functioning, 52–53, 283, 284, 285
 and impulsivity, 53–54
 LGBTQ+ people and, 131–132
 mental health statistics and, 280–281
 as neurodevelopmental label, 21, 22*f*
 student examples of, 33, 84, 113, 128–129, 146, 287–288
 as web, 42*f*
attention regulation, ADHD and, 52–53
attention tunnel, 233
AuDHD (or AuDHDer)
 and depression, 281

 as example of identity-first language, 35
 mental health statistics and, 281
 student examples of, 33, 84
 use of term, 7–8
auditory (hearing) (sensory system), 191, 192*f*–193*f*, 203*f*
Auditory Processing Disorder, 195
augmentative and alternative communication (AAC) devices, use of, 224
authenticity
 as antidote to camouflaging, 130–133
 neurodiversity-affirming supports for, 133–136
 role of privilege in being authentic, 130–131
autism
 characteristics of, 44–52
 consistency and, 46–48
 and depression, 280, 284
 diagnosis of, 50–51, 190
 engagement and communication of autistic students, 222
 "high-functioning" autism, 51
 history of functioning labels for, 50–51
 infantile autism, 50
 and intellectual disabilities, 49–51
 LGBTQ+ people and, 131–132
 as linear spectrum, 40, 41*f*
 mental health statistics and, 280

as neurodevelopmental label, 21, *22f*
"profound autism," 51
and repetition, 46–48
stigma around, 51
student examples of, 33, 46, 84, 182–183, 219, 264, 287, 288
as web, 40, *41f*
autism spectrum disorder (ASD), 17, 50, 255

B

badges, as way to integrate novelty, 245–246
barriers
    difficulty or reluctance in communicating, 81–82
    examining barriers to learning through UDL lens, 114–118
    feeling unwelcome as, 81
    gender biases as, 25
    to identification, 24–25
    identification of, 71, 117
    power imbalances as, 82
behavior
    ABC Model (antecedent-behavior-consequence), 139–140
    adaptive behavior, 64
    all behavior as communication, 139–140, *141f*
    demand avoidance, 156–159
    examples of student-tracked behaviors, 147–148
    moving beyond behaviors and using co-regulation, 139
    nonsuicidal self-injury (NSSI) behavior, 289–292
    Positive Behavioral Interventions and Supports (PBIS), 150–151
    rethinking behavior in the classroom, 137–164
    stimming behaviors, 120–121, 206–208
    use of co-regulation in, 139, 147–149, 152–154
behavior charts, 139, 140, 142–144
belonging, in neurodiversity-affirming schools, 70
Benjamin (student example), 33
"big group/small group teaching," 92–93
big-picture thinking, as strength of nondivergent students, 239
bipolar
    characteristics of, 66
    misdiagnosis of, 67
    as neurodivergent diagnoses and psychological one, 21, *22f*
blindness, category of disability under IDEA, 256
boss levels, as way to integrate novelty, 246–249
Brainovia (RPG), 250
burnout, in neurodivergent students, 85

C

camouflaging
    authenticity as antidote to, 130–133
    educators' role, 132–133
    reasons students camouflage, 120–122
    scripting conversations, 126–127
    short- and long-term effects of, 127–129
    types of, 124
    in unpacking neurodivergence, 122–123
Cardona, Miguel, 172
Carlos (student example), 59
CASEL (Collaboration for Academic, Social, and Emotional Learning) (SEL framework), 167–181, *168f*
CAST (Center for Applied Science Technology), 114
CBT (cognitive-behavioral therapy), 200
challenges
    with neurodivergent people/students in schools, 5
    use of in classrooms, as way to integrate novelty, 246–249
chameleon, as type of camouflaging, 125
Chiyo (student example), 288
choice, provision of as helping to create neurodiversity-affirming culture, 77
clarification, asking for, as neurodiversity-affirming communication, 215
classrooms
    building emotionally competent ones, 165–187
    inclusion in, 70
    rethinking behavior in, 137–164
    student and classroom vignettes, 13
    typical classrooms vs. UDL classrooms, *109f*
    use of challenges in as way to integrate novelty, 246–249
code switching, 16
Cognitive Ability Test (CogAT), 60
cognitive functioning, intellectual disabilities and, 63–64
cognitive giftedness
    characteristics of, 59–61

as neurodevelopmental label, 21, 22f
sensory needs of, 190–191
student examples of, 63, 182
cognitive-behavioral therapy (CBT), 200
collaboration, between staff and co-teaching, 87–94
Collaborative for Academic, Social, and Emotional Learning (CASEL), SEL framework, 167–181, 168f
communication
all behavior as, 139–140, 141f
augmentative and alternative communication (AAC) devices, 224
autism and, 44–45, 222
neurodivergent communication styles, 221–225
nonverbal communication, 224–225
social communication, 61, 290
that is neurodiversity-affirming, 211–228
communication modes, offering multiple ones, as neurodiversity-affirming communication, 216
community education, provision of, 32
community of care, establishment of, 181
competence, presumption of, 34, 79–80
competency-based grading, 243
competition, cautions with, 245
consequences, as not synonymous with punishment, 140
consistency, autism and, 46–48
coping strategies, identifying healthy ones, 181

co-regulation
cycle of, 153f
described, 144–145
examples of student-tracked behaviors, 147–149
before self-regulation, 149, 152, 154
use of to move beyond behaviors, 139
co-teaching, 87–94
counseling interventions, considerations for, 285–289
COVID-19 pandemic
as accelerating neurodiversity movement, 18
impacts of, 1
Cyrus (student example), 182–183

D

DCD (developmental coordination disorder) (dyspraxia), 58–59
deaf-blindness, category of disability under IDEA, 255
deafness, category of disability under IDEA, 255
decision-making
good decision-making as SEL framework core competency, 167, 169f
impact of responsible decision-making on teaching, 177
incorporating responsible decision-making in classroom, 177–178
declarative language, 152, 153f, 154, 155f, 158, 159, 217
deficit-based language, 34

Dell Technologies, recruitment of neurodiverse talent and thinkers, 19
depression
AuDHD (or AuDHDer) and, 281
autism and, 280, 284
learning disabilities and, 281
as not typical, 283
as psychological diagnosis, 22f
as second area of diagnosis for bipolar, 66
design, how it affects students, 79
destigmatization, 11, 16, 19, 31–33
detail-orientation, as strength of nondivergent students, 238
developmental coordination disorder (DCD) (dyspraxia), 58–59
diagnoses. *See also* misdiagnosis
of Asperger's, 17
of autism, 50–51, 190
of disruptive mood dysregulation disorder (DMDD), 67
gender biases and, 284
neurodivergent diagnoses as compared to psychological diagnoses, 21, 22f
of obsessive-compulsive disorder (OCD), 64
sorting out emotions from diagnoses, 281–283
Diagnostic and Statistical Manual of Mental Disorders (DSM-III), infantile autism diagnosis, 50
Diagnostic and Statistical Manual of Mental Disorders (DSM-IV), Asperger's diagnosis, 17

Diagnostic and Statistical Manual of Mental Disorders (DSM-V)
  Asperger's diagnosis, 17
  on assistance required for persons with autism, 51
  autism spectrum disorder (ASD) diagnosis, 50
  on obsessive-compulsive disorder (OCD), 64
  on social communication, 61
  on specific learning disabilities, 55
dice, gamifying with, as way to integrate novelty, 251
differences, use of term, 6, 7
different, use of term, 6, 7
digital badges, as way to integrate novelty, 245–246
Digital Promise
  Learner Variability Project (LVP), 27–28
  Learning Navigator, 28, 29*f*
disability laws, protection for people under, 70
disability/disabilities. *See also* Americans with Disabilities Act (ADA); Individuals with Disabilities Education Act (IDEA); intellectual disability/ies; learning disabilities; specific learning disabilities (SLDs)
  categories of under IDEA, 255–256
  conceptual models of, 71
  definition of under Section 504, 258
  medical model of, 71
  social model of, 8, 71, 72
  stigma around, 72

disruptive mood dysregulation disorder (DMDD), diagnosis of, 67
distractor, as type of camouflaging, 125
Dmitri (student example), 288–289
"don't-do" list, creation of, 181
dopamine, differences of, 231
double empathy problem, 9–10
Double Empathy Problem sections
  adaptable and responsive learning environments, 106–107
  alexithymia, 199–200
  interrupting in class, 174–175
  monotropism, 233–234
  overview, 13
  rejection sensitivity dysphoria (RSD), 162–163
  scripting conversations, 126
  sensory differences and suicidality and self-injury, 293
  social standing among peers, 219–220
Dungeons & Dragons (role-playing game), 249, 251
dyscalculia
  characteristics of, 56–57
  as neurodevelopmental label, 21, 22*f*
dysgraphia
  characteristics of, 57
  as neurodevelopmental label, 21, 22*f*
dyslexia
  characteristics of, 55
  identification of and services for, 54–55
  as neurodevelopmental label, 21, 22*f*

dyspraxia, as neurodevelopmental label, 21
dyspraxia (developmental coordination disorder, DCD), characteristics of, 58–59

E

echolalia, 223–224
educational identification, of neurodivergence. *See* identification
elaboration, asking for, as neurodiversity-affirming communication, 215
Elijah (student example), 241
emotional competence
  building emotionally competent classrooms, 165–187
  as key in neurodiversity-affirming classrooms, 165
  ways to strengthen yours, 180–181
emotional disturbance, category of disability under IDEA, 255
emotional literacy, 180
emotional regulation
  ADHD and, 54
  as compared to emotional competence, 166
  impact of teacher emotional regulation, 166–167
  manifestations of, 139
  and somatic awareness, 200–201
  strategies for, 148
emotions
  sorting out emotions from diagnoses, 281–283

understanding family emotions and concerns, 182

The End of Average (Rose), 27

engagement
- of autistic students, 222
- providing multiple means of, 101–102

equitable education systems, creation of, 2–3, 15

executive functioning
- ADHD and, 52–53, 283, 284, 285
- and demand avoidance, 158
- emotional regulation and, 153f
- and hidden curriculum, 173f
- masking of, 121, 284
- sensory integration differences and, 190, 191f
- as skill toward achieving goals, 268
- student examples of help with, 84, 129
- support for, 105, 174, 232, 236, 238, 244, 247–248, 250

F

families
- engagement of, 81–82
- understanding family emotions and concerns, 182

feedback, giving regular feedback, 110–111

fidgets, use of, 205–206

finger flicking/wiggling, as stimming behavior, 207

504 plans. *See also* Section 504 (Rehabilitation Act of 1973)
- do neurodivergent students need them? 259

making sense of, 260
what to look for in one, 259–260

flexible thinking, as skill toward achieving goals, 268

Four Es Framework, 182–184

free appropriate public education (FAPE), 254, 257

frequent flyer, as type of camouflaging, 125

G

gamification, 245

gender biases
- as barrier to educational identification, 25
- and diagnoses, 284

generalized anxiety, as psychological diagnosis, 22f

getting to know students, questions for, 179

goals
- of neurodiversity movement, 19
- rethinking goals of IEPs to be neurodiversity-affirming, 266–269, 267f, 269f
- sharing of lesson goals, 109–110
- skills toward achievement of, 268
- SMART ones, 262, 262f, 266–267, 270

Goldman Sachs, recruitment of neurodiverse talent and thinkers, 19

grading
- competency-based grading, 243
- standards-based grading, 243

gustatory (taste) (sensory system), 191, 192f–193f, 204f

H

hand flapping, as stimming behavior, 207

hearing impairment, category of disability under IDEA, 255

"hidden curriculum," 172, 173f

hierarchies, recognizing unconventional reactions to, as neurodiversity-affirming communication, 217–218

"high-functioning" autism, 51

hyperactivity, ADHD and, 53

hyperfixation, as strength of nondivergent students, 235

hyperlexia, as neurodivergent label, 49

hypersensitive (overresponsive) sensory reaction, 194

hyposensitive (underresponsive) sensory reaction, 194–195

I

IDEA (Individuals with Disabilities Education Act). *See* Individuals with Disabilities Education Act (IDEA)

identification
- barriers to, 24–25
- diagnostic processes for identification of neurodivergent people, 4
- educational identification of neurodivergence, 23–25
- medical diagnosis vs. educational identification of neurodivergence, 23–24
- and services for students with dyslexia, 54–55

identity-first language (IFL), 8, 35–36

imperative language, 152

impulsiveness/impulsivity
  ADHD and, 53–54
  and suicidality and self-injury, 291
inclusion
  in classrooms, defined, 70
  through mainstreaming, 69–70
inclusive education, vision for, 271–272
Independent Living, 17
individualized education programs (IEPs)
  blending of with SLPs, 271–272
  described, 254–256
  do neurodivergent students need them? 259
  making sense of, 260–263
  rethinking goals of to be neurodiversity-affirming, 266–269, 267f, 269f
  strengths-based ones, 272–273
  as support option, 20, 259
  what to look for in one, 259–260
Individuals with Disabilities Education Act (IDEA)
  categories of disability under, 255–256
  as compared to 504 plans, 257
  described, 254
  on dyslexia, 54
  on LREs, 263–264
  on mainstreaming, 69
  as support option, 71, 253
info-dumping, 221–222
intellectual disability/ies
  autism and, 49–51
  category of disability under IDEA, 255–256
  characteristics of, 63–64
  as neurodevelopmental label, 21, 22f
interoceptive sensory system, 192f–193f, 204f
interruptions, in class, as Double Empathy Problem, 174–175
Intersecting Identities, 13, 76, 131, 160, 196, 213
Iowa Test of Basic Skills (ITBS), 60
Isaiah (student example), 215

J

Javier (student example), 113
Joseph (student example), 264–265
JPMorgan Chase, recruitment of neurodiverse talent and thinkers, 19
Judah (student example), 83, 84

K

Kanner, Leo, 50
Katy ISD, Texas, on school design, 79

L

labels
  history of autism and functioning labels, 50–51
  neurodevelopmental labels, 21–22, 22f
  stopping fear of, 31
  understanding neurodivergent labels, 44
language
  ableist language, 73f
  declarative language. See declarative language
  deficit-based language, 34
  identity-first language (IFL), 8, 35–36
  imperative language, 152
  neurodiversity-affirming language, 16, 34–36, 77
  non-ableist language, 73f, 77
  person-first language (PFL), 8, 35, 36, 71
  speech or language impairment, as category of disability under IDEA, 256
learner variability
  defined, 26–27
  Learning Navigator (Digital Promise), 28, 29f
  vs. neurodivergence, 30–31
  and neurodiversity-affirming schools, 26–30
  recognition of, 28
  stereotype threat and, 29–30
Learner Variability Project (LVP) (Digital Promise), 27–28
learning
  identifying barriers to, 117
  mastery-based learning, 242–243
learning disabilities, mental health statistics and, 281
learning environments. See also classrooms
  adaptable and responsive ones, 106–107
  typical classrooms vs. UDL classrooms, 109f
Learning Navigator (Digital Promise), 28
learning styles, intellectual disabilities and, 63–64
least restrictive environment (LRE), rethinking of, 263–266
lesson goals, sharing of, 109–110
LGBTQ+ people, autism and ADHD and, 131–132
linear spectrum, of understanding neurodivergent diagnosis as too shallow, 40

LinkedIn, skill badge of "Dyslexic Thinker," 19
Lisabeth (student example), 83, 84
listening
  attentive listening, 134
  "whole body listening," 208–209
literal thinking, as strength of nondivergent students, 239–240
logic, as strength of nondivergent students, 237
LRE (least restrictive environment), rethinking of, 263–266
Luca (student example), 287
LVP (Learner Variability Project) (Digital Promise), 27–28

M

mainstreaming, inclusion through, 69–70
mania, as first area of diagnosis for bipolar, 66
masking, 121, 122–123, 284. *See also* unmasking
mastery-based learning, 242–243
Maya (student example), 239
medical diagnosis, of neurodivergence, 23–24
mental health needs
  considerations for counseling interventions, 285–289
  creation of neurodiversity-affirming ones, 293–294
  misdiagnosis of neurodivergence, 284–285
  neurodivergence and mental health, 280–281, 282*f*
  sorting out emotions from diagnoses, 281–283
  suicidal ideation and nonsuicidal self-injury (NSSI) behavior, 289–292
mental health, neurodivergence and, 280–281
microcredentials, as way to integrate novelty, 245–246
Microsoft, recruitment of neurodiverse talent and thinkers, 19
Milton, Damian, 9
Minh (student example), 238
mirror, as type of camouflaging, 125
mirror neurons, power of, 167
misdiagnosis
  of bipolar, 67
  of neurodivergence, 284–285
  of obsessive-compulsive disorder (OCD), 285
  under previous diagnostic criteria, 51
modifications, accommodations vs., 257–258
monotropism, as strength of nondivergent students, 232–234
multiple disabilities, category of disability under IDEA, 256
mutism, situational, 225

N

Naglieri Nonverbal Ability Test (NNAT3), 60
negative attention, avoidance of, as reason students camouflage, 120–121
negative thoughts, challenging of, 181
neural connectivity, differences of, 231
neurodevelopmental labels, 21–22, 22*f*
neurodivergence
  can you "grow out" of it? 86–87
  destigmatizing of. *See* destigmatization
  vs. learner variability, 30–31
  medical diagnosis vs. educational identification of, 23–24
  and mental health, 280–281
  misdiagnosis of, 284–285
  overlapping neurodivergence and mental health needs, 282*f*
  stigmatization of. *See* stigma
  understanding labels for, 44
  unpacking of, 42–43
  as variation of "normal," 20
neurodivergent, use of term, 8
neurodivergent communication styles, 221–225
neurodivergent diagnoses, as compared to psychological diagnoses, 21, 22*f*
Neurodivergent Learner's Bill of Rights, 77, 78, 82, 87
neurodivergent people/students/learners
  burnout in, 85
  challenges for schools, 5
  characteristics of, 3
  classification of, 20, 22*f*
  diagnostic processes for identification of, 4
  do they need IEPs and 504 plans? 259
  impact of ableism on, 74–75
  support for, 104–106, 138
  waning stigma around, 4
neurodivergent traits, deficit-based vs. strengths-based perspective for, 275*f*–276*f*
neurodiverse, use of term, 8

neurodiversity
  frequency of Google searches for, 17f, 17
  labels that fit within definition of, 21
  vs. neurodivergence, 19
  use of term, 17
Neurodiversity Audit of Classroom Environment Checklist, 202
neurodiversity movement
  goals of, 19
  history of, 17–19
  promoting awareness of, 19
  as recognizing values of all people, 20
  those leading charge in, 4
The Neurodiversity Podcast, 3, 14
Neurodiversity University Educator Hub, 14
neurodiversity-affirming clinical practices, 287–289
neurodiversity-affirming communication
  described, 212–213
  neurodivergent communication styles, 221–225
  setting stage of, 214–220
neurodiversity-affirming culture, 70, 76–80, 87
neurodiversity-affirming language, 16, 34–36, 77
neurodiversity-affirming practices, 25
  competency-based grading as aligning with, 243
  described, 2
  push for in schools, 5–6
  setting the stage for, 214–218
  trauma-informed and, 82–84
  Universal Design for Learning (UDL) as. *See* Universal Design for Learning (UDL)

neurodiversity-affirming safety plans, creation of, 293–294
"Neurodiversity-Affirming Teachers' Compact of Shared Beliefs" (webinar), 14, 87–88
neuro-normative, use of term, 6–7
neurotypical, use of term, 6
NNAT3 (Naglieri Nonverbal Ability Test), 60
non-ableist language, 73f, 77
nonsuicidal self-injury (NSSI) behavior, 289–292
nonverbal communication, 224–225
noradrenaline (norepinephrine), differences of, 231
novelty
  preference for, as strength of nondivergent students, 241–242
  as survival mechanism, 243–244
  ways to integrate, 244–245
nypical, use of term, 7

O

obsessive-compulsive disorder (OCD)
  characteristics of, 64–65, 190
  diagnosis of, 64
  misdiagnosis of, 285
  as straddling space between neurodivergent diagnoses and psychological ones, 21, 22f
obsessive-compulsive thinking, 64–65
Office of Special Education and Rehabilitative Services (OSEP), 54–55

olfactory (smell) (sensory system), 191, 192f–193f, 203f
one teach, one assist, 94
one teach, one observe, 95
Opai, Keri, 76
oppositional defiant disorder (ODD), diagnosis of, 67
organizing materials, strategies for, 148
orthopedic impairment, category of disability under IDEA, 256
other health impairment, category of disability under IDEA, 256
overresponsive (hypersensitive) sensory reaction, 194

P

PANDA acronym, 157–158
parallel teaching, 92
Pascal (student example), 154–155
pathological (pervasive) demand avoidance (PDA), 48, 156–159
peer support, fostering of, 225–226
personal growth, intellectual disabilities and, 64
person-first language (PFL), 8, 35–36, 71
pervasive and development disorders (PDD), 50
PLAAFP (present level of academic achievement and functional performance), 261
PLEP (present level of educational performance), 261
PLOP or PLP (present level of performance), 261

Posey, Allison, 114
positive attention, gaining of, as reason students camouflage, 121–122
Positive Behavioral Interventions and Supports (PBIS), 150–151
positive intent, assumption of, as neurodiversity-affirming communication, 214
post-traumatic stress disorder (PTSD), as straddling space between neurodivergent diagnoses and psychological ones, 21, 22f
present level of academic achievement and functional performance (PLAAFP), 261
present level of educational performance (PLEP), 261
present level of performance (PLOP or PLP), 261
processing, cognitive giftedness and, 60–61
"profound autism," 51
proprioceptive sensory system, 192f–193f, 204f
psychological diagnoses, as compared to neurodivergent diagnoses, 21, 22f
PTSD (post-traumatic stress disorder). *See* post-traumatic stress disorder (PTSD)

Q

questions, to get to know students, 179

R

reaction vs. response, 171f
reasoning, as strength of nondivergent students, 237
rejection awareness. *See* rejection sensitivity
rejection perception. *See* rejection sensitivity
rejection sensitivity, 160–162
rejection sensitivity dysphoria (RSD), 160, 162–163
relationship skills
 impact of on teaching, 178
 incorporating of relationship-building skills into classroom, 178–179
 as SEL framework core competency, 167, 169f
repetition, autism and, 46–48
representation, providing multiple means of, 102–103
risk assessment, 293–294
rocking, as stimming behavior, 207
role-playing games (RPGs), as way to integrate novelty, 249–250
Rose, Todd, 27
routine
 autism and, 46–48
 comfort with, as strength of nondivergent students, 240
RSD (rejection sensitivity dysphoria), 160, 162–163
rule follower, as type of camouflaging, 124

S

safety plans, creation of neurodiversity-affirming ones, 293–294
Section 504 (Rehabilitation Act of 1973), 20, 71, 253–254, 257–258. *See also* 504 plans
SEL framework (CASEL), 167–181, 168f
self-advocacy
 encouragement of, as neurodiversity-affirming communication, 217
 as skill toward achieving goals, 268
self-awareness
 impact of on teaching, 170
 incorporating of into classroom, 170–171
 as SEL framework core competency, 167, 168f
self-care, importance of, 166, 180
self-disclosure, 6
self-management
 impact of on teaching, 172
 incorporating of into classroom, 174
 as SEL framework core competency, 167, 168f
self-reflection, practice of, 180
self-regulation, co-regulation before self-regulation, 149, 152, 154
sensorimotor differences, 195
sensory craving, 195
sensory differences, and suicidality and self-injury, 291
sensory discrimination differences, 195
sensory integration differences, 194–195
sensory modulation differences, 194–195
sensory needs
 accommodations and tools for, 203f–204f

building awareness of sensory integration differences, 190–200
impact of unmet sensory integration needs, 191f
meeting of, 189–209
as skill toward achieving goals, 268
support of in schools, 201–206
sensory systems
auditory (hearing), 191, 192f–193f
gustatory (taste), 191, 192f–193f
olfactory (smell), 191, 192f–193f
proprioceptive, 192f–193f, 204f
tactile (touch), 191, 192f–193f
vestibular, 192f–193f, 204f
visual (sight), 191, 192f–193f
serotonin, differences of, 231
shapeshifter, as type of camouflaging, 125
silent student, as type of camouflaging, 124
Simone (student example), 128–129
Singer, Judith, 17
situational mutism, 225
SLDs (specific learning disabilities). *See* specific learning disabilities (SLDs)
SLPs (student learning plans), 269–278
SMART goals, 262, 266–267, 270
social acuity, over social skills, 226–227
social anxiety, as straddling space between neurodivergent diagnoses and psychological ones, 21

social awareness
impact of on teaching, 175–176
incorporating of into classroom, 176
as SEL framework core competency, 167, 168f
social communication differences, and suicidality and self-injury, 290
social interaction, as skill toward achieving goals, 268
social model of disability, 8–9, 71, 72
Sol (student example), 216
somatic awareness, emotional regulation and, 200–201
Sophie (student example), 56
"special interests" (SpIns), 232–233
specific learning disabilities (SLDs)
category of disability under IDEA, 256
dyscalculia. *See* dyscalculia
dysgraphia. *See* dysgraphia
dyslexia. *See* dyslexia
speech or language impairment, category of disability under IDEA, 256
spinning, as stimming behavior, 207
standards-based grading, 243
station teaching, 93–94
status quo, questioning of, 32–33
stereotype threat
and learner variability, 29–30
ways to mitigate for neurodivergent learners, 30
Stevenson High School (Lincolnshire, Illinois), on school design, 79
stigma. *See also* destigmatization

around autism, 51
around disabilities, 72
around intellectual disabilities, 63
as barrier to educational identification, 25
cautions about, 48
dealing with neurodivergence as compared to dealing with learner variability, 30–31
elimination of, 35
influence of, 285
of LBGTQ+ people, 131
of neurodivergence, 36, 42, 76, 211
reduction of, 2, 4, 21, 106, 118
reinforcement of, 128
role of in misdiagnosis, 284
stimming behaviors, 120–121, 206–208
strengths-based instruction
defined, 230
neurology as justifying strengths-based supports, 230–231
starting with strengths, 231–242
stress-management tool kit, importance of, 180
student and classroom vignettes, 13
student examples
Alyssa, 219
Amari, 62–63
Amina, 46
Anika, 287–288
Anya, 237
Benjamin, 33
Carlos, 59
Chiyo, 288
Cyrus, 182–183
Dmitri, 288–289
Elijah, 241

Isaiah, 215
Javier, 113
Joseph, 264–265
Judah, 83, 84
Lisabeth, 83, 84
Luca, 287
Maya, 239
Minh, 238
Pascal, 154–155
Simone, 128–129
Sol, 216
Sophie, 56
Trevor, 146–147
Zenia, 273
student learning plans (SLPs), 269–278
suicidal ideation, 289–291
swaying, as stimming behavior, 207

T

tactile (touch) (sensory system), 191, 192f–193f, 203f
tapping, as stimming behavior, 207
TAS-20 (Toronto Alexithymia Scale), 196–197
task, staying on, strategies for, 147
teacher emotional regulation, impact of, 166–167
teaching
    alternative teaching, 92–93
    "big group/small group teaching," 92–93
    co-teaching, 87–94
    impact of relationship skills on, 178
    impact of self-awareness on, 170
    impact of self-management on, 172
    impact of social awareness on, 175–176
    parallel teaching, 92
    station teaching, 93–94
    team-teaching, 91–92
tech industry, and neurodiversity, 5
"think aloud" strategy, 171
Toronto Alexithymia Scale (TAS-20), 196–197
Tourette syndrome
    characteristics of, 65
    as neurodevelopmental label, 21
trauma-informed practices, 82–84
traumatic brain injury, category of disability under IDEA, 256
Trevor (student example), 146–147
TRUE strategy/method, 135–136
twice-exceptionality/twice-exceptional (2e) learners, 59, 61–63, 122

U

underresponsive (hyposensitive) sensory reaction, 194–195
understanding, fostering of, 225–226
unhelpful thoughts, challenging of, 181
universal design
    influence of on UDL, 98–99
    principles of, 99f
Universal Design for Learning (UDL)
    benefits of understanding of, 6
    in the classroom, 108–111, 109f
    defined, 98
    examining barriers to learning through UDL lens, 114–118
    how it supports neurodivergent learners, 104–106
    principles of, 100–104
    universal design's influence on, 98–100
    use of, 177
    ways all students benefit from, 111
    why use it, 118
unmasking, neurodiversity-affirming supports for, 133–136
Unpacking Neurodivergence, 13

V

verbal ability, as strength of nondivergent students, 235–236
vestibular sensory system, 192f–193f, 204f
visual (sight) (sensory system), 191, 192f–193f, 203f
visual impairment, category of disability under IDEA, 256
Visual Processing Disorder, 195
visual-spatial ability, as strength of nondivergent students, 236–237
vocal stimming, 207
voice memo, as type of camouflaging, 125–126

W

Weschler Intelligence Scale for Children (WISC-V), 60
"whole body listening," as not neurodiversity-affirming, 208–209
workspaces, having flexible ones available, 110

Z

Zenia (student example), 273

About the Authors

Emily Kircher-Morris, M.A., M.Ed., LPC, inspired by her own experiences as a neurodivergent learner, is dedicated to supporting neurodivergent individuals in a way she wasn't during her academic years.

With a background in both education and mental health, Emily has worked across multiple settings including gifted and general education classrooms and school counseling, and now maintains a private practice as a licensed professional counselor. Her practice focuses on supporting neurodivergent individuals, including those who are autistic, ADHD, twice-exceptional (2e), gifted, and more, helping them navigate their unique challenges and embrace their strengths. She frequently provides professional development and continuing education training for educators, clinicians, and other professionals, sharing insights on neurodiversity-affirming approaches to education, mental health, and personal development. As host of The Neurodiversity Podcast, she explores topics related to the development of neurodivergent people throughout their lifespan, featuring conversations with experts and individuals from the neurodivergent community.

Emily lives near St. Louis, Missouri.

Amanda Morin is a neurodivergent neurodiversity activist, award-winning author, early childhood specialist, and nationally known speaker, deeply committed to fostering accessible and inclusive environments for neurodivergent individuals. She leverages her expertise in learning and child development, Universal Design for Learning (UDL), special education, advocacy, and mental health to distill complex data into easily digestible information for parents, educators, and employers who want to advance the mission of creating inclusive content, programs, and strategies to make the world accessible to all.

Amanda played an integral role in launching Understood.org in 2014 and has worked with other organizations and publications, including Bright & Quirky, Edutopia, Association for Supervision and Curriculum Development (ASCD), Education.com, *Parenting Special Needs Magazine*, and Popsugar Moms. During her years as an early childhood educator, she taught kindergarten and worked with disabled infants, toddlers, and preschoolers.

Amanda lives near Portland, Maine.